LOUIS SULLIVAN

The Function of Ornament

LOUIS SULLIVAN

The Function of Ornament

Edited by
WIM DE WIT

Text by
DAVID VAN ZANTEN, WILLIAM JORDY, WIM DE WIT, ROCHELLE BERGER ELSTEIN

With a contribution by
ROBERT TWOMBLY

CHICAGO HISTORICAL SOCIETY

THE SAINT LOUIS ART MUSEUM

W. W. NORTON & COMPANY · NEW YORK & LONDON

Published simultaneously in Canada by
Penguin Books Canada Ltd., 2801 John Street, Markham, Ontario L3R 1B4.
The text of this book is composed in Monotype Bell.
The composition is by Michael & Winifred Bixler.
This book was printed and bound in Italy
The design is by Katy Homans, with Mark La Riviere.

Library of Congress Cataloging-in-Publication Data

Louis Sullivan: the function of ornament.
Catalog of an exhibition.
1. Sullivan, Louis H., 1856–1924—Exhibitions.
2. Decoration and ornament, Architectural—Middle
West—Exhibitions. I. Sullivan, Louis H., 1856–1924.
II. Wit, Wim de. III. Van Zanten, David, 1943–
IV. Chicago Historical Society. V. St. Louis Art
Museum.

NA737.S9A4   1986   720'.92'4   86–12536

W. W. Norton & Company, Inc., 500 Fifth Avenue, New York, N. Y. 10110

W. W. Norton & Company Ltd., 37 Great Russell Street, London WC1B 3NU

2 3 4 5 6 7 8 9 0

ISBN 0-393-02358-3

Contents

Exhibition Tour

Chicago Historical Society
September 2, 1986 – January 4, 1987

Cooper-Hewitt Museum
March 24 – June 28, 1987

The Saint Louis Art Museum
August 28 – October 25, 1987

Foreword

TODAY WE VIEW THE ORIGINS OF CONTEM-
porary architecture with a renewed interest in
nineteenth-century historicism and in Beaux-Arts
classicism. The controlled, monumental vision of
ancient Greco-Roman building which materialized
in the World's Columbian Exposition of 1893, for
example, again has sparked our curiosity and admiration. We have begun to study the classical architectural tradition taught at the great Parisian Ecole
des Beaux-Arts in order to understand that art
at its source.

One result of this has been a reevaluation of
many nineteenth-century designers who once had
been dismissed—especially Beaux-Arts classicists
like Charles Follen McKim, Cass Gilbert, and John
Russell Pope. But it also has resulted in the realization that our old heroes were still remarkable
men, although in a broader sense. We have come
to understand that the Beaux-Arts tradition was
far more elastic and fertile than we had formerly
wanted to believe and that in America it had given
birth to the work of Richard Morris Hunt, Henry
Hobson Richardson, and even Frank Furness.
Furthermore, we have come to recognize and
appreciate the impressively monumental Beaux-
Arts qualities in the designs of the leaders of
Chicago architecture—Daniel Burnham, of course,
but Louis Sullivan and Frank Lloyd Wright as
well.

Until recently, Sullivan has been a figure with a
chiefly professional following. Widely known to
architects and historians, his reputation has been
eclipsed in recent years by that of his famous pupil,
Frank Lloyd Wright. The general audience seems
to have forgotten that Sullivan was himself a tow-
ering figure in the history of American building
art. While Wright has been treated frequently in
books and popular publications, Sullivan has stayed

"underground," mainly known to practitioners or
to those who might have taken a course in American art or architecture in recent years. Our inten-
tion is to change that perception, promoting Sullivan's life and works to a larger audience once
more. The enduring beauty and inspiration that
his buildings provide are still a valid resource for
practitioners, as Mr. Obata's introduction indicates. But they are also objects worthy of our renewed respect and admiration, for their quality,
and for their traditional regard for the human values of decoration, monumental form, and historical
reminiscence.

In the spring of 1980, the present exhibition
was proposed to David and Ann Van Zanten in
discussions which began with the director of The
Saint Louis Art Museum, James D. Burke. The
participants knew that it had been more than
twenty-five years since the publication of Vincent
Scully's article on Louis Sullivan and that most
publications on this seminal American architect
had appeared in scholarly or trade journals, not
before the general public. The restoration of the
Wainwright Building in St. Louis was just then
completed, ensuring the preservation of one of
America's most important historic buildings. The
three discussants could scarcely have imagined the
great interest in the preservation and reuse of
historic American buildings that would occur in
the next five years, owing to substantial changes
in tax law. They simply looked for recognition for
Louis Sullivan and for those who had labored so
hard to preserve the Wainwright.

As planning proceeded, Ann Van Zanten was
appointed curator of architectural collections at
the Chicago Historical Society. Like her husband,
she held a doctorate in architectural history from
Harvard University, and had already begun a

productive career as a scholar in American architectural studies. Ellsworth Brown, director of the Chicago Historical Society, then proposed that the project be undertaken as a joint venture between the two museums. After a few additional commitments were determined, the Van Zantens began their work in earnest. The shocking and tragic death of Ann in August 1982 delayed the exhibition for some time, but only served to continue the commitment of the participants toward the realization of the exhibition and the book. With the arrival of Wim de Wit as curator of architectural collections at the Chicago Historical Society in the spring of 1983, the project went forward again as other authors were contacted and venues settled. For the authors and museum staffs of the two collaborating institutions, the book and exhibition which appear now reinforce our commitment to carry out the work that Ann herself intended.

This publication is made possible by a generous grant from the Luce Foundation for Scholarship in American Art, a program of The Henry Luce Foundation, Inc. The authors and organizers are also indebted to the following for their substantial assistance in realizing the project: the National Endowment for the Arts, a federal agency; Johnson & Higgins; Consolidated Aluminum Corporation; and Prudential Associates, a Limited Partnership owning the Guaranty Building, Buffalo, New York, Arthur Collins, Arthur D. Emil and John J. Ferchill General Partners.

ELLSWORTH BROWN
Chicago Historical Society
JAMES D. BURKE
The Saint Louis Art Museum

Introduction

THIS LOUIS SULLIVAN RETROSPECTIVE IS significant to practicing architects for several reasons. For one, I think it's reassuring to see Sullivan's works and papers at a time when there are so many winds of change blowing in the architectural world. Sullivan's work is vibrant with integrity, consistency, wholeness, and harmony. Secondly, he reminds us that the structural intent of a building can be an integral part of a building's design. We see this in his high-rise buildings like the Guaranty Building in Buffalo and the Wainwright Building in St. Louis. We see it also in mixed-use centers like the Chicago Auditorium and even in small one- or two-story commercial buildings like the Owatonna Bank in Minnesota.

The exhibition is also important for what we can learn from Sullivan, about the careful integration of form, structure, and ornamentation—particularly as more and more architects endeavor to make buildings richer in detail. Sullivan himself never used ornamental details from the past but created his own and made it a part of the whole. His ornamentation never looked applied or like an afterthought. It is always part of the total design.

More than eighty years ago, Sullivan was solving many of the very same urban design problems that architects face today. Even if the solutions are ultimately different, we can still learn much from the way he went about solving these common problems. As a practicing architect, it has given me—and I'm sure many of my colleagues —great pleasure to go back to Sullivan's buildings in Chicago, St. Louis, Minnesota, or Iowa. They're still meccas of learning.

Much has been written about Sullivan, his personality and psyche. To some extent, today he is even controversial. But if you look at his buildings, you will see they speak to us in a universal language of design that is unequalled. Therein lies his genius.

GYO OBATA
Hellmuth, Obata & Kassabaum
St. Louis

Acknowledgments

WORK ON THE EXHIBITION AND CATALOGUE, *Louis Sullivan: The Function of Ornament,* has been an exciting experience, especially because of the collaboration of scholars and collectors, many of whom made essential contributions to the conceptual framework of the project. We are grateful to all those who offered their help.

Chicago, the city where Louis Sullivan worked for most of his life, is also the city of Sullivan specialists. No one knows more about this seminal American architect than Tim Samuelson and John Vinci. Both have opened their collections to us and answered numerous questions without hesitation. In addition, Tim Samuelson gave much of his time to help us with the conservation of many of the items in the exhibition; John Vinci kindly allowed us to consult the Richard Nickel collection, a source of documentation on many unknown Sullivan buildings. Kathy Cummings made it possible to locate particular items in this collection, and we appreciate all her time on this endeavor. We are also grateful to Sue Tindall for her willingness to share her knowledge of terra-cotta, a material Sullivan used extensively.

No exhibition of Sullivan's work could be made without the collaboration of many collectors, the foremost of which are in Chicago and New York. Sincere thanks go to John Zukowsky, curator, and Pauline Saliga, assistant curator of the Architecture Collection at The Art Institute of Chicago; Susan Godlewski, head of Special Collections, and Paul Glassman, former architectural librarian, both in the Burnham Library there; and Janet Parks, curator of drawings at the Avery Architecture and Fine Arts Library of Columbia University in New York. We also thank the other collectors and institutions who allowed us to borrow from their extensive Sullivan collections: Robert Furhoff and Wilbert Hasbrouck in Chicago; Jane Tammen in Newark, Ohio; Francis X. Blouin, director, and Marjorie Barritt, librarian, the Bentley Historical Library at the University of Michigan, Ann Arbor; Alan Lathrop, curator, Northwest Architectural Archives at the University of Minnesota, St. Paul; John D. Randall in Williamsville, New York, and the United Founders Life Insurance Company, Oklahoma City, Oklahoma; David Huntley, director, and Michael Mason, curator, Office of Cultural Arts and University Museums, Southern Illinois University at Edwardsville; and Evan Maurer, director, and Hilarie Faberman, curator, University of Michigan Museum of Art, Ann Arbor. Many other institutions, too numerous to list individually, have supported the exhibition by lending items from their collections.

The following directors and presidents of banks designed by Sullivan took the time to meet with us and assist with research on the history of these buildings: Kenneth Wilcox in Owatonna, Minnesota; John Sagers, Ted J. Welch, and William Crawford in Cedar Rapids, Iowa; Lawrence Mindrup and Max Smith in Grinnell, Iowa; James Posthauer in Lafayette, Indiana; Douglas Stewart in Sidney, Ohio; and John S. Pratt in Columbus, Wisconsin.

Kate Roberts's research on Owatonna and Sullivan's bank there provided a solid basis for the model included in the exhibition. Joan Papadopoulos, business volunteer for the arts, helped with fund-raising in the Chicago area. We thank her for all her work.

Both the exhibition and the catalogue are a co-production of the Chicago Historical Society and The Saint Louis Art Museum. Many people in these institutions helped enormously throughout the planning and implementation periods. Michael Shapiro, curator of nineteenth and twentieth century art at The Saint Louis Art Museum was an important link between both museums. He spent many hours discussing the exhibition and catalogue and was crucial to the success of the project as a whole. This book reflects the sensitivity and careful attention to detail of Mary Ann Steiner, director of publications at The Saint Louis Art Museum. At the same institution the registrar, Helene Rundell, did a masterful job of organizing a complex transportation schedule and caring for the objects. Patricia Cadigan Tucker and Patricia Manthei, public relations officers at both museums, performed the important task of ensuring that this Sullivan exhibition receives the attention it deserves. At the Chicago Historical Society Andy Leo, director of design, Lisa Ginzel, designer, and Paul Madalinski, chief preparator, together with their staff, did a wonderful job designing and installing the exhibition; Russell Lewis, director of publications, and Meg Walter, assistant editor, were alert editors of the exhibition labels; and Walter Krutz made many photographs for the catalogue. Finally, Kitty Hannaford was a very capable and persistent research assistant without whose help many deadlines would not have been met. During her work locating photographs for the catalogue she received a great deal of help from Anne Steinfeldt, assistant curator of Prints and Photographs at the Chicago Historical Society. We are indebted to all of them.

Sullivan to 1890*

David Van Zanten

Introduction

ABOUT 1880 THE TWENTY-FOUR-YEAR-OLD Louis Sullivan joined the firm of Dankmar Adler as chief draftsman and designer; on May 1, 1883, he became Adler's partner.[1] Immediately upon his arrival, the firm's work was transformed. Their first major design was the Borden Block (fig. 1), an extremely simple stone and brick box with large windows and distinctive floral ornament cut deep into the spandrels to bring out the bones of the building's structural frame. This was followed by the Revell Building (1881–1883), the Jeweler's Building (1881–1882) and the Rothschild Store (1881) (figs. 2–4). In the first work, the Revell Building, the ornamental motifs flatten and enlarge on the limestone lintels showing themselves to be elegantly stylized flowers. In the second these start to extend evenly across the surface, balancing the window openings so that the whole façade becomes a sheet of ornament. The ground floor piers are carved as huge, single sunflowers. Finally, in the Rothschild Store, the stone and ironwork of the façade is steadily more elaborately formed into stylized lotus forms as it rises, floor by floor, to culminate in a cut-out floral skyline[2]

The firm's interior decorations, like those in the Grand Opera House (1880), one of their first commissions, and later those of Hooley's Theatre (1882) and McVickers' Theatre (1885), seem to have been similarly articulated with huge, flattened floral patterns (see fig. 47). A small but important decorative fragment survives in the firm's sandblasted door window of 1883 (fig. 5) with its pattern of rigid geometric divisions and free, curving organic forms looking like abstractions of the botanical plates of Asa Gray.

Contemporary observers found it difficult to grasp this art. In 1882 a reporter for the *Daily Inter Ocean* interviewed Sullivan about the decorations in Hooley's Theatre. "Mr. Sullivan is a pleasant gentleman," he wrote, "but somewhat troubled with large ideas, tending to metaphysics. . . . He refers to that work you will see about the stage opening as the differentiation of an absolute truth having something to do with Spencer's first principles and Darwin's doctrine of evolution, with the predicate [sic] of a flower and an ordinary staircase for an hypothesis." He goes on to quote the twenty-six-year-old designer, "These are unclassified forms and stock terms will convey no adequate idea of the successful treatment under a new formula that is a new phase in the art of architecture."[3] Fifty-four years later, in 1936, with the advantage of hindsight and professional nomenclature, Sullivan's younger architect-contemporary, Thomas Eddy Tallmadge, categorized this early work as "a strange combination of Victorian Gothic, English 'Eastlake,' and French Neo-Grec."[4]

Crude as these façades and interiors might appear to us today with the Wainwright Building and the late banks in mind (and confusing as these efforts to categorize them might appear), they were profoundly distinctive and prophetic of what was to come. Sullivan had already created something new in 1880. He was obviously struggling to transform this into something still more extraordinary, which he would accomplish ten years later. The subject of this essay is the evolution of that ideal from Sullivan's introduction to architecture, as a student at the Massachusetts Institute of Technology in September 1872, to its initial culmination in the Wainwright Building, the Getty Tomb, and the Transportation Building at the Columbian Exposition, all designed in the fall and winter of 1890–1891.

Figure 1
Dankmar Adler & Company (Louis Sullivan, designer), Borden Block, Chicago, 1880. Courtesy Chicago Historical Society ICHi–19454.

Figure 2
Dankmar Adler & Company (Louis Sullivan, designer), Revell Building, Chicago, 1881–1883. J. W. Taylor, photographer. Courtesy David Van Zanten.

Figure 3
Dankmar Adler & Company (Louis Sullivan, designer), Jewelers' Building, Chicago, 1881–1882. Kitty Hannaford, photographer.

Figure 4
Dankmar Adler & Company (Louis Sullivan, designer), Rothschild Store, Chicago, 1881. Demolished. Courtesy Harold Allen.

Figure 5
Adler & Sullivan, office door, Western Sand Blast Manufacturing Company, 1883. Courtesy Chicago Historical Society.

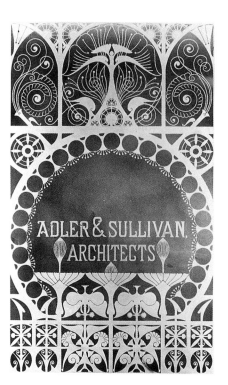

Sullivan's Architectural Education, 1872–1883

Just before his death in 1924 Louis Sullivan published his *Autobiography of an Idea*, depicting his youth and early manhood. Three of its later chapters are devoted to his architectural education, first for a year as a "special student" at the Massachusetts Institute of Technology (1872–1873), then as a draftsman in the offices of Frank Furness in Philadelphia and William Le Baron Jenney in Chicago, and finally for a year at the Ecole des Beaux-Arts in Paris (1874–1875).

Sullivan does not put much store by this "education" in his autobiography, but even in its barest outline it has a certain unity and significance. Proximity might have originally led the Bostonian Sullivan to M. I. T., but once there he let that program's particular character determine what followed. M. I. T. was the first formal architectural school in the United States and followed the French system of the Ecole des Beaux-Arts in Paris. The director, William Robert Ware, had been trained in the atelier opened in 1857 in New York by Richard Morris Hunt, the first American architect trained at the Ecole. In 1871, Ware hired as the teacher of design Eugène Letang, a product of the Ecole. When, after his year at M. I. T., Sullivan repaired to New York, he presented himself to Hunt, sought advice in his office about attendance at the Ecole, and was advised by another Ecole product there, Sidney Stratton, to look up a former student in Hunt's atelier, Frank Furness, in Philadelphia. Sullivan seems to have been uninterested in the English and Anglophile, apprentice-trained architects in New York, like Vaux, Withers, Upjohn, Renwick, and the Potters. Sullivan went to Philadelphia, worked for Furness, then on to Chicago, where he sought employment with the only French-trained architect in the city, William Le Baron Jenney (*diplômé* of the Ecole Centrale des Arts et Manufactures), in preference to the Anglophile Neo-Gothicist Peter B. Wight and the apprentice-trained Americans, Van Osdel, Boyington, Wheelock, and others. Finally, in 1874 he went to Paris, straight to Letang's old atelier, that conducted by Emile Vaudremer. He was clearly following a thread, a newer French thread, in the woof of American culture, in preference to the more traditional English one.

At M. I. T. Sullivan had been trained by Ware and especially Letang in the French system of composition, or architectural reasoning.[5] We can follow this in the thesis designs of his fellow students, especially those of Henry A. Phillips and Charles M. Baker, presented in 1873 and 1878 respectively. Sullivan also gloried in Richardson's Brattle Square Church just erected three blocks from M. I. T. in the Back Bay.

Letang's training in composition at the Ecole des Beaux-Arts is evident in his own school projects, several of which he brought to M. I. T. to serve as models (fig. 6), and their influence is clear in the theses. Phillips's Pumphouse of 1873 (figs. 7 and 8) is elaborated into a monumental composition by the positioning of the reservoir and the addition of mediating stairways and terraces. The arrangement of separate, clearly defined volumes of Letang's Thermal Bath of 1868 reappears in Baker's Town Hall of 1878 (fig. 9) with its dominant octagonal meeting room, subordinate rectangular library and office spaces, and its tall clock tower marking the entry. The text of Baker's thesis begins with "History of the Design" in which he explains step by step, using block diagrams, how he conceived and refined his volumetric composition.[6]

The configurations of these M. I. T. theses do not follow any specific historical models: they are not based on those of Greek temples, Gothic churches, or Renaissance *palazzi*. Rather they have been generated from the immediate requirements stated in the programs by a method of compositional reasoning that, beginning at least in 1878, had to be stated in the thesis text. These students were being taught to "make buildings out of their heads," as Sullivan said of several architects he admired, not to copy from books. Similarly the details are not in any immediately recognizable

historical style. The designs are composed of masonry boxes congruent with their interior functional volumes: the engine room and standpipe of the Waterworks; the meeting room, library, and offices of the Town Hall. The stonework of the plinths, cornices, buttresses, and openings is hefty and exposed, unadorned except for incisions, bevels, and long unconventional curves acknowledging the texture of the material. The result suggests on a modest scale Letang's Thermal Bath, an elegantly modulated composition of volumes, as one would expect at the Parisian Ecole, but one unadorned with conventional historical motifs. Instead its bare surface is emphatically articulated by its structural skeleton and pierced with utilitarian arched openings. The "style" of the building is indefinite, if it could be said to have a style in the historicist sense: the two principal spaces have thermae windows and suggest a Roman bath, while the arcaded forecourt seems Italian Renaissance, and the wings French eighteenth century. All these reminiscences, however, have been reduced to abstract geometric forms, stripped of their identifying details, and unified by a treatment in which each element is shown

to be simply one or another way of building with masonry.[7]

Letang's project and the contemporaneous work of his master, Vaudremer, were products of French "rationalisme classique" which by the 1860s had come to dominate the teaching at the Ecole des Beaux-Arts, finally receiving highest academic approval in 1864 when it was embodied in the winning Grand Prix design by Julien Guadet. The movement had commenced in the 1830s with Henri Labrouste's Bibliothèque Ste.-Geneviève (fig. 10) and had spread to inform much French institutional architecture during the second Empire: Félix Duban's Quai Malaquais façade of the Ecole des Beaux-Arts itself (1858–1862), Victor Baltard's church of St.-Augustin (1862–1868), and Léon Vaudoyer's Marseilles Cathedral (1856–1893), to select three examples on which Vaudremer himself worked at the beginning of his career around 1860. All were compositions of masonry volumes, baresurfaced with utilitarian arched openings, their ornamentation restricted to bevels, incisions, and occasional broad concave curves. In a word, their volumes and surfaces were rendered in their entirety and each element adjusted to the others, all abstracted according to the consistent, embracing principle of spatial and structural expression. Nothing was copied directly from a historical source; no element was added without modification to harmonize it with the whole.

In Europe this French rationalist classicism was paralleled in the English Gothic Revival when first Pugin, then Ruskin, deprecated precise historical reproduction and demanded similar volumetric and structural expression. In ornamental design Owen Jones and his pupil Christopher Dresser were likewise preaching and demonstrating the functional abstraction of all the historical styles—and nature as well—for application in modern design.

Although Letang's and Phillips's designs may have been before Sullivan's years at M. I. T. in 1872–1873, it was not these that he remembered to cite and praise in his autobiography fifty years later, but instead Richardson's Brattle Square Church (fig. 11).[8] "His thought was mostly on the tower of the new Brattle Street [sic] Church, conceived and brought to light by the mighty Richardson, undoubtedly for Louis' special delight; for was not here a fairy tale indeed!"[9] At first glance, this is a puzzling reminiscence since the building almost immediately was overshadowed by Richardson's Trinity Church begun two blocks away, in April 1873, and the great event of Boston architecture during Sullivan's year at M. I. T.[10] But the Brattle Square Church must have made sense to a student of Letang. Richardson had studied at the Ecole from 1859 to 1865 and was a friend of Guadet. The church was one of the clearest examples in America of French rationalist classicism. Its extraordinary tower ends with a surprising flat, Italianate top below which there is a huge frieze of angels, some singing, those on the corners blowing trumpets that extend far out into space. It had been sculpted by the Frenchman Bartholdi. The meaning is clear: as the bells supported in the tower call the worshippers so also do these figures, but more beautifully with voice and trumpet. The frieze brings out the function of the tower it ornaments, but now imaginatively, metaphorically, by sculptural representation. This is specific, however, and very

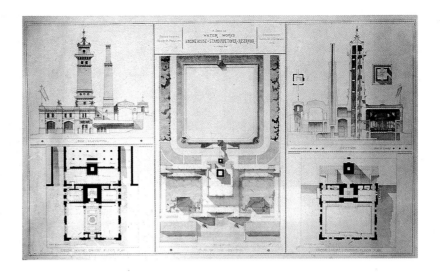

Figure 7
Henry A. Phillips, Thesis Design for a Water Works, Engine House, Standpipe and Reservoir, Massachusetts Institute of Technology, 1873, plan, section and side elevation. Courtesy, M. I. T. Historical Collections.

Figure 8
Henry A. Phillips, Water Works, Main Elevation. Courtesy M. I. T. Historical Collections.

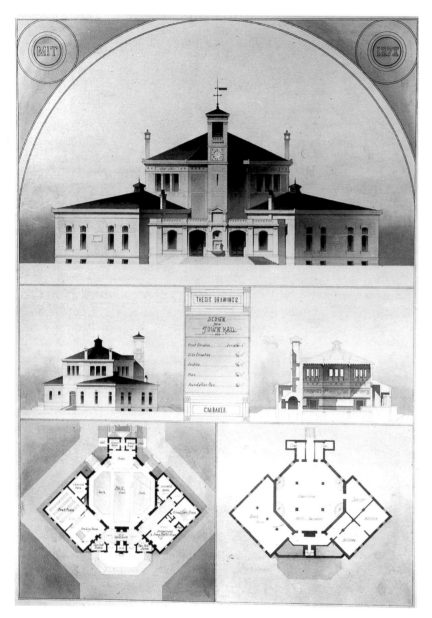

Figure 9
Charles M. Baker, Thesis
Design for a Town Hall,
Massachusetts Institute of
Technology, 1878. Cour-
tesy, M. I. T. Historical
Collections.

different from a historicist reminiscence, as for example, the equation of ecclesiastical and traceried Gothic that the Anglophile Richard Upjohn used in his contemporaneous Central Church (1866) nearby in the Back Bay. The transformation of functional expression into metaphor was the last, most important and most difficult step in the rationalist classicist enterprise; it is appropriate that Sullivan picked out the Brattle Square tower as the great memory of his stay at M. I. T.

Sullivan was by no means the only one in Boston to struggle with metaphorical as well as literal expression in architecture. On Phillips's Waterworks thesis project a series of bulls' heads are set diagonally at the corners of the standpipe spouting jets that cascade down the shaft, reminding one of the joy of the play of pumped water. His is both a giant ornamental fountain and a utilitarian pumphouse. Indeed, Professor Ware's partner, Henry Van Brunt, had been writing about the "poetry" of function in architecture since 1861.[11] With a vagueness compounded by conviction he discoursed on the expressive power of the shapes of a building if handled in the spirit of the Greeks. "Like the gestures of pantomime, which constitute an instinctive and universal language, these abstract lines, coming out of our humanity and rendered elegant by the idealization of study, are returning to architecture its highest capacity of conveying thought in a monumental manner." He was very specific that the originators of this idea were the French designers of the circle of Labrouste.

Editing his essays on the "poetry" of architecture for publication in 1893, Van Brunt employed the term "Néo-Grec" to designate this philosophy.[12] He edited that term into his essay, "Greek Lines," replacing the original, vaguer term "romantic." He was making a distinction that had come to be clear between the functionalist and the poetic descendants of Labrouste, between those (like Vaudremer and Letang) who were satisfied with the elegant statement of the facts of a building, and those who pushed on to elaborate it into an imaginative "fairy tale." This group by Sullivan's day were called the Néo-Grecs because of their exquisite, archaicizing touch. They were led in Paris by Labrouste's admirers, among them Charles Chipiez and Victor-Marie Ruprich-Robert.[13]

There was a profoundly decorative impulse in these men's work and appropriately from 1850 to 1887 Ruprich-Robert was the professor of the history and composition of ornament at the Ecole des Arts Décoratifs in Paris. Between 1866 and 1876 he published in fascicles a beautiful and influential folio volume of plates and text entitled *Flore ornementale*. There he demonstrated methods for the decorative abstraction of real plant types and the elaboration of these into painted and carved ornamentation (figs. 12–14). His last plate, a "Monument to Agriculture" in the form of an exotic temple (fig. 14), exhibits a further quality of the Néo-Grec: its fascination with reconstructions of ancient monuments, oftentimes fantastic (whether intentionally or not). Indeed, it is this visionary archeological tendency which gave the movement its name. What we see in Ruprich-Robert's plate is a statue enclosed in an aediculum of a seemingly Greek archaic sort. But its plan and proportions as well as the brittle style of carving are those of the propylaea at Persepolis, while the decorative motifs that cover its surfaces are not conventional ones, but show their sources in nature and their attachment to the structural surfaces: the cloth around the column shafts; the bees on that cloth; the palm fronds belted to the columns to serve as capitals. Ruprich-Robert here takes a leap beyond his considered text on ornamental design to suggest the origin of the Greek vocabulary in some unplaced, undated Eastern source. He thus makes manifest the impelling idea of a group of Néo-Grec archeologists who explored the exotic Eastern monuments for the sources and ramifications of Greek architecture and produced a series of volumes that contain many of the movement's most compelling images: Pascal Coste's *Voyage en Perse* (1851–1854) and *Monuments moderne de la Perse* (1867); Victor Place and Félix Thomas's *Ninive et l'Assyrie* (1867); Melchior de Vogüé's *Temple de Jérusalem* (1864) and *Syrie centrale* (1865–1877);

and especially Charles Chipiez's *Origines des Ordres Grecs* (1876)—almost a direct explanation of what we see in Ruprich-Robert's plate—*Histoire de l'art dans l'antiquité* (10 volumes, 1881–1914) and *Temple de Jérusalem* (1888–1889; figs. 15 and 16).

Figure 10
Henri Labrouste, Bibliothèque Ste.-Geneviève, Paris, 1838–1851. Courtesy James Austin.

In June 1873, Sullivan arrived in Philadelphia. Having admired a house on South Broad Street he sought out the architect, Frank Furness, and went to work for him. He remained with Furness for five months, until November, when he was let go because of the economic panic which had struck Philadelphia in September with the closing of Jay Cooke's bank. Furness had been recommended to him at Hunt's office in New York, but he had wished to decide for himself. Clearly Ware, Letang, and Richardson had prepared him to recognize good work of a certain sort.

The residence that so struck Sullivan was the Bloomfield Moore House at 510 South Broad Street, first appearing on the city maps in 1874.[14]

Figure 11
Henry Hobson Richardson,
Brattle Square Church,
Boston, 1869–1872. Cour-
tesy Houghton Library,
Harvard University.

Photographs of its interior were published in *Artistic Homes* (1883–1884; fig. 17) but none exists of its exterior due to its refacing by the architect Charles Burns later in the century. This is frustrating because it was precisely in 1873 that Furness's characteristic style was maturing and his work was rapidly evolving, thus preventing conjecture of its appearance. Indeed, there were two other Furness buildings on Broad Street to be seen in 1873: the Rodeph Sholom Synagogue of 1869–1871 (fig. 18) and the Pennsylvania Academy of the Fine Arts of 1872–1876. Why did Sullivan not say that it was the sight of these that sent him to Furness? He is very specific, as he was in picking out the Brattle Square rather than Trinity Church when writing of Richardson in Boston. In the case of the Pennsylvania Academy the reason must have been that there was, as yet, very little of the building to inspect. The cornerstone had only been laid

BAS-RELIEF

MONUMENT A L'AGRICULTURE

Figure 12
V.-M.-C. Ruprich-Robert,
Flore ornementale, *Paris,*
1866–1876, plate 108.

Figure 13
V.-M.-C. Ruprich-Robert,
Flore ornementale, *plate*
129, "Architectural Orna-
ment Carved in Relief."

Figure 14
V.-M.-C. Ruprich-Robert,
Flore ornementale, *plate*
150, "Monument to Agri-
culture."

in December 1872, and construction could not have gotten far beyond the ground floor masonry by the following June. Furthermore, the stone work, even when in place, would not have been cut.[15] Furness's drawings, evidently of 1873, show carved ornament very different from that executed and too summary to be anything more than a general indication of intentions. The synagogue is a more interesting omission on Sullivan's part because it was complete inside and out in 1873 and certainly calling attention to itself. But it was too obviously Moorish, not yet in Furness's personal style.

One must conclude that it was not extravagance that attracted Sullivan's attention, especially since extravagance of many sorts was well represented on Broad Street in that year. James Windrim's confectionary Masonic Temple stood at the corner of Filbert, Edward Tuckerman Potter's Baptist Church at Spruce, Supplee's Lutheran Church at

Arch, to mention only a few. Out of this Mummers' parade of buildings Sullivan had eyes only for a little house far down at the end. He knew what he was looking for, and it was something unrelated to size and elaborateness; it also was something that was just then appearing in Furness's work.

Furness today is chiefly remembered for the Pennsylvania Academy and a series of banks, all finished between 1875 and 1880. It has only recently come to be recognized by David Hanks that before this he had executed a number of large houses for intelligent and influential clients that involved elaborate interior decorations and furniture designs.[16] These included a large house with furniture on Rittenhouse Square for Thomas McKean (1869), interiors and furniture for Fairman Rogers in Newport (ca. 1873–1875), Bloomfield Moore's dwelling, and a dining room for Theodore Roosevelt, Sr. in New York (1876), to

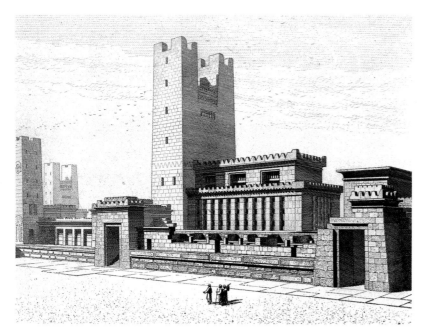

Figure 15
Charles Chipiez, Restitution du Temple de Jerusalem, *Paris, 1889, plate V. Courtesy Regenstein Library, University of Chicago.*

Figure 16
Charles Chipiez, Restitution du Temple de Jerusalem, *plate VI. Courtesy Regenstein Library, University of Chicago.*

mention only those for which we have solid documentation (fig. 20).[17] One should add to this the transformation of the Franklin Market into the Mercantile Library (1867–1869) and the interiors of the Pennsylvania Academy of the Fine Arts itself (finished in 1876).

All of these were neither ignorant nor passive clients, and were active in the movement to found formal design education in Philadelphia. They wanted something specific and explicable and thought that Furness could provide it. Their movement in 1873 caused the local chapter of the American Institute of Architects to open its rooms, newly decorated by Furness, for public exhibitions of architectural drawings and photographs and for *conversazione*.[18] In 1875 the movement brought the theorist and design educator Walter Smith to lecture, both Furness and Fairman Rogers signing the invitation.[19] In 1876 it led to the founding of the Philadelphia Museum and School of Industrial Art (the parent of the Philadelphia Museum of Art) where the English designer and design educator Christopher Dresser was immediately invited to deliver a series of lectures.[20] What these people, the progressive intellectuals of Philadelphia, were thinking about is still clearer in the pages of the *Penn Monthly*, a journal published by the University of Pennsylvania from 1870 to 1882 in an effort to broaden the school's public impact. In 1871, together with articles on literature and science, it published the 1870 address of the Rev. William Henry Furness (father of the architect) to the American Institute of Architects calling for a new style appropriate to modern materials and knowledge of history.[21] In the following year there appeared a laudatory dissertation on Charles Eastlake's *Hints on Household Taste*; in 1873 an essay on the A. I. A. as an organization to educate the general public in the science of design; in 1875 remarks on the principles and personality of the French Gothic rationalist Viollet-le-Duc and the text of Walter Smith's address on design education; in 1876 an essay on architectural principles by Henry Augustus Sims; in 1877 Christopher Dresser's three lectures. The thrust of all this was the deprecation of direct copying in design and the formulation in its place of an approach based on the abstraction of principles from history and the application of these to the specific social and technical problems of America in the 1870s. This was not just the English ecclesiological Neo-Gothicism of Pugin or Ruskin. Eastlake, Smith, and Dresser represented a broader, less moralizing conception of a new style based on science and adapted to the practical improvement of industrial design and design education. Nor was the *Penn Monthly* narrowly Anglophile, presenting the ideas of the Frenchman Viollet-le-Duc and pressing for a unique "American" style. It was an intellectual, not a sentimental, movement that assumed one could reason design through, or, as Sullivan had said of Furness, he could "make buildings out of his head."

Although Furness was at the center of this movement, he left no declaration of what it meant to him. But there is instead the essay of his good friend Sims. After swiftly reviewing the styles of architecture and deprecating the copyism of the Renaissance and Neoclassicism, Sims sets out the principles of English neo-Gothic rationalism: ". . . . The subordination of the exterior of a building to the interior . . . truth of purpose and of construction throughout . . . allowing the mode of construction to show itself, directly or indirectly in the work . . . ornamentation of the construction rather than construction of ornamentation." These principles, however, he sees as also informing the Néo-Grec in France.

. . . . Many clever artists in Paris were moulding and modifying ancient Greek ideas, to adapt them to modern requirements, modern cities and modern purses.

Throwing aside the fixed rules which governed Greek architecture, and reversing the Greek rule, by making the interior of the building the first consideration rather than the exterior, they simply inspired themselves with the Greek feeling and severity, and uniting them with medieval common sense, the result is the style which we now know as the Néo Grec.

Sims goes on to imagine that in the future American architecture will be a combination of the English Neo-Gothic rationalist and the Neo-Gréc, a combination conceivable because of their common emphasis on principle rather than form.

The popular architecture of today in Great Britain is unquestionably the medieval. . . . In France the Néo Grec is without doubt the national style, more or less marked with distinctive peculiarities. I think there can be no doubt that our American architecture of the immediate future will be tinctured to a certain extent by both these schools— for although an architect cannot practice both successfully for the interests and well-being of his art, still a whole generation can consciously and imperceptibly merge the two into one, and partake of some of the distinctive characteristics of each.[22]

In the pages of the *Penn Monthly* and in the homes of enlightened Philadelphians an attitude toward design was coalescing not unlike that which Sullivan had first encountered in Boston. Principle

Figure 17
Frank Furness, Bloomfield Moore House, Philadelphia, c. 1873, Library. Photograph from Artistic Homes, *New York, 1883– 1884. Courtesy The Art Institute of Chicago.*

*Figure 18
Frank Furness, Rodeph
Sholom Synagogue, Phila-
delphia, 1869–1871. Cour-
tesy Historical Society of
Pennsylvania.*

replaced precedent as a basis of design. The ideal was a controlled, scientific exercise of the imagination. In Philadelphia, however, this new art of principle was being practiced, impurely, rather than taught with the mixture of sources Sims predicts, but also imaginatively.

From the furniture surviving from the McKean house of 1869 through the Rogers interior of about 1873 Furness's development as a decorator culminates in the Moore house, the Pennsylvania Academy interiors, and the Roosevelt dining room (see figs. 17–20). The McKean and Rogers designs are relatively restrained and clearly based on English Neo-Gothic models, but are distinctive in the exuberance of their flat incised decorative passages. David Hanks has compared these to the abstract, eclectic patterns published by Christopher Dresser in his illustrated volumes, *Unity in Variety* (1859); *The Art of Decorative Design* (1862); and especially his chromolithographic folio, *Studies in Design* (1874–1876; figs. 21 and 23).[23] Dresser's doctrine of the elaboration of principle rather than the imitation of form was reminiscent of the Gothicists, but he disagreed with their preference for medieval sources and, like his teacher Owen Jones, deduced more abstract rules of pattern design from the whole history of decoration, especially that of Oriental civilizations. This was the doctrine taught by Jones, Dresser, and their friends at the school of the South Kensington Museum in London that Walter Smith had brought to Boston in 1870 and which Rogers, Mrs. Moore, and Furness wished to establish in Philadelphia in 1876. Indeed, Rogers's seemingly Gothicist interior already shows one profound disjunction: instead of the woodwork being left in its natural hue, it has been painted white with touches (of red and blue?) to harmonize it, evidently, with a collection of Chinese porcelain displayed there.

By the time of the Moore, Roosevelt, and Pennsylvania Academy interiors, Furness had taken a step further. His decorative patterns now are much larger in scale and thicker in texture, even more like Dresser's designs (the Moore house cornices, for example), but based on real plant types which he enjoyed sketching.[24] This heightening of key is accompanied by an enlargement of decorative elements to architectural scale: the archway on the Pennsylvania Academy stair landing with its corbelled, squashed columns foretells his later bank façades; the Moore house fireplace with its columns and griffins is a precursor of the Academy archway. James O'Gorman has noted the influence of Ruprich-Robert on Furness, and Neil Levine has convincingly traced this tendency toward overscaling and animation to the French Néo-Grec models Furness had first been trained in at Hunt's atelier in 1859–1861.[25] These French sources are especially evident in Furness's Kensington National Bank of 1875. This exterior as well as the table of the Roosevelt dining room owe little to England: in their heavy, archaic forms they derive from exotic Néo-Grec archeological reconstructions, from the Néo-Grec backgrounds of the paintings of Gérôme and from Ruprich-Robert (figs. 12–14).[26] But more important than an evolution away from English toward French sources, these designs show how thoroughly a fertile imagination like Furness's might combine the two. Starting from the shared principles of stylized natural form and structural expression, he has taken advantage of his American perspective to create designs which are free elaborations of both. What in the end is most French about Furness's work is his avoidance of English archeology and exclusiveness and his unabashed enthusiasm, exoticism, and exaggeration.

From Philadelphia Sullivan went to join his parents who had moved from Boston to Chicago. Again he walked the streets, as he relates in his *Autobiography of an Idea*, looking for a building he liked. Admiring the Portland Block, he sought employment with its architect, William Le Baron Jenney, and there commenced his Chicago career. Before really settling in, however, he left again in July for a year of further formal education at the Ecole des Beaux-Arts in Paris—"headquarters" as he called it.

The Ecole records show that he passed the entrance examination on September 24, 1874, as a student of Letang's master, Vaudremer.[27] Although in his autobiography Sullivan presents himself as the solitary American in his foreign milieu he was, in fact, one of four Americans in Vaudremer's atelier that fall. Alfred Greenough had been there since 1868, Walter Cook since March of 1874, and Arthur Rotch since April.[28] All three had been educated at Harvard, and Rotch has been at M. I. T. as well from 1871 to 1873; Sullivan mentions having known him there.[29] Indeed, between 1868 and 1880, eight former M. I. T. architecture students attended the Ecole as students of Vaudremer, including from March 1875 (thus overlapping Sullivan) William Rotch Ware, Professor Ware's nephew, whom Sullivan also mentions having known at M. I. T.[30] Six other M. I. T. architecture products attended the Ecole during the same period, one respectively in the ateliers of Daumet, Coquart, Pascal, and Guadet, and two in that of Moyaux.[31] Only four Americans in Vaudremer's atelier had not passed through M. I. T., but three of these had either been born or educated in Boston: Alfred Greenough, Walter Cook, and Theophilus Parsons Chandler.[32] Obviously Vaudremer's was the place to go for Bostonians.[33] This is significant not only in that it implies that Sullivan was more methodical than he pretends in his autobiography, but also because it might explain why the experience in the atelier was so anticlimactic. He would have found there little that he had not been acquainted with when he had left M. I. T. fourteen months before. The sheets of paper were bigger, the plans more complicated, the drawing techniques more refined, but the ideas being applied were the same rationalist classicist ones with which he was familiar. Furthermore, these ideas were here being applied in the presence of the actual masters and monuments of the rationalist classicist tradition and had become academic. Instead of working out the logic of a form or building for themselves, Vaudremer's students (or at least the successful ones whose drawings were published or kept by the Ecole) followed earlier rationalist classicist examples close at hand. Projects for a hospital thus tended to be a combination of Gilbert's Asylum at Charenton and Diet's Hôtel Dieu; those of a "Maison pour un riche amateur" were a pastiche of Labrouste's Hôtel Fould.[34]

Vaudremer is described as diffident in his personal relations as well as in his teaching and art.[35] He embodied the cautious side of his movement; his church of St.-Pierre-de-Montrouge (1865–1870) is only a circumspect rationalist modification of its Romano-Byzantine type. A slip Sullivan makes in his autobiography shows that he saw Vaudremer as a compromiser: he calls him the architect of the Sacré-Coeur, a neo-Romanesque pastiche by Paul Abadie that was decided upon in competition in 1874. (Vaudremer served on the jury.) The atelier was never especially brilliant or successful. There were relatively few students, and not many won more than *mentions* in the Ecole competitions (even though Vaudremer was a member of the jury during most of the 1870s). None ever won the Grand Prix de Rome, although

students in his atelier were *en loge* nine times between 1870 and 1880. During these years the school prizes were going to students of Daumet, André, Questel, Ginain, and especially the flamboyant Ernest-Georges Coquart. This last was the star among the *maîtres d' ateliers* just then and when Sullivan's old companion at M. I. T., Henry A. Phillips, arrived in Paris in the summer of 1875, it was to his atelier that he chose to go (joining there George Healy of Chicago—he and his future partner, Louis Millet, would become Sullivan's friends and collaborators.)

None of the Sullivan drawings that survive from these years relates to his work in Vaudremer's atelier but a dozen are tracings from the plates of Ruprich-Robert's *Flore ornementale* (figs. 12 and 24).[36] It is not at all surprising that a young design student should be concerned with the Néo-Grec that winter since it was experiencing another spurt of popularity just then and the courtyard walls of the Ecole building itself had just been painted in garish Néo-Grec patterns by Coquart. But there is evidence that Sullivan's interest in it was more than passing curiosity. The room he rented, which he describes as being two miles from Vaudremer's atelier (and whose location at 17 rue Racine, the Ecole records confirm), was just around the corner from the Ecole des Arts Décoratifs where Ruprich-Robert was teaching the course on ornamental design (and also one Christian-Victor Clopet who appears tangentially in Sullivan's autobiography was to teach mathematics).[37] Can we not assume that Sullivan took the trouble to walk those few steps to attend?

The records of the Ecole des Arts Décoratifs show that Sullivan never formally enrolled.[38] Interestingly, they do show that in 1867 several American architecture students at the Ecole des Beaux-Arts had enrolled, specifically, Charles McKim, Robert Peabody, and Alfred Thorp. They were followed in 1868 by Alfred Greenough from Harvard, Boston, and Vaudremer's atelier. There was only one thing unique and attractive to architecture students that could have drawn them there: Ruprich-Robert's course. In his class Ruprich-

Robert drew ornamental motifs on large canvases in front of the students and explained his principles of decorative abstraction at each step while the students copied them. Beginning in 1866 and finishing in 1876, Ruprich-Robert published his demonstration drawings in groups of plates forming his book, *Flore ornementale*. The book was almost complete by the time the Franco-Prussian War broke out in 1870,[39] so that by 1874–1875 Sullivan would have been able to copy Ruprich-Robert's drawings from the plates of the *Flore ornementale*, perhaps attending just a few lectures now and then to see how the master worked the designs out. (Indeed, only about half the classes were conducted by Ruprich-Robert himself; his assistant, Delaroque, taking charge of the rest).[40] Certainly Sullivan preferred to read Taine, professor of esthetics at the Ecole, rather than to sit and listen to him at the appointed hour each week.[41]

Sullivan was back in Chicago by June 1875.[42] He entered Adler's office five years later, in 1879 or 1880. It is clear that he had learned a great deal during the three years of his architectural education—more than he cared to admit. His decorative inclinations had emerged and been given form by the examples of Furness and Ruprich-Robert. One wonders what there was left to do. Why do we have to wait until 1881 for the Rothschild Store? What was Sullivan designing during those five years? He is much more summary in his treatment of this in his autobiography than he had been in his depiction of his architectural education, but he nonetheless gives us the three important hints: he tells us that he started in the office of William Le Baron Jenney; he relates that he was drawn there by the sight of the Portland Block (fig. 25) which he subsequently discovered to have been the design of Adolph Cudell, he tells us at great length of his friendship stemming from that office with the one-time foreman, John Edelmann. He probably worked as a freelance designer during these years, as Robert Twombly extrapolates, but what he was doing we can only project from these friendships.

Jenney, as has been pointed out, was a great deal more than just a busy commercial architect of the 1880s and 1890s.[43] When he had arrived in Chicago in 1868 he had a grander social standing and a higher education than his predecessors in the profession there, John Van Osdel, William Boyington, Otto Matz, and the rest. He was the son of a New Bedford shipowner, had attended Exeter and Harvard, and had earned a diploma at the Ecole Centrale des Arts et Manufactures in Paris in 1856. More an international businessman and engineer than a designer, he had been named engineer of a projected railway across Mexico at the Isthmus of Tehuantepec, Paris agent of the Bureau of American Securities, engineer on the staff of William Tecumseh Sherman in the Civil War, gaining the title of Major that he enjoyed henceforth at the Union League Club (which he designed in 1886). Upon his arrival in Chicago he went into partnership, not as an architect, but as a planner, with Louis Y. Schermerhorn and John Bogart, both of whom went on to distinguished careers in engineering and business. As planners, they laid out the West Side parks and the boulevards connecting

them—the most important Chicago urban and real estate development around 1870—and they were Olmsted, Vaux and Company's agents for the development of Riverside. When Jenney soon after set up business as an architect it was with Sanford Loring, also of good New England lineage. Loring left the firm in 1872 to become the president of the Chicago Terra Cotta Company, the first business established in the city to develop what was to become the favored material of Sullivan, Root, Burnham, and the Chicago School. From 1875 to 1876 Jenney was professor of architecture at the University of Michigan. He lectured and wrote in Chicago on the history of architecture.[44]

Jenney was also a man of culture. Sullivan admitted this, somewhat deprecatingly, in his autobiography: "The Major was a free-and-easy cultured gentleman. . . . He lived at Riverside, a suburb, and Louis often smiled to see him carry home by their naked feet, with all plumage, a brace or two of choice wild ducks, or other game birds, or a rare and odorous cheese from abroad."[45] But his contribution extended beyond the culinary arts to design and domestic architecture. In the fall of 1875, a few months after Sullivan's return from France, Jenney together with Peter B. Wight organized a display of "Artistic Furnishings and House-Fittings" at the annual Inter-State Industrial Exposition, exhibiting as examples of the best and most upright taste several of their own furniture designs as well as wallpapers by the Englishmen William Burges, Charles Eastlake, and William Morris.[46] Importantly, Jenney and Wight were collaborating with or patronizing several craftsmen whom they established in Chicago: Giovanni Meli at the Chicago Terra Cotta Company; John Legge, an English carver and modeller; and especially Isaac Scott, a furniture maker from Philadelphia who executed most of Jenney's and Wight's designs and worked on his own in the English Neo-Gothic style, espe-

cially for the Glessner family.[47] This establishment of "art furniture" by Jenney and Wight gave courage to young designers recently arrived from the East—Asa Lyon, John Addison, and particularly John Wellborn Root—and it was soon taken up by furniture makers like August Fiedler and Frederick W. Krause.[48] Harriet Monroe remembers Burnham and her brother-in-law Root, who had worked for Jenney and Wight, as fanatic Gothicists upon the founding of their firm in 1873. " . . . They called themselves Gothicists, and made countless drawings of mouldings and other details. They would make each other guess the period of details published in architectural publications, until at last they could place them within ten years in the nation to which they belonged.[49] Their first design, the Sherman House on Prairie Avenue, was a thoroughly Neo-Gothic job and one that Sullivan called, "the best designed residence he had seen in Chicago."[50]

The importance for us of "art furniture" is not just social appeal, but that it was formulated on the basis of rational structural principles rather than the imitation and combination of forms. It was thus applicable to far more than furniture and house architecture; it was an entire theory of design, and as such, it provided a rational basis for design education. In England, it appeared less spectacularly—although more influentially—in the design educational system of the South Kensington Museum and its schools which were established after the Great Exhibition of 1851 following the ideas of Owen Jones and Christopher Dresser. In this form, as a body of principles formulated for design education, it arrived in the Midwest during the 1870s.

We have noted how Frank Furness, Fairman Rogers, and Mrs. Bloomfield Moore participated in the founding of the Philadelphia Museum and School of Industrial Art after the Centennial Expo-

William Le Baron Jenney,
Portland Block, Chicago,
1872. Photograph c. 1878,
before later extensions.
Courtesy Chicago Historical
Society ICHi–01052.

Andreas Adolph Cudell,
Abner Smith residence,
Aldine Square, Chicago,
1873–1875. Courtesy Chi-
cago Historical Society
ICHi–19459.

sition of 1876, inviting Walter Smith, a product of the South Kensington Museum, and Christopher Dresser, professor there, to speak. This was but part of a general movement to establish industrial design education on the English model in the United States.[51] In 1870 the State of Massachusetts had created the office of State Art Education Director and appointed the Englishman Smith to the position. His task was to establish a Normal Art School, organize the art classes at the Boston Museum of Fine Arts, and organize evening classes for artisans in all cities with a population greater than 10,000.[52] Smith was tremendously active, successful, and admired. He published a series of influential volumes: _Art Education: Scholastic and Industrial_, 1873; _Examples of Household Taste_, 1875; _Masterpieces of the Centennial Exposition_, 1876–1878. There developed a movement in the emerging industrial cities of the Midwest to establish the South Kensington-Massachusetts model there. In the early 1870s George Ward Nichols, a one-time collaborator of William Cullen Bryant on the _New York Post_, organized music performances, art education, and the museum in Cincinnati.[53] In St. Louis, Halsey Cooley Ives, a New Yorker trained at the South Kensington Museum, was appointed professor of art and art education at the Polytechnic School of Washington University in 1874, and in 1879 made director of that program in a greatly expanded form as the St. Louis School of Art.[54] Until Ives's retirement in 1909 this was the most highly regarded art school in the Midwest.[55] Finally, and most importantly, in 1878 William M. R. French, an engineer (trained at Harvard and M. I. T.), landscape gardener, and art critic (as well as older brother of the sculptor Daniel Chester French), was appointed secretary of the Chicago Academy of Fine Arts. In 1880 he was appointed its director and in 1882 changed its name to the Chicago Art Institute.[56] Here decorative design appeared in the curriculum in the 1880s taught by Louis Millet, who, from 1880, had been George Healy's partner in the firm of decorators, Healy and Millet. Both were Sullivan's contemporaries at the Ecole des

Figure 27
Andreas Adolph Cudell,
Cyrus McCormick House,
Chicago, 1874–1879. Cour-
tesy Chicago Historical
Society ICHi–01235.

Beaux-Arts as well as his close friends and collab-orators from the Auditorium to Owatonna.[57] What we see here is the pedagogical equivalent of the synthesis that marked Furness's style of decorative design: the broader, functionalist part of the Eng-lish tradition mixed with the French. The problem for men like Jenney, Ives, French, and Millet was the establishment of a whole system of decorative and architectural design to serve industry and real estate development.

Jenney's office was clearly the doorway to advanced design in Chicago in 1875. And Jenney himself was a patron as much as an employer. Among the many other bright young men that Jenney collected in his office were Adolph Cudell and John Edelmann.[58]

Cudell appears fleetingly in Sullivan's autobiog-raphy. Sullivan had sought employment in Jenney's office, he wrote, because he was so struck by Jenney's Portland Block. "Louis learned inciden-tally that the Portland Block had in fact been designed by a clever draftsman named Cudell. This gave him a shock. For he supposed that all archi-tects made buildings out of their own heads, not out of the heads of others."[59] He also appears, more intriguingly, in Thomas Tallmadge's *Architecture in Old Chicago* (posthumously published, 1941).

Of the lesser luminaries who shone through the dying smoke of the Fire, none was more interesting than Adolph Cudell, who hailed from Aix la Chappelle [Aachen], and came to Chicago imme-

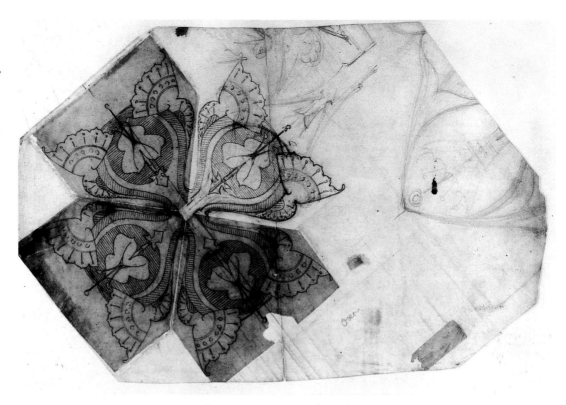

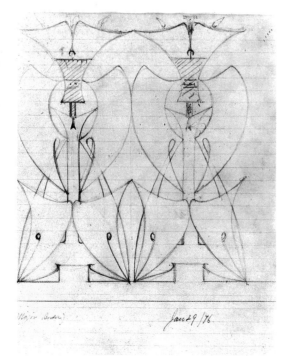

*diately after the fire. . . . Richard E. Schmidt
began his distinguished architectural career in
Cudell's office as a draftsman. He describes him as a
handsome man with black hair in Apollo-like ring-
lets, and as a draughtsman of ability with metic-
ulous technique. . . . The stone columns [at Aldine
Square, fig. 28] had capitals of Greek Ionic ances-
try, and all of the carvings and mouldings had a
crispness and snap that could have come only from
one place, and that was Paris. As I see it, Aldine
Square in style was a melange of the work of the
distinguished Frenchmen of the time of Napo-
leon III—Hittorf, Labrouste, and Garnier all
looked down at us from the façades. . .*[60]

Born Andreas Adolph Cudell in Aachen, Germany on December 5, 1850, he appeared in Chicago in 1871.[61] The next year he founded a partnership with August Blumenthal and later, in 1893, with Arthur Hercz.[62] He had an important practice as a house architect and decorator, using various styles, all of them exuberantly, starting with the Néo-Grec of the large Aldine Square development for Hiram Smith of 1873 and the Cyrus McCormick house of 1874–1879 (figs. 26 and 27). These along with Richard Morris Hunt's Néo-Grec Marshall Field house of 1871–1873 were the most striking domestic designs to be seen in Chicago in the late 1870s and must have made the public vividly aware of the Parisian fashion. But they probably did not seem so new to Sullivan after Furness and Ruprich-Robert, especially since they were basically renditions of the common Néo-Grec of provincial European and New York mansions with all their characteristic (and soon to be clichéd) motifs, rather than explorations of the abstract principles of design.[63]

These principles of design were what concerned Edelmann and brought him together with Sullivan. They were great friends, as Sullivan related in his autobiography, as Frank Lloyd Wright and Irving K. Pond reaffirm, and as Paul Sprague and Donald Egbert have documented.[64] They were actually architectural collaborators for a moment in 1875–1876, decorating the interiors of Moody's Tabernacle and the Sinai Temple. Although both buildings have been destroyed, descriptions and a few drawings survive, as well as several other drawings by Sullivan related to these, some inscribed to Edelmann (figs. 28 and 29).[65] These drawings constitute Sullivan's earliest preserved independent designs.

Edelmann was from Cleveland. He had served as a draftsman there before going to Chicago in 1872, working first for Adler, then for Jenney as foreman. When Sullivan arrived in that office in November of 1873 they became close friends, exercising together at their "Lotus Club" on the Calumet River, talking, and attending performances of Wagner's music.[66] Edelmann practiced on his own from 1873 to 1876 with Joseph S. Johnston, then moved back to Cleveland, farmed in Iowa, and agitated for populist and socialist political causes. In 1879 he was back in Chicago as Adler's foreman and he there introduced Sullivan to his future partner. Then in 1881 he returned to Cleveland, covering the buildings of Coburn and Barnum with Sullivanesque ornament, came back to Chicago to work on the Pullman Building (and perhaps Sullivan's Auditorium), before settling in New York in 1887 (where, according to Frank Lloyd Wright, Sullivan visited him).[67] There he worked for large offices, apparently being responsible for a certain exotic, Sullivanesque decoration that characterized the work of Alfred Zucker.[68] He participated actively in the anarchist movement and died of a heart attack in 1900.

Irving K. Pond depicted Edelmann in his unpublished autobiography. When he had first arrived in Chicago, Pond roomed with two college friends, Ossian Simonds and Clarence Arey. Arey brought Edelmann home one evening,

Having discovered him in the office of the architect for whom both of them were working at the time— or perhaps he discovered Arey. At any rate Edelmann discovered Simonds and me. With Simonds he talked transcendentalism of a sort, with me he talked anything. . . .

While John was talking all his happy nonsense to me and my companions, he would be using his pencil semiconsciously on scrap paper and on the backs of envelopes—on anything that came handy. The scrawls would be destroyed immediately, in the same inconsequential way in which they had been produced. After a time I became sufficiently interested to inquire into the nature of these sketchy objects. John showed them freely and jokingly said their underlying motif was what he called 'the Lotus of the Calumet'. They were the spikey shapes and bud-like things with twisted tendrils which I began to recognize [in more sophisticated form] in the ornament which the young architect Louis Sullivan was employing[69]. . . . John said that was only natural, "as originally he had given Louis the idea."[70]

But it is clear from comparison with the designs of Furness, Ruprich-Robert, and especially Dresser that Sullivan had all the inspiration he needed by 1875 to produce such compositions. They are by no means copies of these sources, however. His designs take off from natural forms, (as his botanical studies prove) as Furness's also had, and as Jones, Dresser, and Ruprich-Robert insisted they should. What is remarkable is how successful Sullivan already was in his original geometric elaboration, as we see in the later pencil drawings for the synagogue decoration of 1876. These drawings are designs for stencilled painted decorations and thus are flat, resembling certain plates in Dresser's *Studies in Design* (see figs. 21–23) which are almost exclusively for two-dimensional wall decoration. (The plates in Ruprich-Robert's *Flore ornementale* were principally for three-dimensional, carved decoration.) Sullivan's basic floral motif, however, with its triangular leaves, lotuslike blossoms, pistils, stamens, and seed pods, seems too close to the later carved motifs in Furness's work for the resemblance to be coincidental. We might assume that Furness's lost stencilled decorations, like those around the edges of the library ceiling in the Moore house which are discernible in figure

17, already in the time that Sullivan was in his office, had developed Dresser's patterns in this way.

These designs also seem to have been applied on a scale and in a manner that must have made even Furness seem cautious. The *Chicago Tribune* published a description of the Moody Tabernacle decoration, probably written by its then art critic, William M. R. French:

Radiating from a skylight 36 feet in diameter, are a series of sprigs, executed in glass and cast iron, in green, yellow, blue and white. Bounding this is an altar circle of rosettes of white glass with blue centre. Outside this circle is a wide band of maroon with gold beads. . . . Then comes the cove, passing at the bottom into an octagonal lintel. The problem then became the unity of the two features, solved by the introduction of huge plant forms starting from the columns, and throwing out from each two leaves, 16 feet long, crossing each other and extending to the skylight. This formation leaves a triangular space between the edge of the maroon band and the point of intersection of the two leaves. The triangles, eight in number, are filled each with an immense flower, 7 feet 6 inches across the top, resting on a gold background.[71]

Some hint of the effect of these huge floral patterns perhaps may be gotten from Sullivan's 1885 treatment of the "funnel" around the proscenium of the Chicago Opera Festival Theatre (see fig. 47).

Critics found these decorations "peculiar," "startling," and exotic, the *Chicago Times* stating of the synagogue work, "To this temple belongs the distinction of being the only church edifice in the city decorated in the Egyptian Style."[72] Sullivan and Edelmann were already formulating "a new style in the art of architecture." What is important about them is that, not only do they demonstrate Sullivan's receptivity to the ideas of Furness, Dresser, and Ruprich-Robert, but the way in which they are applied presages his efforts after 1880 to to treat whole façades as single unified fields of flat ornamentation.

These decorations and the drawings contemporaneous with them are the more tantalizing for the lack of evidence about what Sullivan was doing between 1876 and when he becomes identifiable as Adler's designer around 1880. What else we have from these years is a series of nine drawings of nudes, dated between September 28, 1879, and November 17, 1880 (figs. 30 and 31). All but two were executed on Sundays (and one of those two is dated Christmas Day, December 25, 1879) when he would have had time for sketching at a life class. His touch is exquisite, as one might have supposed. Some are simple *academies* (one includes a chinstrap to help the model keep her pose), but exoticisms appear in several: anatomical exaggerations, transformations into Michelangelesque half-humans, and decorative *staffage*. Among the last is an Ionic column, three vases of svelte archaic shape, and what seems to be a stair baluster of the most elegant Néo-Grec form with a turned base, flairing shaft, and spikey volute top penetrated by a stalklike finial. These show what Sullivan had learned from the plates of Ruprich-Robert and his Parisian contemporaries. That stair baluster is the first hint of the three-dimensional ornament Sullivan began to produce for Adler around 1880, resembling, for example, the baluster of the Selz house (1883) now in the University of Southern Illinois at Edwardsville. In Adler's office Sullivan could elaborate it to cover whole façades, like that of the Rothschild Store, or to inhabit whole theatre interiors, like that of Hooley's which so amazed the reporter for the *Daily Inter Ocean*. By 1884 it was manifested in the monumental crowning of the Troescher Building and in the front of the Ryerson Building where four-story lotus forms hold in panelled bay windows above and below Hindu colonnades elaborately carved in stone.

Between 1886 and 1890 Sullivan passed through a sudden phase of imitating the severe Romanesque style of H. H. Richardson. This commenced abruptly with the design of the Auditorium Building in late 1886 and ended equally abruptly with that of the Walker Warehouse of 1888–1889 (figs. 32–36 and 63).[73] At least by the time of the Walker project this had become a cathartic experience for him: a thing he seems to have felt he had to do and get past. Irving K. Pond remembers, "When sometime after the completion of that building

[the Auditorium], Sullivan was called upon to design the Walker Warehouse at Adams Street near the river (and in sight of the Field Wholesale) he remarked in my presence, 'I'm going to show 'em in the Walker building more than Richardson ever knew.'"[74] Frank Lloyd Wright later wrote of that building in *Genius and the Mobocracy* (1949): "The master brought the manila sketch with the elevation penciled upon it, laid it over my board with the remark, 'Wright, there is the last word in Romanesque.' I puzzled over that remark a lot.

Figures 32 and 33
Adler & Sullivan, Auditorium Building, Chicago, 1886–1889. Cervin Robinson, photographer.

What business had he with the Romanesque?"[75] After the Walker Warehouse, in the fall of 1890, came the Wainwright Building and Sullivan's completely individual "new" style.

During this Richardsonian episode, Sullivan's façades ceased to be thin sheets of ornament and were transformed into thick, massive walls of stone enlivened only by their shape, proportions, pattern of openings, and rendered surfaces. His picturesque skylines were replaced by the severe cubic geometry that was to characterize his work henceforth.

Inside these structures the geometry of his spaces became firm and dramatic while his ornament—transformed by the impact of Richardson—found a cogent relationship to architectural form and surface. This episode coincided with the design of the Auditorium, the largest structure yet erected in Chicago and the one that made Adler and Sullivan's reputation.[76] Sullivan's initial designs were more elaborate and tentative than the final, decisively Richardsonian design, the execution of which began on January 28, 1887. For the first time in his

career Sullivan faced a truly huge challenge. Prophetically, his response was to simplify, but not only to simplify in the sense of abstracting, as in the case of the Wainwright where he seemed to follow his maxim, "Every problem . . . contains and suggests its own solution."[77] In 1886, he simplified by retreating from his own Furnessic ornamental fantasizing and accepted the tutelage of another master, Richardson.

An episode so dramatic could not pass without inspiring certain myths. Sullivan's Auditorium design is particularly close to that of Richardson's Marshall Field Wholesale Store, erected in the west Loop in 1885–1887 (see fig. 62).[78] From this it has been inferred that the promoters insisted upon the imitation.[79] Likewise John Wellborn Root is supposed to have criticized Sullivan's first projects, saying, "he was going to smear another façade with ornament,"[80] and Sullivan is supposed to have reacted in pique. But the fact that Sullivan carried on the Romanesque after the Auditorium design and the tremendous importance of it for his later work belie any simple, anecdotal explanation: this was the watershed and we must examine it closely.

Irving K. Pond, S. S. Beman's chief draftsman from 1880 to 1887, wrote in his *Autobiography* of the Richardsonian style arriving in Chicago around 1885.[81] The Marshall Field Wholesale Store and the Glessner and MacVeagh Houses were the local examples of his work, all begun in 1885 and finished in 1887.[82] But Richardson had died young in April 1886; his stylistic cloak was suddenly empty and thus one that a competitive man like Sullivan could put on, if only momentarily. The real competitor Sullivan had to best was John Wellborn Root who, in the mid-1880s, was demonstrating that Richardsonianism was a whole way of thinking and one that invalidated the established system which Sullivan had so carefully learned and was so vigorously applying.

Root too died five years later, at the age of 41 in January 1891.[83] His partner, Daniel Burnham, carried on the firm as an urbanist and public personality, eclipsing his former partner. We perhaps have forgotten how formidable the firm of Burnham and Root already was in the 1880s, and how the designer, Root, rather than the administrator, Burnham, dominated it. While firms like Adler & Sullivan were erecting large lofts of the sort of the Borden Block and Ryerson buildings in the 1880s, Burnham & Root were refining the high elevator office building, beginning with the Montaulk Block of 1881. They erected a host of these, culminating in the Masonic Temple of 1890–1892, at twenty-two stories the tallest skyscraper in the city. Before the skyscraper boom of 1890–1893, only token opposition to the firm's dominance was offered by S. S. Beman with his Pullman Building (fig. 40), Jenney with his Home Insurance Building, Cobb with his Chicago Opera House, and Holabird & Roche with their Tacoma Building (fig. 57). The red walls of the Loop, and especially LaSalle St., were Root's creation.

Furthermore, Root was well-born, well-educated, and well-connected. "He knew . . . the value of social prestige," Sullivan wrote of him. "To be the recognized great artist, the center of acclaim and *reclame* was his goal."[84] He was cosmopolitan and self-confident. He equalled his East Coast confreres in the quality of his work and was calmly studying what he hoped were the beginnings of a bare, western "commercial style" when he died.[85] This commercial style was in brick, granite, and terra-cotta with the round arches, thick, simple masses, and primitive Romanesque detailing of Richardson, but independently and imaginatively manipulated. The Rookery Building, the design of which was begun in April 1886 (figs. 37 and 38), was its great expression and a monument of which Sullivan, as he started to formulate the Auditorium, must have been profoundly aware. Henry Van Brunt in 1891 described Root as the most original of the Richardsonians.

It was his fortune to contribute to this great America-Romanesque experiment nearly or quite as much as Richardson did. The latter introduced the revival, and, through the unexampled vigor of his personality, had already led it on to an interesting

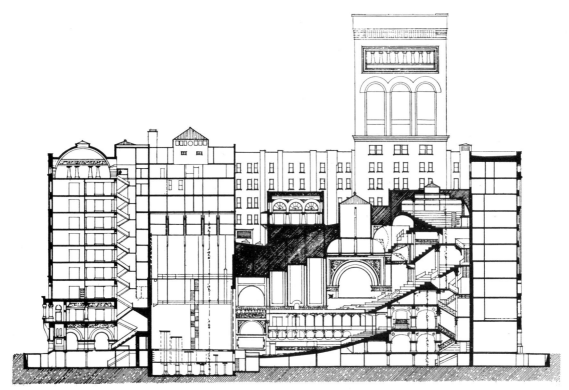

THE AUDITORIUM, CHICAGO—LONGITUDINAL SECTION.

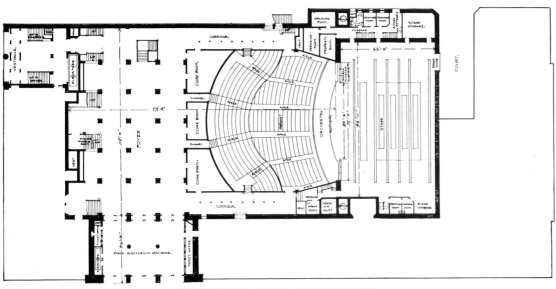

THE AUDITORIUM, CHICAGO—PLAN OF FIRST STORY.

Figure 34
Adler & Sullivan, Audi-
torium Building, Chicago,
1886–1889, section. From
Engineering News, 1894.
Courtesy University of
Chicago Library.

Figure 35
Adler & Sullivan, Audi-
torium Building, Chicago,
1886–1889. Plan From:
Engineering News, 1894.
Courtesy University of
Chicago Library. Plan is
reverse of section pictured
above.

point of development, when his career was interrupted by death; the former [Root] carried it still further toward the point of its establishment as the characteristic architectural expression of American civilization. The latter conferred upon it power, the former, variety, and both, with their trained coadjutors in the profession, have already proved that the experiment is not merely a revival, barren of results, like the neo-Gothic, the free classic or Queen Anne, and other numerous English trials, but the introduction and probable acclimatization of a basis of design, *established upon Romanesque round-arched elements, which elements have never been carried to perfection, and were, consequently, capable of progression* [Van Brunt's emphasis].[86]

Wright in *Genius and the Mobocracy* (1949) wrote: "H. H. Richardson (great emotionalist of the Romanesque Revival) was the only one whose influence the master most felt. And John Root, another fertile rival of that time who knew less than the master but felt almost as much. The master admitted he sometimes shot very straight indeed. They were his only peers."[87] Root, nonetheless, must have been demonstrating something Sullivan already knew. Richardson's Romanesque was an elaboration of the round-arched vocabulary of the Ecole des Beaux-Arts. His Brattle Square Church, which Sullivan remembered so clearly when writing his *Autobiography of an Idea* in 1922–1924, was an early work and clearly showed its derivation from the French tradition in its smooth masonry surfaces, its sometimes mannered arrangement of openings, and its insinuated Greco-Roman details, the most prominent of which was Sullivan's beloved tower frieze. In Trinity Church, designed in 1873–1874, Richardson dressed this up in a more archeological and picturesque Franco-Spanish Romanesque style that was mistaken by some as the essence of his art.[88]

It was not only Richardson who was practicing this French round-arched architecture in New York and Boston in the 1870s and 1880s.[89] A number of Ecole students were producing impressive examples: Alfred Thorp (student of Daumet,

1864–68) in his New York Racquet Club (1875–1876); Cady, Berg (student of André, 1877–1879), and See with their Metropolitan Opera House (1881–1884), the Auditorium's immediate competitor; McKim (student of Daumet, 1867–1870); Mead, and White with their Goelet and Judge Buildings of 1886–1887 and 1888–1889. The vocabulary had been established by Hunt with his Tenth Street Studio Building of 1858, carried on by his student, George Post, in his Long Island Historical Society of 1878–1880, and in 1885 given magisterial expression in Walter Cook's De Vinne Press Building (fig. 39).[90] In this last, a powerful compactness and simplicity of shape are combined with an elegant, if mannered, pattern of openings and an exquisite brick and terra-cotta surface—French enough to be quite free from Richardsonianism. Cook, of course, was Sullivan's old colleague in Vaudremer's atelier. His design was greatly admired and widely published. The smooth-faced, Beaux-Arts Italianate vocabulary was clearly defined, paralleling that of Richardson's Romanesque in the 1880s. It received its definitive statement in McKim's Boston Public Library of 1887–1898, facing Richardson's Trinity Church of ten years earlier across Copley Square in Boston as a sort of challenge or, better, correction. It arrived in Chicago with the New Yorker, S. S. Beman, in 1879, commencing in his great Pullman Building on Michigan Avenue in 1883 (fig. 40) which Pond correctly is at pains to describe as not merely Richardsonian.[91]

It was in the midst of this that Sullivan designed the Auditorium. He seems to have been inspired by the example of his more receptive Ecole colleagues to reconsider what he had glimpsed in Paris but had, at first, put aside as irrelevant to his essentially decorative purposes. Now he must have felt he should reconsider. What is deceptive is that his first step was to imitate the recently dead master, H. H. Richardson, rather than to experiment, like Thorp or Cook. Next, he quickly began exploring Richardson's sources and working out his own ideas about form, vocabulary, interior space, and ornament. He bested Root by going to his

source, Richardson, and Richardson by going to his source, France.

What Richardson and Root enjoyed in the round-arched Romanesque was its primitive, elemental quality, which they emphasized in their rough surfaces, over-scaled details, and barbaric ornament. They justified it as a primitive style for the raw young American nation.[92] At its origins, however, in Paris, and especially in Labrouste's seminal Bibliothèque Ste.-Geneviève (see fig. 10),

the round-arched style was remarkable for the subtlety of its modulation and the exquisiteness of its decorative passages, passing, as we have seen, into the Néo-Grec. It had been this quality that Cook had reintroduced in the De Vinne Press Building. It was also this quality—more Labroustian and Néo-Grec than Romanesque—that Sullivan brought out in the later, upper portions of the Auditorium, particularly in the tower where his own office was to be established. Significantly, he

Figure 36
Adler & Sullivan, Auditorium Building, Chicago, 1886–1889, interior, modern condition. Cervin Robinson, photographer.

published the tower separately in the *Inland Architect* in October 1888. Its smooth surfaces recall those of the Bibliothèque Ste.-Geneviève; its compressed corbelled cornice is like the Egyptoid compositions of the Néo-Grecs, as also is its row of stocky, splayed archaic Doric columns.

The most overtly Néo-Grec of Sullivan's designs at this time is the Ryerson Tomb in Graceland Cemetery of 1887 (fig. 41). It has the smooth surfaces, the heavy proportions, the simplified Egyptoid details and even the diminutive pilistrade and pyramidal top of the Auditorium tower. But here these features have expressive meaning. The basic element—the tomb chamber with a pyramidal termination—reproduces a typical common ancient Egyptian tomb type that also appeared in the Levantine cultures.[93] This exotic but elemental symbol of death is elaborated and exaggerated in the Ryerson Tomb by thickening and simplifying the mouldings, by pressing against each side two closed, mastaba-like masses articulated only with

long, earthward curving surfaces, and by building the whole of polished black granite.

This is a profoundly lithic structure, not in the sense of Richardson or Root, in the roughness of its surfaces, but in the squareness of its forms, the precision of its assembly, and in the sharpness of its mouldings. One understands that it is made of blocks, carefully cut and neatly fitted. The quality of *assemblage*—of stone decoratively and structurally cut with infinite, primitive precision—was a basic characteristic of the French Néo-Grec, especially as it appeared in the great archeological volumes of the years around 1870–1880 that must have been Sullivan's chief sources in his reconsideration of his French experiences: those of Coste, de Vogué and Chipiez mentioned earlier (see figs. 15 and 16). The sense of *assemblage* together with specificity of symbolism likewise characterized the Néo-Grec of the Paris ateliers, especially as it was represented in journals like the *Revue générale de l'architecture* and *Croquis d'architecture*, the volumes

Figure 39
Babb, Cook & Willard,
De Vinne Press Building,
399 Lafayette St., New
York, 1885. Courtesy
Museum of the City of
New York.

Romanesque vocabulary. To Sullivan, that vocabulary's attraction lay in its reductivism and here it was reduced to almost nothing. It opened a vista, nonetheless, into a whole world of primitive, elemental forms that he had first glimpsed in Paris and that soon, by 1890, he would master.

Sullivan's exteriors of the years 1886–1890, however, are less telling than his interiors. One of the clichés of Sullivan scholarship is that he was not a good planner.[94] In spite of his Beaux-Arts education and in spite of the inspiration he gave Frank Lloyd Wright—the most brilliant spatial planner of the epoch—Sullivan is depicted as having displayed his talent only in the design and ornamentation of façades. In 1977 Paul Sprague challenged this view by examining Sullivan's house plans, especially that of his own vacation dwelling at Ocean Springs, Mississippi of 1890, with its axes and modulated volumes.[95] More recently, the material presented in Narciso Menocal's chapter on Sullivan's houses after 1893 makes him emerge as one of the most symphonic, if sometimes overly enthusiastic, manipulators of space working in the years around 1900, even in this modest genre.[96] He may not have been able to find full play for himself in the skyscrapers that seem to constitute the central monuments of his mature oeuvre, but there was most certainly a planner in Sullivan trying to fight its way clear.[97] The late banks with their urbanistically shaped volumes and monumental arrangements of geometric openings clearly reflect Sullivan's fascination and skill with three-dimensional composition.

There was, however, one genre in which Sullivan's facility as a spatial planner showed itself, a genre of basic importance from the very beginning of his career with Adler: that is theatre interiors. In a series of at least eleven striking designs, from the Grand Opera House interior of 1880 through the Auditorium of 1886–1889 to the Schiller Theatre of 1891–1892, Sullivan worked out a distinctive style of spatial composition as well as his celebrated ornament, the latter integrated at the beginning with architectural form.[98] Such designs are, of course, the most ephemeral of architectural types

of Ruprich-Robert, and César Daly's *Architecture privée* (1864–1877) and *Architecture funéraire* (1871). The latter was a publication of tomb designs, which brings us back to a basic point: for all the Frenchness of Sullivan's touch, he is not copying any specific French model. There are no close parallels to the Ryerson design among Daly's plates. Sullivan has gone back into history—as the French would have insisted he do—and constructed a powerful fantasy from the primitive, lithic imaginings of the Néo-Grec archeologists.

Sullivan accepted the simplicity of a primitive source but not its crudity and insouciance. This is Greek (or sometimes Byzantine), not Romanesque. The picturesque quality in Root's work, which Harriet Monroe excuses as the reflection of still developing taste and haste, is very different from the clean-shaven precision of Sullivan's. In this sense the Walker Warehouse is the "last word": one could not squeeze any more delicacy of window arrangement and surface out of the

Figure 40
Solon S. Beman, Pullman
Building, Chicago, 1882–
1884. Courtesy Chicago
Historical Society ICHi–
19460.

and with the sole exception of the Auditorium all of these are now destroyed, many within a few years of their construction. It has always been known that Adler was highly regarded as a theatre designer. What we need to acknowledge and explore is just how basic theatre design was to the firm during the formative years, 1880–1892 (accounting for $4,572,948 of work out of a total of about $9,000,000, according to Morrison's list),[99] and of what great importance this series of projects was for Sullivan's artistic evolution. Down to the Schiller Building, Adler and Sullivan were theatre architects, and Sullivan himself a theatre decorator. When they addressed the newly invented steel frame office building in 1890–1893, Sullivan turned his theatre solution inside out and began to apply to façades what he had already worked out in monumental interiors.

Adler had established his reputation with the Central Music Hall of 1879, once on the corner of State and Randolph Streets (figs. 42 and 43) where he had erected a fairly bald rectangular space across the back half of his lot, behind a block of offices facing on State Street and had constructed two superimposed balconies above a slightly ascending orchestra. The ceiling was flat, with a cove, and the space was narrowed toward the stage by two diagonal walls bearing the organ pipes. It was a simplified version of the conventional theatre layout with tiers of balconies ascending from the well of the orchestra.

This spatial paradigm was continued in the earlier, smaller theatres from the beginning of the Adler and Sullivan partnership: the Grand Opera House of 1880 (figs. 44 and 45), the Kalamazoo Academy of Music of 1881–1882, and the first McVickers Theatre of 1885 (fig. 46).[100] Something new, however, appeared with the Chicago Opera Festival Theatre hastily thrown up in the spring of 1885 inside the shell of Boyington's Inter-State Industrial Exposition building (fig. 47).[101] Adler and Sullivan were obliged to transform a long, narrow space roofed with semicircular iron arches into an opera house. They were tremendously successful by enframing the stage with a

Figure 41
Adler & Sullivan, Martin
Ryerson Tomb, Graceland
Cemetery, Chicago, 1887.
Courtesy The Art Institute
of Chicago.

vast, funnel-like surface, decorated with one of Sullivan's biggest and most dramatic Furnessic floral bursts. The excessively elongated shape was thus counteracted both acoustically and esthetically and a new type of Opera space created.

The Auditorium (1886–1889), the Pueblo Opera House (1888–1890), and the Milwaukee Stadt Theater (1890) were larger in capacity than the earlier theatres and in larger structural envelopes (figs. 34–36, 48–51).[102] Here Adler & Sullivan developed the implications of the Opera Festi-

val design on a more elaborate, permanent scale. They took advantage of this paradigm to spread the seating longitudinally down the axis from the proscenium and to shape a series of contrasting acoustical and architectural volumes along that axis. Acoustically, these compositions start with an arched or square funnel-like space expanding away from a relatively small proscenium opening. Then, where the first balcony cuts across, the funnel ends and the ceiling is carried up to define a self-contained architectural volume. Finally, the second

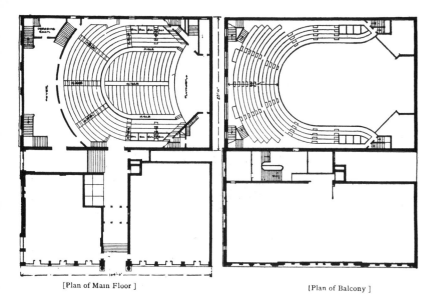

[Plan of Main Floor]   [Plan of Balcony]

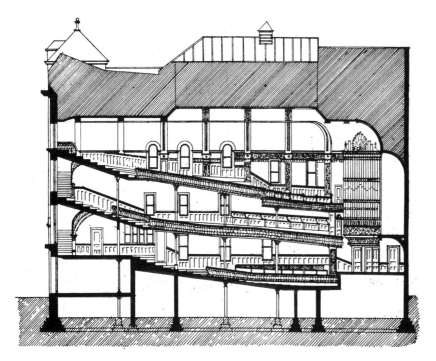

Figure 42
Dankmar Adler & Com-
pany, Central Music Hall,
Chicago, 1879, plans.
From Engineering News,
1894. Courtesy University
of Chicago Library.

Figure 43
Dankmar Adler & Com-
pany, Central Music Hall,
Chicago, 1879, section.
From Engineering News,
1894. Courtesy University
of Chicago Library.

balcony is excavated out of the far wall of this volume. The result is as if a small theatre of the conventional sort were linked to the stage by a sort of telescope and levitated one story above the orchestra: there is a strange disassociation from the stage that permits the geometry of the theatre space to make itself felt. Acoustically, however, each building was made a kind of amplifier and the results were greatly acclaimed.

Sullivan's problem was how to articulate and unify this strange and novel arrangement of spaces. He could do so freely because while the shapes were acoustical they were not structural, resembling the interiors of Baroque churches or Beaux-Arts' student projects: thin shells suspended inside a protecting exterior envelope.[103] Sullivan experimented with several solutions, the most complex of which is at Pueblo. There he defines an octagonal space by continuing the first balcony around the space to embrace the boxes enframing the proscenium and cutting out one of the eight sides as the stage opening. Above this, at the level of the first balcony, the space is brought to a square and three huge Richardsonian arches are thrown across the two sides and the proscenium. The two lateral arches open into deep, lush landscape paintings. To this point his composition is a powerful Beaux-Arts scheme of big forms and simple, strongly contrasting shapes—like the central *salle des pas perdus* of a French student design. But then the practical exigencies of a theatre space break in and muddy things. The fourth, back wall of the space, instead of being closed with another great arch, opens up into a series of ill-defined spaces around the second balcony. The ceiling of the room furthermore, instead of resting on the arch tops, climbs down the stage side to form the funnel-like sounding board around the proscenium opening and opens up on the other side toward the second balcony. The ceiling surface, nonetheless, is magnificently shaped and coffered in the Roman manner.

The Milwaukee Stadt Theater interior (figs. 50 and 51), coming just after Pueblo, was simpler but more effective. Sullivan eliminated the centralized composition of the first level, which at Pueblo had implied a point of attention in the middle of the orchestra rather than on the stage, but kept the motif of a monumental volume at the second level, above the balcony. Here it is a square volume, with its lateral faces defined by huge, single ornamental panels, covered with a dramatic barrel vault which acknowledges the axis of the proscenium. This square, vaulted volume floats above the first balcony and is attached to the stage by a smooth, relatively shallow funnel-shaped space.

The Auditorium (figs. 34–36), however, was Sullivan's first and biggest effort to solve the problem of space and in it were the seeds of both Pueblo and Milwaukee, as well as of his greatest triumph of theatre composition, the Schiller. In the Auditorium for the first time, he had given the seating space independent, monumental definition by placing at the first balcony level two great arches, leading into deep painted landscapes (with inscriptions from his own poem, "Inspiration") supporting a coved ceiling and a broad skylight. This tall space, however, is linked to the proscenium by the acoustical funnel that is extended halfway down the length of the space in the form of a series of arched segments rather than as a slanting surface.[104] As a result, instead of a static, centralized composition as at Pueblo, this is a crescendoing composition, one moving away along the proscenium axis as the floor rises like a natural hillside (rather than an openwork of balconies as in conventional theatres).[105]

The culmination of this development was Sullivan's last theatre, in the Schiller Building, which opened on October 17, 1892 (figs. 52–53). Here he returned to the segmented funnel of the Auditorium, realizing that its shape permitted the unification of the high central volume of the auditorium space and the immediate forestage area. The entirety of the walls and ceiling is a modulated series of broad arches telescoping out from the proscenium until, at the front of the second balcony, they culminate in a shallow, barrel-vaulted space marked by a monumental panel in relief. Here is a

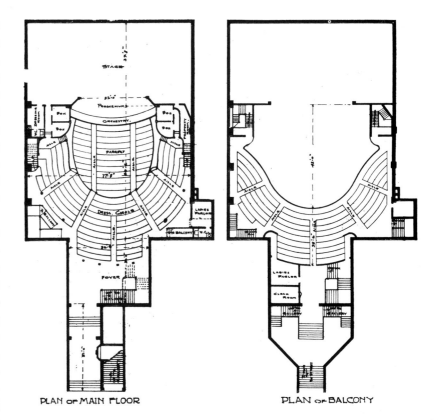

PLAN OF MAIN FLOOR   PLAN OF BALCONY

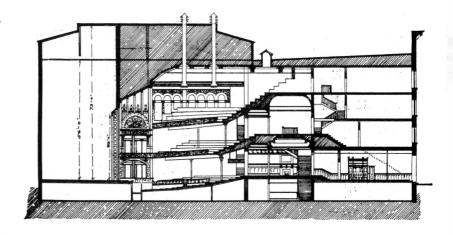

Figure 44
Dankmar Adler & Company (Louis Sullivan, designer), Grand Opera House, Chicago, 1881, plans. From Engineering News, *1894. Courtesy University of Chicago Library.*

Figure 45
Dankmar Adler & Company, Grand Opera House, Chicago, 1881, section. From Engineering News, *1894. Courtesy University of Chicago Library.*

magisterial orchestration of volumetric shapes, but not of the arbitrary sort that so often characterized the French student designs as well as Sullivan's Pueblo project. Instead Sullivan uses a single form, the segmented barrel vault, determined by the sight lines and acoustics of the space, simply and powerfully elaborated.

One of the most important achievements in Sullivan's theatre interiors is his application of an ornament that is both omnipresent and unobtrusive.[106] His symphonic compositions of form read clearly through veils of color and ornament that seem to grow from their surfaces. Historicist ornament—columns, pediments, traceried arches— would have disrupted the purity of his geometric combinations. It is as if the simplicity of his Richardsonian treatment of exteriors had been turned outside in and rendered in colored, carefully worked materials rather than textured stone.

During the early 1880s Sullivan's Furnessic ornament had been a continuous pattern laid over and imposed on a façade, as in the Rothschild Store. Unity was achieved by continuity of pattern and largeness of scale, most dramatically in the "funnel" of the Chicago Opera Festival Theatre. This was a two-dimensional, angular, applied ornament, best when flattest. In order to conceive his new Auditorium ornament Sullivan had to recognize the mass of the architecture underneath, and again the model that helped him to do so was Richardson's.

Richardson's ornament is not much discussed today. Indeed, since the 1920s his strength has been seen to lie in his relative eschewal of ornament.[107] But this was not so much an eschewal as a reintegration of ornament with mass: a basically new concept. Richardson's ornament, beginning with Trinity Church, was less Romanesque than Byzantine, based on the massed acanthus leaves of the decoration in Hagia Sophia and San Marco in Venice. It permitted broader, flatter ornamental surfaces than had been possible with the natural or crocket carving of the Gothic and the Gothic Revival. It could be carved in grainy materials and sunk into surfaces to bring out their bulk or spread across planes to enrich them. His interiors for the New York State Capitol in Albany are among the earliest, most varied, and most splendid demonstrations. The Byzantine acanthus pattern was simple, abstract, and without canonical form so that it could be blended with his rock-faced masonry and seem an equivalent. In a word, Richardson's seemingly modest ornament continued the simplification, emphasis upon mass, and novel combinations of his work in general and was basic to it.

The opportunities for imaginative elaboration in English Neo-Gothic design lay chiefly in flat panels within a structural framework of one sort or another. The basic skeleton remained set. Suddenly, with Richardson, the whole surface became a field to be rendered in various qualities of plain and rich, hard and soft. Architecture became sculptural. Architecture and ornament became the same, the latter growing out of the former.

In Chicago, Root gloried in these new opportunities. The Rookery, and especially its Syrian-arched doorway, proves Van Brunt's characterization of Root as the most imaginative of the Richardsonians: its rock-faced masonry flattens to Islamic diapering in the spandrels and to over-scaled Celtic belting around the opening, with strange Byzantine half-columns growing out of each side (see fig. 38). The Rookery still stands for us to enjoy, but Root achieved similar effects in his Insurance Exchange (1884–1885), his Phenix Building (1885–1887), Rand-McNally Building (1880–1890), Masonic Temple (1890–1892), and Women's Temple (1890–1892). His plans for the Columbian Exposition in steel and polychrome terra-cotta suggest that he there would have made the ultimate display of Richardsonian decorative fantasy. Significantly Henry Ives Cobb's Fisheries Building at the Exposition was regarded as the most faithful to Root's projects and was remarkable for its decorative surface of diminutive sea animals (fig. 54).[108] The French architect R.-J. Hermant (student of Vaudremer, 1874–1880), writing on the Exposition in the *Gazette des Beaux-Arts*, admired the ornament of

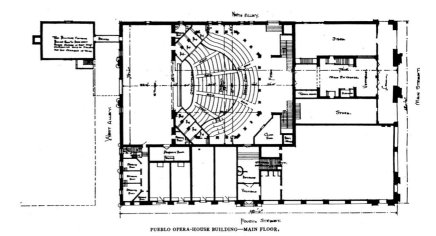

PUEBLO OPERA-HOUSE BUILDING—MAIN FLOOR.

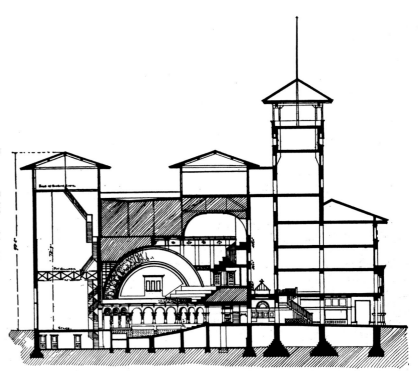

PUEBLO OPERA-HOUSE BUILDING.
[Longitudinal Section.]

Figure 48
Adler & Sullivan, Opera House, Pueblo, Colorado, 1888–1890, plan. From Engineering News, 1894. Courtesy University of Chicago Library.

Figure 49
Adler & Sullivan, Opera House, Pueblo, Colorado, 1888–1890, section. From Engineering News, 1894. Courtesy University of Chicago Library.

Figure 50
Adler & Sullivan, Stadt Theater, Milwaukee, 1890. plans and section. From Engineering News, *1894. Courtesy University of Chicago Library.*

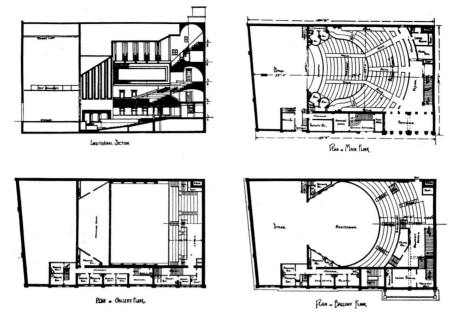

DEUTSCHES STADT THEATER, MILWAUKEE, WISCONSIN.

Figure 52
Adler & Sullivan, Schiller Building, Chicago, 1891– 1893, plans. Demolished. From Engineering News, *1894. Courtesy University of Chicago Library.*

Figure 53
Adler & Sullivan, Schiller Building, Chicago, 1891– 1893, section. Demolished. From: Engineering News, *1894. Courtesy University of Chicago Library.*

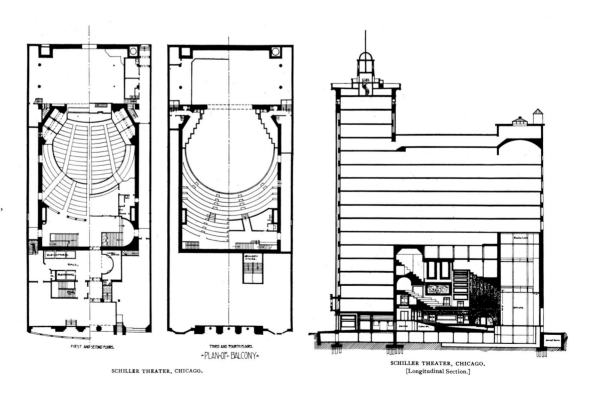

Figure 51
Adler & Sullivan (Redecorated by Arthur Hercz),
Stadt Theater, Milwaukee,
interior, 1890. Courtesy
Milwaukee County Historical Society.

the Fisheries Building even more than Sullivan's own Transportation pavilion.[109]

Sullivan too was clearly looking at Richardson's ornament at that date.[110] The flattened acanthus appears in his drawings already in 1885 and is everywhere in the Auditorium ornament of 1888–1889. Like Root's, Sullivan's ornament takes on a richness and three-dimensionality that permits it to seem hard or soft, expressing the mass of the architectural forms to which it is now closely related. Yet almost at once it starts to become abstract, flat, and fantastic—sometimes overtly Islamic—as Sullivan's Néo-Grec touch asserts itself and everything becomes precise, delicate, and beautifully mannered in its curves.

What in Richardson, Root, and Cobb is thick and three-dimensional, is flattened out in Sullivan and run across clearly defined surfaces. Indeed, to start with the ornamental motifs in Sullivan's work —attractive and exotic as they are—misses the point, for they are but the infilling of compositions of flat panels and surfaces. In Sullivan's early work, like the Jeweler's Building façade or the McVicker's vestibule (see figs. 3 and 46), these panels are a flat, abstract organizing grid laid over the surface. In the Auditorium, where he starts to develop spatial shape in the acoustical interior, the panels become the edges of volumetric facets and his whole ornamental undergrowth is shaped and molded to form the animated surface of symphonically responding spatial shapes.

During the fall and winter of 1890–1891 Sullivan designed the Getty Tomb (October 1890)[111] near the Ryerson Tomb in Graceland Cemetery, the Wainwright Building in St. Louis (November 1890–April 1891),[112] and the Transportation Building for the Columbian Exposition (January–April 1891),[113] in that chronological order (see figs. 41, 66, 67, 70). In these designs Sullivan's mature and profoundly individual style appears.

This was clearly another decisive moment in his career. The Auditorium had been inaugurated on December 9, 1889 (although interior work continued for a year after that), leaving both Adler and Sullivan exhausted, as well as famous and fairly wealthy. Sullivan took a long vacation during January and February 1890. He described it in his autobiography:

Louis's case was one of utter weariness. He went to central California. The climate irritated him. Then he moved to Southern California—the climate irritated him. . . . He had friends in San Diego and stayed there a while. . . . Then on to New Orleans. That filthy town, as it then was, disillusioned him. Here he met Chicago friends. They persuaded him to go with them to Ocean Springs, Mississippi, eighty odd miles to the eastward on the eastern shore of Biloxi Bay. He was delighted and soothed by the novel journey through cypress swamp, wide placid marsh with sails of ships mysteriously moving through the green, and the piney woods. . . .

Here, in this haven, this peaceful quiescence, Louis's nerves, long taut with insomnia, yielded and renewed their life. In two weeks he was well and sound.

He bought property and began to build the shingled vacation house with its rose gardens that was to be so dear to him.

'Twas here Louis did his finest, purest thinking. 'Twas here he saw the flow of life, that all life became a flowing for him, and so the thoughts the works of man. 'Twas here he saw the witchery of nature's fleeting moods—those dramas gauged in seconds. 'Twas here he gazed into the depths of that flowing, as the mystery of countless living functions moved silently into the mystery of palpable or imponderable form. 'Twas here Louis underwent that metamorphosis which is all there is of him, that spiritual illumination which knows no why and no wherefor, no hither and no hence, that peace which is life's sublimation, timeless and spaceless.

He ends this reverie: "Arrived in Chicago, Louis at once went to work with his old time vim. . . . The steel-Frame form of construction had come into use . . . and in St. Louis it was given first authentic recognition and expression in the exterior treatment of the Wainwright Building, a nine-story office structure, by Louis Sullivan's own hand."[115]

Sullivan's chapter ends here. The story of the invention of the skyscraper ended here as well in critical opinion well before Sullivan wrote these words in 1922–1924. But the events of 1890–1891 were only half over. On November 29 the Wainwright plans were announced: some three weeks later, on December 13, Burnham named a panel of five East Coast architects to design the buildings of the Columbian Exposition, added five Chicago designers (including Adler & Sullivan) shortly thereafter, and brought the ten firms together for a grand meeting on January 10, 1891. Richard Morris Hunt presided as president of the Board of Architects, Sullivan as secretary. And it was at this moment that Root disappeared from the scene, struck down by pneumonia. Burnham and McKim took charge and conceived the classical confection of the Court of Honor. This episode of the winter of 1890–1891 Sullivan later placed in a separate chapter in his *Autobiography of an Idea* as a tragedy unfolding beyond his ken or control: "A small white cloud no bigger than a man's hand was soon to appear above the horizon."[116] But this was not separate nor beyond Sullivan's control during those busy months. The "White City" was formulated without models and precedents while he created his own new vocabulary and his invention was in part a critique of Burnham's. To Chicagoans and to visitors from all over the world, the Transportation Building was the first revelation of Sullivan's great ideal. A neat skyscraper away in St. Louis was a footnote.

There was a general transformation of American architecture around the time of that winter extending beyond both the Wainwright Building and the Fair. Richardsonianism had died. Every bright young architect in the nation acted: McKim in New York; Cass Gilbert nearby in Minneapolis; Eames and Young nearer by in St. Louis with the great Cupples Station development begun in 1890.[117] Sullivan had to act too, and he did so along lines parallel to his contemporaries. He adopted a lighter, more lyrical style, classical with certain exotic undertones, rendered most often in terracotta which permitted him to extend his ornament broadly across his surfaces. The basic similarity in touch and compositional simplicity between Sullivan and McKim at this moment has been noted,[118] yet it only serves to make more striking the originality and power of Sullivan's solutions, which intrigue where McKim's reassure.

The modern critical emphasis upon the Wainwright Building as the watershed has allowed critics to see it as a transparent revelation of the steel frame and its vocabulary as specifically invented for this.[119] That vocabulary, however, had already appeared in the entirely masonry Getty Tomb (the drawings for which are dated to October 1890) and reappears in the Transportation Building, of wood and staff. It is clearly a vocabulary initially unrelated to the material in which it was executed and conceived in a broader context than that of the tall office building.[120]

The first and smallest of Sullivan's buildings of that winter, the Getty monument, is a gloss on the earlier Ryerson Tomb. We noted of that earlier design its consciousness of assemblage from carefully cut blocks. In the Getty Tomb this becomes even more emphatic: the three lower courses read as a base for the rainbowlike arches that occupy the faces, and the voussoirs of the arches are set off by diapered spandrel zones. Three huge slabs sit on top like lids distinguished at the sides by the wavelike cutting of their end profiles. The whole rests on a wide plinth cut into a broad Néo-Grec curve. What is interesting, however, is that the symbolic specificity of the black, Egyptoid Ryerson design is gone. The Getty Tomb is merely a sober stone box. It is a system of architectural form, a solution "so broad as to admit of no exception." In the Transportation Building the demonstration of such a system would become his expressly stated objective. Indeed, in the case of the Getty Tomb, Sullivan himself may have felt that he had gone too far. In his next and last tomb, that for Ellis Wainwright in St. Louis of 1892, he returned to symbolism, adding a dome internally clothed in magnificent mosaics.

The Wainwright Building was the next step. The solution is the same, but on a larger scale: a box with a lid on top; one structural motif on each face, in this case a primitive pilistrade. Nothing is permitted to disturb the regularity of the system, not even the door. As in the Getty Tomb, the surfaces are flat and distinguished by their patterning (or lack of it). Although clothed with terra-cotta above the second floor, the structure is boxy, as if in big pieces, with square piers and a lintel.

In so treating the Wainwright Building, Sullivan transformed it into the great Néo-Grec fantasy: the primitive temple form where the primordial origins of architectural elements are decipherable. We see this type in the last plate of Ruprich-Robert's *Flore ornementale* and in Chipiez's reconstructions, especially his most famous, that of Solomon's Temple (1889) (see figs. 14–16). De Vogüé and Viollet-le-Duc had depicted Levantine and Byzantine architecture as a later return to primitive Greek principles.[121] Vaudremer's Byzantine was Néo-Grec in this sense as it evolved during the 1870s and 1880s.[122] Basic in all of this was the reconstitution of the conventional capital as a pier top with recognizable botanical or sacrificial items attached, then abstracted to acknowledge the material and structural situation. Sullivan's Wainwright pilistrade is another in this series.

In the Transportation Building Sullivan also seeks to bring forward a single image, in this case by detaching and emphasizing one element, the huge arched doorway rendered in gold, red, blue, and green. The Frenchman J.-R. Hermant assumed that this had symbolic force as an evocation of a railroad tunnel. In the context of the Fair, however, it is one of the first of Sullivan's Syrian arches enframed in a square taking up Root's great *trouvaille* at the Rookery Building. Designed immediately upon Root's death, it is a gesture of homage to the multicolored terra-cotta and steel vision of the Fair he had been proposing,[123] and also a correction, as Sullivan renders it in lush, controlled ornament instead of Root's primitive Celtic belting, and even brings it closer to a historical source, the spreading *liwan* façades of the mosques at Isphahan.[124]

After the revolutionary designs of the winter of 1890–1891 came Sullivan's skyscrapers of 1891–1892: the Schiller Building (January 1891), the Fraternity Temple project (September 1891), and the Union Trust Building in St. Louis (March 1892). In these he develops his solution, but not directly from the Wainwright.

In two aspects—Sullivan's emphasis on shape and his use of a masonry, arched vocabulary—these skyscrapers hark back more to the Getty Tomb and the Transportation Building as well as to the Walker Warehouse and the Auditorium interior. What distinguishes the Schiller Building and the Union Trust is their emphatically molded three-dimensional massing, the U-shape of the latter stepping back as it rises above the street, and the tower and haunch of the former, affirming a new façade line along Randolph Street, then rocketing above it as a freestanding element. The indented, stepped volume of the Fraternity Temple would have been the full elaboration of these two smaller statements of Sullivan's idea and would have towered above the Loop like a Babylonian ziggurat.

Donald Hoffmann has pointed out that at this moment Sullivan was formulating a system of urban composition with these new steel-frame elevator buildings, achieving symphonic form through setbacks and towers.[125] This first series of designs, from the Getty Tomb to the Schiller Building, were not the light steel cages Chicago architects were beginning to design at the time: Root's Rand McNally and Reliance; Beman's second Studebaker; Holabird & Roche's Pontiac and McClurg Buildings. Sullivan's were volumetric, masonry structures. It was only beginning with the thinner surfaces of the Guaranty Building of 1894–1895, then with the grill-like treatment of the Carson Pirie Scott Store, and the Condict and Gage Buildings of 1898–1901 that Sullivan really comes to express the elasticity and lightness of the steel frame. In 1892 he was still the great French composer who had emerged with his theatre interiors after 1886.

The assumption of all that I have tried to indicate is that Sullivan was profoundly French during his formative years. He had to discover French design bit by bit and at first combined it with the Anglo-American ideas of Ruskin, Jones, Dresser and Furness. But by 1890 he had emerged as the last great Néo-Grec. In Rand McNally's *A Week at the Fair* of 1893 Adler & Sullivan sign a description of the Transportation Building which commences: "The style is somewhat Romanesque, although to the initiated the manner in which it is designed on axial lines, and the solicitude shown for good proportions and subtle relation of parts to each other will at once suggest the methods of composition followed at the Ecole des Beaux-Arts." This may seem perverse because until recently French design has been categorized as that of the Ecole des Beaux-Arts and that has been seen as equivalent to Burnham's vision of the Columbian Exposition: white copies of Greek and Roman temples. Neither Burnham nor McKim, however, felt the French to be correct or exemplary, because of their licenses (especially those of the Néo-Grecs) and they sometimes equated the Beaux-Arts with the bizarre. In the last ten years historians led by Neil Levine have come to appreciate the basic Néo-Grec current in French nineteenth-century architecture which emphasized principle over form and exotic, primordial sources over conventional models. These Néo-Grec French principles were also Sullivan's. He understood the deeper, inner lesson of the French tradition and advocated it in America.[126]

Before the Columbian Exposition of 1893 Sullivan seems to have sought to project a French image. He had learned his French from his Genevan grandmother. He dropped the "s" in the pronounciation of his first name and enunciated his middle name "Henri," not Henry. Frank Lloyd Wright tells us his closest friends were the two half-Frenchmen Healy and Millet, and that his habits were very Parisian.[127] He had the most important French journals in his library, the *Revue générale de l'architecture*, the *Encyclopédie d'architecture* and the Néo-Grec student publication, *Croquis d'architecture*.[128] He was appreciated by the French; casts of his ornament were installed in the Musée des Arts Decoratifs.[129] But this was all in the 1890s. By the time he wrote his *Autobiography of an Idea* in 1922–1924, the Néo-Grec Beaux-Arts he had known had faded from memory, replaced by the pleasant, picturesque, "correct" vision of the younger American students there. The riveting visions of the Néo-Grec, in which exoticism com-

Figure 54
Henry Ives Cobb, Fisheries Building, World's Columbian Exposition, Chicago, 1891–1893, detail. Courtesy Chicago Historical Society. From James B. Campbell, Campbell's Illustrated History of the World's Columbian Exposition, *Chicago, 1894.*

bined with the science of design and the truth of construction, were no longer anything anyone would recognize. So Sullivan wrote it out of his story and made his architectural education sound like a kind of Huckleberry Finn ramble instead of the focused pursuit of the Néo-Grec, one of the most general and characteristic goals of the age.

Tentative as this text is, it represents work pursued continually for most of my career and I am deeply indebted to a number of good friends and colleagues for inspiration and help. First of all Paul Sprague who, when I was a freshman in college, showed me his masters' thesis on Sullivan and first awakened my fascination with this subject and with architectural history in general. Second, Neil Levine whose lengthy study of the Néo-Grec strand in nineteenth-century architecture has formed the foundation of my own understanding of the epoch. Third, my late wife, Ann, with whom I discussed this project frequently and upon whose good sense and factual knowledge I have been gratefully dependent. The group assembling this exhibition and catalogue have been wonderfully close and helpful—Wim de Wit, Rochelle Elstein, William Jordy, Cervin Robinson, Robert Twombly, Sabra Clark. Many others have been helpful with advice and information: John Vinci, Tim Samuelson, Sally Chappell, John Zukowsky, Susan Rossen, David Gebhard, Peter Goss, Theodore Sande, Nancy Bartlett, Baryl Manne, Doris Sturzenberger, as well as the students in my seminar at Northwestern University, Barbara McClosky, Holly Dankert, Kitty Hannaford, and Paula Hutton. A generous Northwestern University research grant aided my study of several buildings. Finally, I must happily acknowledge the helpfulness of David Huntley in charge of the Sullivan project at the University of Southern Illinois, Edwardsville, and the information, counsel, and cheerfulness of my colleague, Carl Condit.

1. Sullivan states in his *Autobiography of an Idea* (American Institute of Architects, 1924) that he first met Adler early in 1879 and that soon Adler offered him a one-third partnership for the first year, fifty percent thereafter, starting on May 1, 1880. "On the first day of May, 1880, Adler & Co. moved into a fine suite of offices on the top floor of the Borden Block aforesaid. On the first day of May, 1881, the firm of Adler & Sullivan, Architects, had its name on the entrance door" (pp. 256–57). Paul Sprague, however, states that the firm first appeared under the dual name in 1883 and so must have been founded on May 1, 1882 (*The Drawings of Louis Henry Sullivan* [Princeton: Princeton University Press, 1979], 28). Robert Twombley confirms the 1883 date (announced on the first page of the *Chicago Tribune* of May 1) but proposes that Sullivan had been working in Adler's office in some part-time capacity since at least as early as 1879.

2. The documentation of Sullivan's early work began, of course, with Hugh Morrison, *Louis Sullivan: Prophet of Modern Architecture* (New York: Norton, 1935) and with Willard Connely's biographic research (*Louis Sullivan: the Shaping of American Architecture* (New York: Horizon, 1960). Paul Sprague focused upon these problems in his doctoral dissertation, *The Architectural Ornament of Louis Sullivan and his Chief Draftsmen*, (Princeton, N.J.: Purdue University Press, 1968) and his volume cited above. Important analytical insights were added by James O'Gorman, *The Architecture of Frank Furness* (Philadelphia: Philadelphia Museum of Art, 1973) and Theodore Truak, "French and English Sources of Sullivan's Ornament and Doctrine," *Prairie School Review* 4th quarter XI, No. 4, [1974]: 5–28). Robert Twombly's *Louis Sullivan: His Life and Work* clarifies things further, as will the publication of the Richard Nickel-John Vinci list of Sullivan's oeuvre.

3. *Daily Inter Ocean*, August 12, 1882: 13. I owe this fascinating reference to Robert Twombly.

4. *Dictionary of American Biography* XVIII (New York: Scribner's, 1936) 196.

5. On the M. I. T. program: M. Shillaber, *Massachusetts Institute of Technology School of Architecture and Planning, 1861–1961* (Cambridge, Mass.: M. I. T. Press, 1963). The organization of the M. I. T. Historical Collections now permits much more specific study of this matter and I have profited greatly from it. J. A. Chewning, a graduate student at M. I. T., is working on this topic, and has found a photograph of one of Sullivan's student projects, among other things. Several parallel histories of American architectural education and schools have been published: Spiro Kostof,

The Architect: Chapters in the History of the Profession, (New York: Oxford University Press, 1961); T. K. Rohdenburg, *A History of the School of Architecture* [of Columbia] (New York, 1954); K. C. Parsons, *The Cornell Campus* (Ithaca: Cornell University Press, 1968).

6. M. I. T. Historical Collections.

7. Our understanding of the methods and character of French Beaux-Arts architecture has been focused and reformulated during the last ten years by a series of volumes, among them: D. D. Egbert, *The Beaux-Arts Tradition in French Architecture* (Princeton, N.J.: Princeton University Press, 1980); A. Drexler, ed. *The Architecture of the Ecole des Beaux-Arts* (New York: Museum of Modern Art, 1977); Robin Middleton, ed., *The Beaux-Arts and Nineteenth Century Architecture* (London: Thames & Hudson, 1982). What follows in this essay is an extension of this reevaluation and is most specifically dependent upon the work of Professor Neil Levine at Harvard who, from the commencement of his work, has picked out the fundamental importance of the Néo-Grec strain: his Master's thesis, *The Idea of Frank Furness' Buildings*, Yale University, 1967; his doctoral dissertation, *Architectural Reasoning in the Age of Positivism: the Neo-Grec Idea of Henri Labrouste's Bibliothèque Ste.-Geneviève* (Yale University, 1975); and his essays in Drexler's and Middleton's volumes.

8. Jeffrey Karl Oechsner, *H. H. Richardson: Complete Architectural Works*, (Cambridge: M. I. T. Press, 1982) cat. no. 29. Begun in 1869 and dedicated in December 1873.

9. Sullivan, *Autobiography*, p. 188.

10. Oechsner, *op. cit.*, no. 45.

11. Henry Van Brunt, "Greek Lines," *Atlantic Monthly* VII, no. 44 (June 1861): 654–67. See also William A. Coles, *Architecture and Society* (Cambridge, 1969), a publication of Van Brunt's writings with basic biographical information.

12. Henry Van Brunt, *Greek Lines and other Architectural Essays* (Boston: Houghton Mifflin, 1893).

13. On the Néo-Grecs, see the publications of Neil Levine cited in note 7, above.

14. The house first appears in *Jones' Atlas of Philadelphia*, which was certified correct by the City on July 28, 1874. It is indicated as having a cut stone façade. Moore listed this as his address first in *Gospill's Business Directory* in 1876. The

later façade is published in Moses King's *Philadelphia and Notable Philadelphians* (New York: Moses King, 1902). In 1916 John G. Johnson purchased it to house his celebrated art collection, where it was open to the public from 1922 to 1933.

15. O'Gorman, *The Architecture of Frank Furness*, 80–85. Extensive documentation and drawings survive at the Academy.

16. D. Hanks and Page Talbot, "Daniel Pabst—Philadelphia Cabinetmaker," *Bulletin of the Philadelphia Museum of Art* LXXIII, no. 316 (April 1977).

17. Hanks and Talbot document the McKean house (whose façade is reproduced in Moses King's *Philadelphia*); the Rogers interior is reproduced in C. W. Eliot, *The Book of American Interiors*, (Boston, 1876), facing p. 113; the Roosevelt room was documented by David Hanks after the table was purchased by the High Museum in Atlanta, Georgia (D. Hanks and D. C. Pierce, *The Virginia Carroll Crawford Collection: American Decorative Arts, 1825–1917* (Atlanta: High Museum of Art, 1983), 78–79. Charles Moore in his *Life and Times of Charles Follen McKim* (Boston: Houghton Mifflin, 1929), 37, describes Furness as he appeared in 1870: "Frank Furness, one of the first architects of the city (whose recent successes were the Tom McKean house at Walnut at Twentieth, and the conversion of the Market House into the Mercantile Library) wanted McKim to come into his office. He had seen a photograph of a casino McKim had done and had pronounced the opinion that the boy had learned to draw."

18. *Penn Monthly*, IV (July 1873): 503–505; O'Gorman, *Frank Furness*, 200.

19. The letter was printed as part of the lecture publicity and a copy survives in the archives at the Philadelphia Museum of Art. The lecture itself was published in the *Penn Monthly* VI (1875): 492–510.

20. All three lectures were published in the *Penn Monthly* VIII (1877): 12–29, 117–129, 215–25. Dresser was visiting the Centennial Exposition on his way to Japan (R. Dennis and J. Jesse, *Christopher Dresser, 1834–1904* [London, 1972]).

21. *Penn Monthly* II (1871): 295–308; republished by Don Gifford, *The Literature of Architecture* (New York: Dutton, 1966), 390–404.

22. Sims's diaries survive, proving a close acquaintance between the two, and have been the subject of a Master's thesis at the University of Pennsylvania by Leslie Beller. See Sims's essay, "Architectural Fashions," *Penn Monthly* VII (1876): 700–711.

23. See Simon Jervis, *High Victorian Design* (London: National Gallery of Canada, 1985). On Dresser: Dennis and Jesse; *Christopher Dresser: ein viktorianischer Designer, 1834–1904* (Cologne: Kunstgewerbe Museum, 1981); Stuart Durant is completing a definitive work. On Owen Jones, see Michael Darby, *Owen Jones and the Oriental Influence in Nineteenth Century Design*, doc. diss. (Reading University, 1974); *The Islamic Perspective* (London: Islam Festival Trust, 1983). On the South Kensington Museum: H. Cole, *Fifty Years of Public Work* (London: G. Bell & Sons, 1884); Shirley Bury is completing a definitive monograph. See also R. Redgrave, *Manual of Design* (London: Chapman & Hall, 1876); Ralph Wornum, *Analysis of Ornament* (London: Chapman & Hall, 1856). Most recently, W. Herrmann, *Gottfried Semper: In Search of Architecture* (Cambridge: M. I. T. Press, 1984).

24. Such sketches survive among his papers. See O'Gorman, *op. cit.*, 34–37.

25. Levine, *The Idea of Frank Furness' Buildings*.

26. V.-M. Ruprich-Robert, *Flore ornementale* (Paris: Dunod, 1866–1876). This parallel has been pointed out by O'Gorman and Turak.

27. Archives Nationales, Paris, Aj^{52}383. He was presented by Vaudremer on 11 September 1874, sat for the examination on 24 September and was admitted to the school on 22 October. His record notes no awards in the competitions.

28. Archives Nationales, Paris, Aj^{52}367, 360, 381. See Greenough's obituary, *American Architect and Building News* XVI (August 16, 1884), 73. He was thoroughly committed to the Ecole, spending most of his short life there and in Europe. He had been offered Ware's old position at M. I. T. when Ware went on to Columbia in 1883, but Greenough declined due to poor health. On Rotch: Harry L. Katz (with Richard Chaffee), *A Continental Eye: The Art and Architecture of Arthur Rotch* (Boston: Atheneum, 1985).

29. Sullivan, *Autobiography*, p. 185.

30. The others were: William Marcey Whidden and Louis A. Sonrel (admitted 1878), William Everett Chamberlain and Edmund R. Wilson (admitted 1879) and Alexander W. Longfellow, Jr. (admitted 1880). Clearly this breaks down

into two waves, one comprised of Rotch, Ware and Sullivan in 1874–75 and a second comprised of Whidden, Sonrel, Chamberlain, Wilson, and Longfellow in 1878–80.

31. William Bigelow, admitted in 1873 as a student of Pascal; Henry A. Phillips, admitted in 1875 as a student of Coquart; William Appleton Burnham and Henry Sargent Hunnewell, both admitted in 1877 as students of Moyaux, and A. D. F. Hamlin, admitted in 1879 as a student of Guadet.

32. Theodore Sande informs me that it is a "family tradition" for Chandler to have attended the atelier of Vaudremer while in Europe after graduating from Harvard. Chandler's name does not appear in the Ecole records.

33. Certainly the more numerous American painters at the Ecole in the 1870s concentrated in certain ateliers, namely those of Gérome and Bougereau. (See *Chicago Times*, February 13, 1876, where a writer describes Gérome's atelier as principally made up of Americans and Englishmen.)

34. A project for a "Hôtel pour un riche amateur" by Vaudremer's student L.-F. Beauvais that was awarded a *première medaille* in October 1873, is published in *Croquis d'Architecture* X, 4 (1873). A number of projects from later in the decade survive at the Ecole in Paris: hospital projects by J.-R. Hermant and Antoine Leconte; a restaurant in a park and a city gate by J.-A. Ruy. In 1880 Hermant and Ruy won the *Second Grand Prix* and the *Premier Second Grand Prix* with designs for a hospital, published in A. Guérinet, *Les Grands Prix de Rome d'architecture, 1850–1900* (Paris, n. d.).

35. Walter Cook, "Emile Vaudremer," *Journal of the American Institute of Architects* III (1915): 299.

36. Art Institute of Chicago.

37. Clopet's quite thorough dossier survives at the Archives Nationales, Paris: Aj[53]129. He was a Parisian, *bachelier ès sciences*, 1856, trained at the Ecole Centrale des Arts et Manufactures (1859–1862) and the Ecole des Beaux-Arts (1862–1866). From 1863 to 1877 he was *répétiteur* in the *cours scientifiques* at the Ecole and in 1876–1877 *Professeur suppléant* of perspective. In October 1875 he was hired as professor of mathematics at the Ecole des Arts Décoratifs in which capacity he served until his death in 1885.

38. Archives Nationales, Paris, Aj[53]143: records of foreign students enrolled at the Ecole National des Arts Décoratifs.

39. It was reviewed as if complete in the *Moniteur des Architectes* of 1870 just before the outbreak of the War.

40. The school records (Archives Nationales, Paris, Aj[53] 131) show the attendance varying that year between nine and thirty-six. One evidently came when one wished.

41. Sullivan, *Autobiography*, p. 233.

42. Sullivan implied in his autobiography that he had stayed in Paris for two years. Willard Connely established that he was back by July 1875, from dates in a notebook now in the Avery Library (*Louis Sullivan: The Shaping of American Architecture*, 69–73). Sprague notes a reference in Andreas' *History of Chicago* II, 5 (Chicago, 1884) 566, to the effect that he had returned in June 1875 (*The Architectural Ornament of Louis Sullivan*, 26). Twombly located the announcement of his arrival in New York on the *Britannic* the day before in the *New York Times* of May 24, 1875.

43. David Van Zanten "The Nineteenth Century: The Projecting of Chicago as a Commercial City and the Rationalization of Design and Construction," *Chicago and New York: Architectural Interactions* (Chicago: Art Institute of Chicago, 1984) 30–48. The basic source: Theodore Turak, *William Le Baron Jenney: A Nineteenth Century Architect*, Ph.D. diss., (University of Michigan, 1966); Turak is preparing a monograph.

44. For example, the lectures on the history of architecture he delivered at the University of Chicago and published in in the first several volumes of the *Inland Architect and News Record*.

45. Sullivan, 203–204.

46. *Chicago Tribune*, September 26, 1876. See Sharon Darling, *Chicago Furniture: Art, Craft and Industry, 1833–1983* (Chicago: Chicago Historical Society and Norton, 1984) 157–76. On Wight: Sarah Landau, *P. B. Wight: Architect, Contractor and Critic, 1838–1925* (Chicago: Art Institute of Chicago, 1981).

47. Meli: Sharon Darling, *Chicago Ceramic and Glass: An Illustrated History from 1871 to 1933* (Chicago: Chicago Historical Society, 1979), 162; Legge: Peter B. Wight in *Construction News*, January 1, 1910; Scott: David Hanks, *Isaac E. Scott: Reform Furniture in Chicago* (Chicago: Chicago School of Architecture Foundation, 1974).

48. Fiedler published an interesting illustrated pamphlet, *Artistic Furnishing and House Decorating* (Chicago, 1877).

49. Harriet Monroe, *John Wellborn Root: A Study of his Life and Work* (Boston: Houghton Mifflin, 1896) 35.

50. Sullivan, p. 285.

51. Stuart MacDonald, *The History and Philosophy of Art Education* (New York: American Elsevier Publishing Company, 1970).

52. Walter Smith, *Art Education: Scholastic and Industrial* (Boston: J. R. Osgood, 1873).

53. G. W. Nichols, *Art Education Applied to Industry* (New York: Harper & Bros., 1877).

54. Ives was a man of tremendous accomplishments. His papers survive in the Washington University archives and The Saint Louis Art Museum library. See, *Halsey Cooley Ives, LLD. 1847–1911* (St. Louis: Ives Memorial Association, 1915).

55. The school as an institution was awarded the first prize among American art schools at both the Columbian Exposition of 1893 and the Pan American Exposition of 1901 in Buffalo.

56. Only a scattering of French's papers seem to survive at the Chicago Art Institute but a good deal more information will become available when the Daniel Chester French project of the National Trust for Historic Preservation is completed and when the Art Institute archives are catalogued.

57. Millet again is someone we should know much more about (and shall know more when the Chicago Art Institute archives are organized). See David Hanks, "Louis J. Millet and the Art Institute of Chicago," *Bulletin of the Art Institute of Chicago* LXVII, no. 2 (March–April 1973): 13ff.

58. W. B. Mundie, Jenney's younger partner, in his printed lecture *William Le Baron Jenney, 1832–1907* (Chicago: privately printed, 1914) lists among his office staff Burnham, Holabird, Roche, Sullivan, Pond, W. A. Otis, Howard Van Doren Shaw, James Gamble Rogers and Alfred Granger, among others. Pond in his manuscript, *Autobiography of Irving K. Pond* in the American Academy of Arts and Letters, New York, depicts Jenney's office very warmly, as a "springboard" from which he explored various professional options, always with the advice and support of the boss (pp. C13ff.).

59. Sullivan, p. 202.

60. Thomas Eddy Tallmadge, *Architecture in Old Chicago* (Chicago: University of Chicago Press, 1941), 118–120.

61. Letter in the Chicago Historical Society files from the Aachen Standesamt Herzogenrath of April 21, 1977 confirms the birth date and names his father as Dr. Carl Martin Cudell.

62. The papers of Arthur Hercz have been deposited at the Chicago Historical Society.

63. Schmidt, Tallmadge tells us (*Architecture in Old Chicago*, p. 120), felt that Cudell did create his designs from the original sources, so lustily did he go at it.

64. D. D. Egbert and P. Sprague, "In Search of John Edelmann," *Journal of the American Institute of Architects* XLV (February 1966): 35–41.

65. Sprague, *op. cit.*, pp. 2–8. To these should be added five sheets in the Emil Lorch papers at the University of Michigan and one sheet in the Chicago Art Institute (*Ibid.*, figures 8–10). On one of the Michigan sheets the inscription "... chancel ... synagogue ... " is discernible. Just how many of these sheets are related to those two projects is unclear; Sprague thinks none (*op. cit.*, pp. 24–26). Connely, wrongly, felt the earliest were done in Vaudremer's atelier (*op. cit.*, p. 60), although several are dated from when Sullivan was in Paris and are inscribed to Edelmann.

66. Connely depicts these activities very vividly (ibid., pp. 81–94), using a notebook Sullivan kept during these years, now at the Avery Library, Columbia University.

67. Sullivan, p. 102.

68. See the promotional volume by Alfred Zucker, *Architectural Sketches Photographed from Designs for Buildings and from Buildings Erected* (New York: National Chemigraph Company, 1894). Edelmann's hand would seem especially discernible in the Decker Building still standing on Union Square of 1892–1893, as Egbert and Sprague point out (*loc. cit.*, p. 41).

69. Pond, pp. F10–F11. On Simonds see: Mara Gelbloom, "Ossian Simonds: Prairie Spirit in Landscape Gardening," *Prairie School Review* XII, no. 2 (2nd quarter, 1975): 5–18. In 1880 Simonds was William Holabird's first architectural partner.

70. Pond, p. F11.

71. *Chicago Tribune*, June 2, 1876.

72. *Chicago Times*, April 9, 1876. These decorations were destroyed by Sullivan himself when he redecorated and enlarged the synagogue in 1890, but an interior photograph of its later state, brought to my attention by Rochelle Elstein, may show the earlier stencilling still in existence along the cove of the barrel vault (*The Reform Advocate* XXXVI, no. 24 [January 30, 1909]: 765).

73. The principal examples are the Auditorium Building (1886–1890), the Standard Club (1887–1888), the Walker Warehouse (1888–1889), the Opera House Block, Pueblo, Colorado (1888–1890), the Dooley Block, Salt Lake City, Utah (1890–1891) and the Kehilath Anshe Ma'ariv Synagogue (1889–1891), as well as a number of contemporaneous houses.

74. Pond, pp. F13–F14.

75. *Genius and the Mobocracy* (New York: Duell, Sloan and Pearce, 1949), 48.

76. Morrison (*Louis Sullivan: Prophet on Modern Architecture*) devotes an entire chapter to this building (as does Twombly) and the bibliography is extensive. See D. Adler, "The Chicago Auditorium," *Architectural Record* I (April–June 1892): 415–34. Also: Daniel H. Perlman, *The Auditorium Building: Its History and Architectural Significance* (Chicago, 1976). Charles Gregerson and Martha Pollak are pursuing further research on the monument.

77. To quote his phrasing of the idea in his article, "The Tall Office Building Artistically Considered," *Lippincott's Magazine* LVII (March 1896), republished in the Museum of Modern Art Documents of Modern Art series, *Kindergarten Chats (revised 1918) and other writings* (New York: Wittenborn, Schultz, 1947), p. 203.

78. James O'Gorman, "The Marshall Field Wholesale Store, Materials Toward a Monograph," *Journal of the Society of Architectural Historians* XXXVII (October 1978): 174–94.

79. Morrison, *op. cit.*, pp. 88–89. He cites Adler writing in the *Architectural Record*, April–June 1892, who phrases things so that he avoids saying there was any direct influence: "It is to be regretted that the severe simplicity of treatment rendered necessary by the financial policy of the earlier days of the enterprise, the deep impression made by Richardson's Marshall Field Building upon the Directors of the Auditorium Association, and a reaction from a course

of indulgence in the creation of highly decorative effects on the part of its architects, should happen to have coincided as to time and object, . . . " William Jordy analyzes Sullivan's relationship to Richardson very carefully: *American Buildings and their Architects* III (New York: Doubleday, 1972): 83–179.

80. Ibid., p. 88.

81. Pond, ch. 7

82. Oechsner, pp. 133–35.

83. On Root: Monroe, *John Wellborn Root*; Donald Hoffmann, *The Architecture of John Wellborn Root* (Baltimore: Johns Hopkins University Press, 1973).

84. Sullivan, p. 292.

85. Root's sister-in-law, Harriet Monroe, develops this theme at length in her biography. It was a cliché of the 1880s and 1890s, appearing, for example, in the pages of the compendious (but anonymous) volumes *Industrial Chicago*, I (Chicago, 1891–1896): 168. See also Carl Condit, *The Chicago School of Architecture* (Chicago: University of Chicago Press, 1964), 26ff.

86. Henry Van Brunt, "John Wellborn Root," *Inland Architect and News Record* XVI (January 1891): 85–88.

87. *Genius and the Mobocracy*, pp. 78–79.

88. Letter from "C" of Rochester, N. Y., published in *The American Architect and Building News* II, no. 63 (March 10, 1877): 80.

89. The late Carroll Meeks insisted that Richardson was not the only user of the round arch ("Romanesque before Richardson," *Art Bulletin* XXXV, no. 1 [March 1953]: 17–33). Sarah Landau is working to document a whole school of New York round-arch commercial architects (see her "The Tall Office Building Artistically Reconsidered: Arcaded Buildings of the New York School, c. 1870–1890," *In Search of Modern Architecture: A Tribute to Henry-Russell Hitchcock* (New York: Architectural History Foundation/ M. I. T. Press, 1982), 136–64). Morrison himself understood that there was a more complex tradition when, among the possible influences upon the Auditorium, he listed George Post's Produce Exchange (*op. cit.*, p. 88)

90. The building was widely published when it was completed in 1885 (for example, in the *American Sanitary*

Engineer, 1886, pp. 560–561) and was henceforth seen as a paradigm, for example by C. H. Blackall, speaking on "The Legitimate Design of the Casing of Steel Structures" before the A. I. A. in 1899 (*Construction News*, November 22, 1899), Montgomery Schuyler, in his "Warehouse and Factory in Architecture" (*Architectural Record* XV [January 1904]: 1–17), and Lewis Mumford in his *Brown Decades* (New York: Harcourt, Brace, 1931), p. 127.

91. Pond, pp. E1ff.

92. Monroe, *op. cit.*, pp. 244ff, and elsewhere. Cf. John Stewardson, "Architecture in America: A Forecast," *Lippincott's Magazine* LVII (January 1896): 132–37, especially p. 133.

93. G. Perrot and C. Chipiez, *Histoire de l'art dans l'antiquité: l'Egypte* (Paris: Hachette, 1882) (translated as *A History of Art in Ancient Egypt* [London: Chapman & Hall, 1882]). It is the form of the ben-ben or primordial stone.

94. For example, Thomas Hines, *Burnham of Chicago: Architect and Planner* (Chicago: University of Chicago Press, 1974), p. 99.

95. In a lecture delivered in 1976 in Milwaukee in the symposium, "The Prairie School Tradition."

96. Narciso Menocal, *Architecture as Nature* (Madison, WI: University of Wisconsin Press, 1981), pp. 102–127. Most apropos is the A. W. Goodrich project of 1898.

97. There was a very interesting and important incident around 1900 in which a "Sullivanesque" school momentarily appeared among younger Chicago designers who combined his ornament with monumental "Beaux-Arts" planning. It coalesced around the Chicago Architectural Club and the Chicago School of Architecture, the latter conducted by the Art Institute and the Armour Institute in collaboration (Roger Gilmore, ed., *Over a Century* [Chicago, 1982]). Its leaders are the men we call today the "Steinway Hall Group," Frank Lloyd Wright, Dwight Perkins, Robert Spencer, Myron Hunt, Hugh Garden, and Richard E. Schmidt. The students included several later "Prairie School" designers, most notably William Drummond. See George R. Dean, "A New Movement in American Architecture," *Brush and Pencil* V, no. 6 (March 1900): 254–59. Drummond's project of 1902 for an American embassy building, displayed in the Architectural Club exhibition of that year, was a characteristic production.

Wright's own planning during the 1890s was extraordinary in this sense. This group, led by Wright and Sullivan, participated in the founding and brief floruit of the Architectural League of America, beginning in 1899, which they hoped would be a forum for their ideas and a bulwark against revivalism. See Sherman Paul, *Louis Sullivan: An Architect in American Thought*, (Englewood Cliffs: Prentice Hall, 1962), pp. 54ff; and Allen Brooks, *The Prairie School: Frank Lloyd Wright and his Midwest Contemporaries* (Toronto: University of Toronto Press, 1972), pp. 37–42.

98. The buildings were, in chronological order: the Central Music Hall, 1879; the Grand Opera House, opened September 4, 1880; the Kalamazoo Academy of Music, opened May 8, 1882; the redecoration of Hooley's Theatre, opened 1882; the redecoration of McVicker's Theatre, opened 1885; the alteration of the Inter-State Industrial Exposition Building to accommodate the Chicago Opera Festival, opened April 7, 1885; the Auditorium, inaugurated December 9, 1889; the Pueblo Opera House, opened October 9, 1890; the rebuilding of the interior of the Stadt Theater, Milwaukee, opened September 17, 1890; the redecoration of the McVickers Theatre, reopened March 30, 1891; the project for the Seattle Opera House Block, 1890; and finally the theatre in the Schiller Building, opened October 17, 1892. Adler published two important articles on theatre design, illustrated with plans and sections of these buildings, "Theatre-Building for American Cities," *Engineering News* VII (August and September 1894): 717–30, 815–29. Twombly documents these commissions and several more minor ones in his chapter VII. Adler's acoustical theories are analyzed in Michael Forsyth's *Buildings for Music* (Cambridge University Press, 1985).

99. Derived from Morrison's figures (with some additions), *op. cit.*, pp. 294–303.

100. See *Marquis's Handbook of Chicago* (Chicago, 1887), pp. 235ff; *Chicago Tribune* (September 5, 1880) (description of the Grand Opera House); Charles E. Gregerson, "Early Adler and Sullivan Work in Kalamazoo," *Prairie School Review* XI, no. 3 (third quarter, 1974): 5–15.

101. See the brochures from the inauguration of the festival in the Chicago Historical Society, including technical descriptions and the woodcut of the interior. See also "A Mamouth Opera House," *Inland Architect* V (March 1885): 25; A. T. Andreas, *History of Cook County, Illinois* III (Chicago: A. T. Andreas, 1886): 651.

102. See note 76, above; on Pueblo: Lloyd C. Engelbrecht's excellent article, "Adler & Sullivan's Pueblo Opera

House: City Status for a New Town in the Rockies," *Art Bulletin* LXVII, no. 2 (June 1985): 277–95. Charles W. Cooney of the Milwaukee County Historical Society has kindly provided me with basic information on the Stadt Theater and cites Robert J. Burk, *The Birth of the Pabst Theatre*, an unpublished student paper from North Central College of 1971.

103. Frank Lloyd Wright, *An Autobiography* (New York: Longmans, 1933), p. 105, writes of the Auditorium interior as a plastic and acoustical structure, but not as a constructive one: "And while no advantage was taken of the arched elliptical form to carry the loads above, the inner shell itself being carried—suspended from the level trusses above it. Still the form was appropriate, suitable to its purpose and prophetic."

104. Adler's acoustical model was studied and reproduced in a corrected form in the Chicago Civic Opera House of 1929 by Paul E. Sabine, consulting for the architects Graham, Anderson, Probst and White. See Paul E. Sabine, "Acoustics of the Chicago Civic Opera House," *Architectural Forum* LII (1930); 599–604. I owe this information to Sally Chappell.

105. Adler & Sullivan created minor spaces of great interest, too, most particularly the "Apollo Rooms" added to the Central Music Hall around 1890, a barrel-vaulted, sky-lit central space, opening at each side into apsidal, half-domed spaces, showing the geometric versatility of Hadrian's architect at Tivoli.

106. The basic study of Sullivan's ornament is Sprague, *op. cit.* Important recent contributions have been made by Turak, "French and English Sources...," and Jordy. See also the catalogue by David Huntley, *Louis H. Sullivan Architectural Ornament Collection, Southern Illinois University, Edwardsville* (Edwardsville, Ill: Southern Illinois University, 1981).

107. Lewis Mumford, *Brown Decades*, p. 114ff.; Sigfried Giedion, *Space, Time and Architecture* (Cambridge: Harvard University Press, 1941), pp. 360–363.

108. Monroe, p. 245.

109. R.-J. Hermant, "L'Art à l'Exposition de Chicago," *Gazette des Beaux-Arts* X, 3s (1893): 237, 416–25, 441–61; XI, 3S (1894): 149–69.

110. Fiske-Kimball, however, did observe the derivation: *American Architecture* (New York: Bobbs-Merill, 1928),

p. 155. See Menocal, p. 113. It is informative to analyze Louis J. Millet's decoration of the interior of the St. Louis Union Terminal executed in the early 1890s (and just restored) in which he tries to imitate Sullivan in composition, but remain consistently Richardsonian in motif—it is a kind of correction and academicization of Sullivan.

111. Sprague, no. 39, who dates it "about" October 1890.

112. *St. Louis Globe Democrat* and *St Louis Post Dispatch*, November 7, 1890, and *Economist*, November 29, 1890.

113. The most recent and closest study of this much studied subject: T. Hines, *Burnham of Chicago*, pp. 73ff. See also H. Monroe, *op. cit.*, 216ff.

114 Sullivan, pp. 296–98.

115. Ibid., p. 298.

116. Ibid., p. 314.

117. Cupples Station is perhaps the most dramatic of these, being within sight of the Wainwright Building. For Gilbert, see *Architectural Reviewer* I (1897): 42–65.

118. Vincent Scully, *Frank Lloyd Wright* (New York: Braziller, 1960), p. 15.

119. Montgomery Schuyler remarked of the Guaranty Building, "I know of no steel-framed building in which the metallic construction is more palpably felt through the envelope of baked clay." See William Jordy and Ralph Cox, ed. "Architecture in Chicago," II (Cambridge: Harvard University Press, *American Architecture and Other Writings*, 1961), p. 393.

120. In *Genius and the Mobocracy* Frank Lloyd Wright writes, "Material, all alike, were only grist for the marvelous sensuous rhythmic power of imagination he possessed ....Whether executed in stone, wood, or iron, all materials were "clay" in the master's hands. . . . because of this effulgent sense of sympathy he possessed—for all he cared or anything he seemed to want to know materials were pretty much all *one* to him" (p. 58).

121. See especially, Viollet-le-Duc, *Entretiens sur l'architecture* I (Paris: A. Morel, 1863), lecture 6.

122. This is clear in his design of the late 1870s and early 1880s (after Sullivan had returned to Chicago): Notre-Dame d' Auteuil (commissioned 1877, built 1878–1880),

the lycée at Grenoble, and finally the Lycée Buffon in Paris (1887–1889).

123. H. Monroe, *op. cit.*, pp. 245–46.

124. As they are reproduced, for example, in chromolithograph by Pascal Coste in his *Monuments modernes de la Perse* (Paris: A. Morel, 1867).

125. D. Hoffmann, "The Setback Skyscraper City of 1891: An Unknown Essay by Louis H. Sullivan," *Journal of the Society of Architectural Historians* XXIX (May 1970): 186–187; based on Sullivan's article; "The High Building Question," *Graphic 5*, (December 19, 1891): 405.

126. This was the point of the Architectural League of America in its meetings around 1900. In his letters to a younger member of that organization, Claude Bragdon, he states as much (published in his autobiography, *More Lives than One* [New York: Knopf, 1938], pp. 154–59: letter of July 25, 1904, "I believe that I absorbed the real principles the school envelopes, so to speak . . .").

127. Wright, *Autobiography*, p. 102: "Healy and Millet were his companions at this time. The three had known one another in Paris." Healy was the son of G. P. A. Healy, a successful portrait painter who split his time between America and Paris, and had been trained as an architect in the atelier of Coquart from 1874 to 1879. Millet was from New York, a nephew of the successful Paris sculptor Aimé Millet, and also a student of architecture at the Ecole, in the atelier of Train, from 1874 to at least 1878. They set up a successful practice as decorators in Chicago in 1880 (Darling, *Chicago Ceramics and Glass*, pp. 104–10).

128. He also had runs of the *American Architect and Building News*, the *Inland Architect and News Record*, the *Sanitary Engineer* and the London *Building News*. His library was auctioned on November 29, 1909, and a catalogue is preserved at the Art Institute of Chicago. (It is transcribed in David S. Andrew *Louis Sullivan and the Polemics of Modern Architecture* [Urbana and Chicago: University of Illinois Press, 1985], pp. 161–170). It demonstrates great catholicity of interest, including many volumes in history (35 titles), philosophy (28 titles) and science (50 titles) as well as music and art (some 75 titles) and architecture (about 100 titles). There were also about thirty volumes of all sorts in French.

129. See Lauren Weingarden, "Louis H. Sullivan: Investigation of a Second French Connection," *Journal of the Society of Architectural Historians* XXXIX, no. 4 (December 1980): 297–303.

The Tall Buildings

WILLIAM H. JORDY

I received my technical education at the Massachusetts Institute of Technology and the Ecole National des Beaux Arts in Paris. My real education I sought and found alone. That is why I prize it, and why I offer to your service a mind so trained in bold conditions of modern buildings that it is able to distill therefrom a poetic form of expression.

   My business is to grasp the realities of building in all its phases.

—Louis Sullivan, from a letter to a client, 1904

As he threw the "stretch," with the first three bays outlined in pencil upon it, I sensed what had happened. In his vision, here beyond doubt, was the dawn of a new day in skyscraper architecture.*

—Frank Lloyd Wright, *Genius and the Mobocracy*, 1949, on the initial design sketches for the Wainwright Building.

WITH THIS RECORD OF HIS SENSE OF HAVING witnessed a great moment, Frank Lloyd Wright retrospectively celebrated his presence at the event which has characteristically come to represent the birth of an appropriate approach to the design for the office skyscraper. The event presumably occurred sometime in late 1890 or early 1891 in the Adler & Sullivan office, which was then proudly ensconced at the loggia level of the seventeen-story tower of the firm's recently completed Auditorium Building (1886–1889), just under its beetling cornice (fig. 56). The four-sided loggia surrounding the office opened to vistas in all directions, overlooking the city and lake. From this aerie, views of the Loop all around looked down on the initial ventures of what came to be called the "Chicago School," a loose, informal group of architects cooperating and competing in the development of the tall, metal-framed, elevatored office buildings which came to be identified with the city.

The late eighties saw the initial examples of the tall, metal-framed buildings to come. Four especially made the latticed and linear quality of the metal frame apparent on the exterior elevations: Holabird & Roche's Tacoma Building (1886–1889), Baumann & Huehl's Chamber of Commerce Building (1888–1889), William LeBaron Jenney's Second Leiter Store (1889–1891) and Jenney & Mundie's Ludington Building (1891) (figs. 57–59). In all instances, the designs reduce the "wall" to the narrow supporting piers, which metal columns at their core permit, and fill the intervals between with windows. The Chamber of Commerce and Ludington Buildings do so with prosaic directness, by squeezing pairs of normal-sized sash windows between the piers.[1] The bolder Tacoma Building alternates four-windowed projecting bays with paired windows in the plane of the wall to create a window-packed, pleated enclosure, with the vertical piers visually subdued to the fold of the minimal

Figure 55
Adler & Sullivan, Stock Exchange, Chicago, 1893–1894, Trading room (now in The Art Institute of Chicago, restored by John Vinci). Courtesy The Art Institute of Chicago.

Figure 56
Adler & Sullivan, Auditorium, Chicago, Illinois, 1886–1889. Richard Nickel, photographer. Courtesy Richard Nickel Committee.

Figure 57
Holabird & Roche, Tacoma Building, 1886–1889. Courtesy Chicago Historical Society ICHi–01084.

Figure 58
Baumann & Huehl, Chamber of Commerce, 1888–1889. From Industrial Chicago, Chicago, 1891.

Figure 59
William Le Baron Jenney, Second Leiter (later Siegel Cooper and Sears Roebuck) Store, Chicago, 1889–1891. Courtesy The Art Institute of Chicago.

parapeting under the windows. Moldings at the top and bottom of the parapeting cross the supporting verticals at every story, thereby emphasizing the horizontals of the stack of floors over the verticals of the structural columns. Equally bold, if visually less lively than the play of light and shadow across the Tacoma's pleating, the more ponderous Leiter Store squeezes four windows between exceptionally widely spaced piers in elevations organized into a series of fields, which are graduated in size above the astonishingly generous widths of the shop windows below.

For one who came to be popularly credited with "giving form to the skyscraper," Sullivan should have been attracted to these buildings from his elevated vantage point. All the more because Adler & Sullivan, in the middle stories of their modest Troescher Building (1884), had dared as boldly as anyone to employ the skeletal mode of linear piers (without interior metal columns), infilled with windows set on spanning beams (fig. 60). The rusticated base and bristle of ornament at the cornice notwithstanding, Sullivan never surpassed this direct statement of "form following function"—if his familiar motto is to be interpreted literally, as an exhortation that the designer's form should follow the lead of its structure as directly and vividly as possible.

But at the time Sullivan was looking elsewhere. His attention was deflected away from the skeletonized designs which had begun to appear in the Loop, and focused instead on a more traditional image, its exterior walls built of masonry.[2] Only six blocks west of the Auditorium there was the severe granite block of H. H. Richardson's Marshall Field Wholesale Store (1885–1887), which came to have special meaning for Sullivan (figs. 61 and 62). Its base of low, segmental arched openings provides visual support to the tiers of semicircular arching above. Moving up the elevation, a tier of wide arches rising through three stories and two full windows in width becomes a tier of double arches, these rising two stories, one window in width. Together, they recall the small arches riding on the larger arches of a Roman aqueduct.

Figure 60
Adler & Sullivan, Troescher Building (later Chicago Journal Building), Chicago, 1884. Richard Nickel, photographer. Courtesy Richard Nickel Committee.

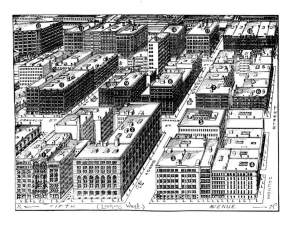

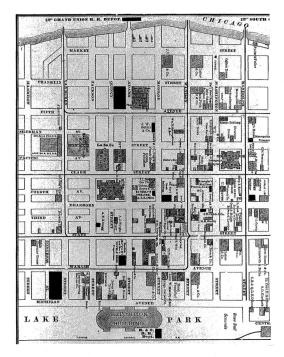

Figure 61
Adler & Sullivan, Auditorium, and H. H. Richardson, Marshall Field Wholesale Store, composite perspective view. Courtesy Chicago Historical Society Map Collection and Frank A. Randall, History of the Development of Building Construction in Chicago, *Urbana, University of Illinois Press, 1949.*

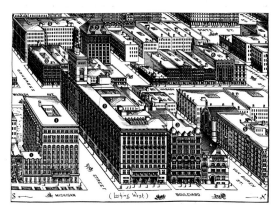

Richardson closes the visual ascent of the stacked arches by the staccato horizontal rhythm of small rectangular windows in close-packed bursts of four, immediately beneath the heavy cornice which barely breaks the compact monumentality of the giant, rough-hewn box. Chicago architects were variously affected by the austere force of Richardson's swan song[3] (he died prematurely, before the box was done), none more so than Sullivan. And none better learned the lesson of Richardson's example than he. So much was this the case that, as he grasped the power of Richardson's box—solely articulated as it was by the repetitive motifs of its openings, and by moldings and textural changes integral with the quarry-faced ruggedness of its masonry walls—Sullivan radically altered his own preliminary schemes for the elevations of the Auditorium, freshly determined just as the Marshall Field Wholesale Store was finishing. In his book on Sullivan, Hugh Morrison illustrates the change in two preliminary drawings for the Auditorium. Sullivan had originally sought to increase the picturesqueness of the larger masonry box by gables, dormers, and turrets at the skyline, and with multi-windowed bays jutting from the walls.[4] Abruptly, he changed course, following the example of Richardson's austerity, progressively simplifying his elevations, until he achieved the severity of what was built (see fig. 56). The young designer was also doubtless attracted, perhaps overwhelmed,[5] by Richardson's bold and direct precedent because of the giant size of the Auditorium commission, filling half a Chicago block, and the largest commission in the city up to its time. Moreover, it is known that the client, Ferdinand W. Peck, was impressed with the large simplicity of Richardson's building, for economic as much as for monumental reasons.[6]

Employing the same rugged, quarry-faced granite for a basement, Sullivan had to bloat the one-story height of Richardson's base to three. Above this base he replicated Richardson's elevation in taller, narrower arches, but more incisively cut and into smooth-surfaced limestone rather than Richardson's textured granite. In this, he followed his

Figure 62
H. H. Richardson, Mar-
shall Field Wholesale Store,
Chicago, 1885–1887. Cour-
tesy Chicago Historical
Society ICHi–01688.

natural inclination toward smoother surfaces with a sharply edged treatment—qualities which would, in fact, be more appropriate to the lightness and precision intrinsic to skeletal construction. However, these qualities are all but lost sight of in the immediacy of contact with the craggy base of the Auditorium which, in scale and assertiveness, competes with Richardson's treatment.

Completion of the Auditorium did not end Sullivan's mesmerization with the Marshall Field Wholesale Store. Some years later, writing his *Kindergarten Chats* in 1901, Sullivan spoke of it as an "oasis" in what he regarded as the desert of mediocre American building. Then, switching metaphors as he often did in his writing, Sullivan saw the Wholesale Store metamorphosed as a person. Among its "paltry" competition it sounds

"a rich, sombre chord of manliness." The Pupil thinks he catches the drift of his Master's high-flown rhetoric, "You mean, I suppose, that here is a good piece of architecture for me to look at . . ." And the Master explodes impatiently at his Pupil's externalizing intelligence in what is perhaps the most familiar section of the *Chats:*

No; I mean, here is a man *for you to look at . . . . a real man, a manly man; a virile force—broad, vigorous and with a whelm of energy—an entire male.*

I mean that stone and mortar, here, spring into life, and are no more material and sordid things, but, as it were, become the very diapason of a mind rich-stored with harmony. . . .

Four-square and brown, it stands, in physical

fact, a monument to trade, to the organized com-
mercial spirit, to the power and progress of the age,
to the strength and resource of individuality and
force of character; spiritually, it stands as the index
of a mind, large enough, courageous enough to cope
with these things, master them, absorb them and
give them forth again, impressed with the stamp of
large and forceful personality; artistically, it stands
as the oration of one who knows well how to choose
his words, who has somewhat [sic] to say and says
it—and says it as the outpouring of a copious,
direct, large and simple mind.

Therefore I have called it, in a world of barren
pettiness, a male; for it sings the song of procreant
power . . . [7]

It was as though this man, gargantuan in presence
both personally and architecturally, overwhelmed
Sullivan at a time when he chose to leave the petty
picturesqueness of Victorianism behind him, as
though Richardson simultaneously intimidated and
inspired Sullivan just as he sought his own voice in
buildings that would speak to a new time in culture
which was just then beginning to assert itself

against mid-nineteenth century attitudes and ideas. Writing to Claude Bragdon in 1903, a younger architect who was himself then attempting to develop a decorative style based on empathetic and kinesthetic approaches to ornament, Sullivan denied much influence from Richardson: "I have admired the fervor and masculinity of Richardson's work; but the absence of logic and common-sense repelled me later. I doubt if Richardson had much influence on my mental growth—if so I have forgotten it, for that is long ago. In my 'Kindergarten Chat' entitled 'An Oasis' I pay tribute to the man."[8]

Whether Sullivan truly forgot what he learned from Richardson, or merely wanted to forget by 1903, the evidence for a profound influence seems incontrovertible.

So caught up was Sullivan in Richardson's Wholesale Store that he quarried it for compositional ideas for about four years, from 1886 through 1890—notably in his Walker Warehouse (1888–1889), Dooly Block in Salt Lake City (1890–1891), Kehilath Anshe Ma'ariv Synagogue (1890–1891), Getty Tomb (1890) and the Transportation Building for the Columbian Exposition (1893) (fig. 63–67), although other designs could be mentioned too. But Sullivan altered his example. Characteristically, he refined, subtlized, complicated, abstracted and, by these very transformations of the bare bones of Richardson's compositional scheme, tended to make more "ornamental" what is logically and hierarchically "architectural" in the Wholesale Store. More precisely, Sullivan treated the plain surfaces of his boxes as fields to be animated, which disclose his proclivities toward ornament, however architectural the terms of the ornamentation.

When the *St. Louis Globe-Democrat* of November 29, 1890 announced the impending Wainwright Building, a crude perspective showed it to be yet another example of Richardsonian Romanesque, generally recalling the format of the Marshall Field Wholesale Store (fig. 62).[9] The announcement gave the design to the local architect, Charles K. Ramsey, without mention of

Adler & Sullivan, who may not yet have been called in to collaborate with him. Although it may represent no more than Ramsey's quick response to the client's need for some kind of visualization for publicity purposes rather than a considered design, it is nevertheless significant that the Wainwright began in an image distantly derived from Richardson's Wholesale Store. Then, a little later, abruptly "As [Sullivan] threw the 'stretch' with the first three bays outlined in pencil upon it . . . here beyond doubt, was the dawn of a new day in skyscraper architecture." Like Wright, Sullivan himself recognized the design of the Wainwright as the watershed design in his career (fig. 70). Again retrospectively to Claude Bragdon, he wrote in 1903,

As to my buildings: Those that interest me date from the Wainwright Bldg., in St. Louis. It was with that that I "broke" (see K.C. Chat "The Tulip") [a reference to his Kindergarten Chats]. It was a very sudden and volcanic design (made literally in three minutes) and marks the beginning of a logical and poetic expression of the metallic frame construction. The Prudential Bldg. [originally the Guaranty] is the "sister" of the Wainwright. All my commercial buildings since the Wainwright are conceived in the same general spirit. . . . The structures prior to the Wainwright were in my "masonry" period. The Auditorium Bldg. and the Walker Bldg., Chicago, are the best of the large ones—the Ryerson, Getty, and Wainwright tombs, among the small.[10]

And nearly twenty years later, when in the last years of his life he wrote his *Autobiography of an Idea*, Sullivan minced no words in self congratulation: "[The steel frame form of construction] was given first authentic recognition and expression in the exterior treatment of the Wainwright Building."[11]

That other architects had expressed the latticed look characteristic for metal skeletal framing before the Wainwright, and especially in Chicago, we have already observed. That the latticed look could even appear in masonry piered construction without the use of metal skeletal framing needs no more confirmation than another glance at Adler & Sullivan's Troescher Building, which, in its openness to glazing, is even bolder than the Wainwright. And other examples were legion in nineteenth-century commercial anticipations in masonry construction of Sullivan's pier-and-spandrel articulation of the metal skeleton in the Wainwright.[12] The Wainwright has become, in Sullivan's words, the mythical "first authentic recognition and expression" of the metal-framed tall office building simply in this: in the decisive expression of "tallness"; in the precision with which the linear opposition of vertical against horizontal characteristic of the metal frame occurs in the crossing of supporting piers over spanning window panels in the Wainwright; in the unswerving directness with which a relatively tall building (very tall for the time in St. Louis) with many windows makes, from this simple and seemingly intractable act of repetition, something architectural; finally, in the realization of this expression in architectural terms which were anti-nostalgic insofar as they evolved directly from the new task and technology at hand.

A stream of critics extending back to the first important critical commentaries on the Wainwright in 1894 and 1895, by two of the leading critics of the day, Barr Ferree and Montgomery Schuyler, have essentially concurred with Sullivan's (and Wright's) assessment of the importance of the Wainwright as *the* cardinal precedent for the *architectural* treatment of the tall, metal-framed office building.[13] Eventually the first full-scale monograph on Sullivan's work by Hugh Morrison in 1935 made the role of the Wainwright decisive indeed. In what is perhaps his key chapter, "Giving Form to the Skyscraper," Morrison used this building as the explanatory example of Sullivan's approach to the tall office building, subordinating all of his other designs "giving form to the skyscraper" to the Wainwright.

It is tempting to do so because the Wainwright Building is not only the first in the series, but the

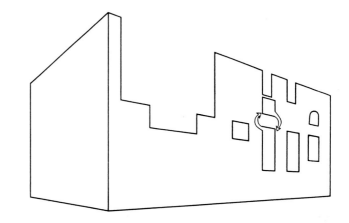

Figure 68
Diagram indicating Sullivan's derivation from the Marshall Field Wholesale Store.

*Figure 69
Preliminary perspective by
Charles K. Ramsey in a
news item announcing the
prospective Wainwright
Building in the* St. Louis
Globe-Democrat, *November
29, 1890.*

WAINWRIGHT BUILDING.

Granite, brick and brown sandstone trimmings will be the building material, and all work will be on fire-proof principles.

physiological in its nature—namely, the attic. In this the circulatory system completes itself and makes its grand turn, ascending and descending. The space is filled with tanks, pipes, valves, sheaves, and mechanical etcetera that supplement and complement the force-originating plant hidden below-ground in the cellar. Finally, or at the beginning rather, there must be on the ground floor a main aperture or entrance common to all the occupants or patrons of the building.[14]

Many office buildings at the time, especially in Chicago, approximated Sullivan's criteria. His statement is not as revolutionary as it was once made out to be. But its straightforwardness (unusual in Sullivan's writings), together with his legendary role in "giving form to the skyscraper," have accorded it special position in the history of American architecture. And in truth, office buildings of the period with pretensions to prestige all too frequently heaped, parfait-style, one historical allusion on another, until this layering of architectural delights filled the investor's cup. Even in less presuming buildings, where budget or inclination encouraged ahistorical plainness, expressions of tallness were often hampered by the two- to five- or six-story heights which historically conditioned many-windowed, multi-partitioned institutional or commercial buildings. Horizontal moldings characteristically interrupt the regularity of tall office buildings in acknowledgment of such precedent. So the Wainwright design substantially follows the functional lead mandated by the uses to which the building will be put: "form follows function," in Sullivan's all too familiar phrase. Put another way, the design essentially meets the "realities of the building," as users and investors in particular would construe these "realities."

He ascends in his essay to a higher plane: "We must now heed the imperative voice of emotion."[15] The first stage in Sullivan's expressive intensification of the material and programmatic criteria for the tall office building is very clear in the Wainwright. It provides another explanation for the use of the Wainwright as the customary starting point

most easily explained. Sullivan himself has contributed to the explanation in his most quoted piece of writing, "The Tall Building Artistically Considered." He published the article in 1896, no doubt (as Morrison observes) with the Wainwright's later Buffalo "sister," the Guaranty, more immediately in mind, since this had just been completed during the previous year. But his comments generally apply to the Wainwright.

Wanted—1st, a story below-ground, containing . . . the plant for power, heating, lighting, etc.; 2nd, a ground floor . . . devoted to stores, banks or other establishments requiring large area, ample spacing, ample light, and great freedom of access. 3rd, a second story readily accessible by stairways —this space usually in large subdivisions, with corresponding liberality in structural spacing and expanse of glass and breadth of external openings. 4th, above this an indefinite number of stories of offices just like all the other offices—an office being similar to a cell in a honey-comb, merely a compartment, nothing more. 5th, the last, at the top of this pile is placed a space or story that, as related to the life and usefulness of the structure, is purely

Figure 70
Adler & Sullivan, Wain-
wright Building, St.
Louis, 1890–1891. Cervin
Robinson, photographer.

toward the illumination of subsequent designs more "difficult" to understand.

The "realities" of the building *per se* provide reinforcing cues for the design: for example, the incisive linear lattice in two planes, verticals against horizontals as a visible surrogate for the concealed reticulated skeletal framing which actually supports the building. The Wainwright also displays an appropriate feeling for the "realities" of the materials that make the building. Smooth-surfaced granite provides a base from which smooth-surfaced red brick piers rise to the cornice. The material itself and the directness of its treatment invoke the metal columns within the brick piers which furnish support for the building. By contrast, most of the ornament appears in terra-cotta, a baked clay which readily receives embellishment in its original ductile state. The sober, structural implications of the brick are set against the fanciful embellishing function of the terra-cotta; the material that *builds* the piers against another that *screens* the parapet area under each window and decorates the cornice in great swirls of tendrils and leaves around oculi openings. In the first important critique of the Wainwright in 1894, Barr Ferree especially praised the appropriateness of the ornament:

A very striking instance of the judicious application of ornament is furnished by the Wainwright Building at St. Louis. . . . The chief lesson taught by this building is the limitation *of ornament, and this notwithstanding that, taken as a whole, a good deal is used. It is employed naturally and where it is most serviceable. This is the principle used by the Greeks, and is the mode that has been used in all the great architectural styles in their best works.*[16]

Ferree went on to add that he liked the sense of solidity about the building and, mindful of the spindliness that had begun to characterize downtown Chicago office buildings, like the Tacoma, he praised the Wainwright for its physical presence. In fact, it was difficult for those of Ferree's generation, brought up on the bulkiness of Victorian wall-ing, to regard the extreme revelation of metal skeletal construction as being truly "architectural."

Of the many fallacies anent the high building and its art that enjoy a sort of vogue in even good circles [Ferree went on], *none is more absurd than the notion that, because it is a skeleton construction, because its weight is carried on a steel framework, and the walls and piers are only curtains or external inclosures of the inner frame, that does the work, therefore the design must express this construction in order to be truthful. . . . It is a preposterous idea, yet one that has a large support. No one will contend that mankind would look better were its skeleton of bone placed outside the flesh rather than within it.*[17]

As early as 1896, in the second major critical assessment of the Wainwright, Montgomery Schuyler was perceptive enough to observe (as did Morrison later, and more emphatically) that the wide piers bounding the corners of the Wainwright and the deep cornice were, in fact, illogical for metal framed construction. And, Morrison added, so was the density of the range of piers across the two fronts of the Wainwright. Only every other member of what appear to be identical verticals contains a structural column, because normal spacing for metal skeletal construction permits such wide-spaced intervals between supports.[18] The close-packed piers, in conjunction with their forceful enframement, indicate that, even at Sullivan's epochal moment of breakthrough toward an appropriate expression for the metal-framed tall office building, the weightiness, the density and the cubic concentration of Richardson's block still unconsciously haunted his design. More precisely perhaps, Sullivan developed the new potential with conscious reference to what had so considerably stirred him in the immediate past. After all, it was Richardson's example that had to be matched and superceded. Sullivan had slighted a number of Chicago office buildings from the mid-eighties onward, that were more responsive to the structural facts of the metal-framed tall office building, choosing instead to drink at the "oasis."

It is also true that the cubic quality of the Wainwright anticipates the sense of the block which permeates all of Sullivan's designs for the tall office building. From beginning to end, their format substantially remains that of the Renaissance palace with a base of one, more often two, or rarely three stories, a window wall for the tiers of offices above, all capped by a prominent, heavily embellished cornice. The palacelike boxiness of Sullivan's buildings has its nineteenth-century roots in the ubiquitous "commercial palaces" which lined the business districts of cities from roughly the 1840s onward. However much Sullivan may have "given form to the skyscraper," the relatively modest height of his tall office buildings preserved something of the blocky quality of the Renaissance palace format. (With one exception, a thirty-six story project for the Fraternity Temple Building, they range between eight and sixteen stories, averaging out to thirteen, whether built or unbuilt). None of them, except perhaps the Schiller, is really designed as a tower, which is quintessentially the form to which skyscrapers aspire in the golden decades of their development during the 1920s and 1930s. Sullivan's single design for a very tall building, the unbuilt Fraternity Temple Building commissioned by the Independent Order of Odd Fellows in 1891 (see fig. 81), is the exception which proves the rule. Although deservedly praised as a vanguard example of the set-back kind of massing characteristic of New York developments in the 1920s,[19] the "tower" essentially remains a pyramidal stack of Wainwright buildings, each with its cornice, heaped and abutted into a polygonal core tower. This is itself capped by a too abruptly attached loggia and polygonal "cupola." Sullivan's finest tower, the Schiller, is a tall block on end (see fig. 83).

Towers were, in any event, more natural to the New York development of the tall building during Sullivan's lifetime and beyond, at least through the period up to World War II. Towers logically take off from the constricted lots typical of New York. The platting of Chicago and other midwestern cities tended toward larger (often *much* larger) lots, as though the expansiveness of the prairie persisted even in the urban centers, and the accumulation of properties to make even larger sites seems to have proceeded more rapidly in Chicago than in New York. Large sites encourage the blocky form of massing with its analogy to the palace shape. So, too, perhaps did the deliberately anonymous approach to Chicago office design of "one office just like all other offices . . . similar to a cell in a honeycomb, merely a compartment, nothing more."[20] Window next to window next to window: window over window over window: if any past architectural form comes to mind, especially in the blocky context of much of Chicago's building around 1890, it is something vaguely comparable to the Renaissance palace, with its sense of power deriving from austerity and repetition.

Large blocks encourage such treatment, whereas towers are assertive entities, and as such encourage the kind of self-congratulatory advertising which corporate headquarters desire in cities like New York. With twenty major railroad lines coming into Chicago resulting in more than fifty major railroad trunk lines, Chicago was a city for processing and trans-shipment, for manufacturing where ease of widespread distribution was important, and for the regional offices of national corporations. Chicago commercial buildings were, by and large, speculative buildings, where anonymity and interchangeability of square footage was foremost in client concern, and where a high proportion of the commercial buildings were the investments of eastern capitalists who were less concerned with regional civic or corporate glory for the remote interior metropolis than for ample return.[21]

If the Chicago business environment encouraged the use of the block as the format for Chicago commercial building, it also derived from a positive exhilaration with large simple forms for Chicago office buildings in the eighties and nineties. The preference was widely noted at the time. Other cities, of course, possessed such down-to-earth business buildings. But visitors to the city were

appear, like them, simply boxes of windows. Who
would suppose that mere lumps of iron and bricks
and mortar could be sublime?

Or from the Scottish journalist, William Archer,
in 1900:

As the elephant (or rather the megatherium) to the
giraffe, so is the colossal business block of Chicago to
the sky-scraper of New York. There is a proportion
and dignity in the mammoth buildings of Chicago
which is lacking in most of those which form the
jagged skyline of Manhattan Island. For one
reason or another—no doubt some difference in the
system of land tenure is at the root of the matter—
the Chicago architect has usually a larger plot of
ground to operate on than his New York colleague,
and can consequently give his building breadth and
depth as well as height. Before the lanky giants of
the Eastern metropolis, one has generally to hold
one's aesthetic judgment in abeyance. They are not
precisely ugly, but still less, as a rule, can they be
called beautiful. They are simply astounding manifestations of human energy and heaven-storming
audacity. They stand outside the pole of aesthetics
like the Eiffel Tower or the Fourth Bridge [which
are now within it]. But in Chicago proportion goes
along with mere height, and many of the business
houses are, if not beautiful, at least aesthetically
impressive—for instance, the grim fortalice of
Marshall, Field & Company, the Masonic Temple,
the Women's Temperance Temple (a structure with
a touch of real beauty), and such vast cities within
the city as the great Northern Building and the
Monadnock Block.

Or the French observer, Paul Bourget:

At one moment you have nothing around you but
"buildings." They scale the very heavens with their
eighteen and twenty stories. The architect, who
built them, or rather, made them by machinery,
gave up all thought of colonnades, mouldings,
classical decorations. He ruthlessly [Bourget's
word is brutalement] accepted the speculator's

repeatedly overwhelmed by the way in which a
straightforward approach to design had taken over
the largest and most expensive business buildings
in Chicago, giving a brutal, assertive, severe, yet
impressive monumentality to the Loop. Their
observations have been too widely reproduced to
need more than a reminder. Differences between
the big masonry blocks and the newer skeletal
construction, for which Chicago was acknowledged
to be the innovating center, were blurred in their
observations. The British journalist, George
Washington Steevens, wrote in 1897:

All about you they rise, the mountains of building
—not in the broken line of New York, but thick
together, side by side, one behind the other. . . .
Broader and more massive than the tall buildings
of New York, older also and dingier, they do not

inspired conditions,—to multiply as much as possible the value of the bit of earth as the base by multiplying the superimposed "offices."

One might think that such a problem would interest no one but an engineer. Nothing of the kind! The simple power of necessity is to a certain degree a principle of beauty; and these structures so plainly manifest this necessity that you feel a strange emotion in contemplating them. It is the first draught of a new sort of art,—an art of democracy made by the masses and for the masses, an art of science, where the invariability of natural laws gives to the most unbridled daring the calmness of geometrical figures.

And the New York architectural critic, Montgomery Schuyler, (now commenting on the newer skeletal buildings) in his often reproduced record of a conversation with a Chicago architect in 1896:

I get from my engineer a statement of the minimum thickness of the steel post and its enclosure of terra cotta. Then I establish the minimum depth of floor beam and the minimum height of the sill from the floor to accommodate what must go between them. These are the data of my design.[22]

If outsiders noted an austerity about Chicago's finest office buildings which gave uniqueness to the Loop, at least as an overall impression, the four-volume compendium on the city's economy, *Industrial Chicago*, went so far in 1891 as to boast of these buildings as having a collective style. "The Commercial style is the title suggested by the great office and mercantile buildings now found here. Light, space, air and strength were demanded . . . as the first objects and exterior ornament as the second. Thus the severity in many buildings, ornamentation in a few, and massiveness in all portrayed the varied ideas of owners on art matters as well as their determination to build strong and large." After more awkward, but vigorous, bragging in this vein, *Industrial Chicago* concluded that the tall business buildings of the city represented a "new style."[23]

All of these factors in his environment and their implications for design undoubtedly played a role in the blocklike format of Sullivan's designs.

For one whose self-inflicted motto was "form follows function," the almost belligerent assertion of the block in Sullivan's commercial style was the more paradoxical because few of his office buildings are blocks in actuality (see fig. 72). Most contain hollowed light courts unseen from the street—as, in fact, did Richardson's U-shaped Marshall Field Wholesale Store (see fig. 62).[24] The courts were extensively windowed, usually painted white, or, most lavishly, lined with white enameled brick. Brochures advertising the buildings to potential renters featured the availability of natural light from courts, as well as from windows in the street walls, as in the rental brochure for the Wainwright Building: "The plan of the building . . . is of the form of the letter U, with a wide and light court to the north and a widening of the alley toward the west. . . . the building is so well lighted that every office or room in the building will have direct outside light and air."[25]

Indirectly, the light courts indicate something of the hold which the compact block had on Sullivan's creative imagination, and therefore merit a short digression. As in most office buildings of the period, windowed courts cut their way through the blocks, frequently down to skylights over lobbies and store space on the ground floor. In the Wainwright and Guaranty Buildings, these terminate in stained glass skylights over portions of the lobbies. The light court of the Guaranty was perhaps the most lavish. Walls of glazed white brick were banded with narrow inset decorated moldings in terra-cotta. They provided decorative rulings on which the windows sat, and prefigure a similar treatment for the wall of the Carson Pirie Scott Store. Newspaper reports at the time of the Guaranty's erection waxed enthusiastic about the glazed bricks of the light court, which were indeed treated as one of the expensive features of the design.[26] (It was filled in for additional office space during its restoration just prior to 1983, so that the grid of the dished domes comprising the stained glass skylight over the magazine stand in the lobby, each containing an abstracted seed pod, now requires fluorescent sunshine; as does the larger, adjacent skylight over part of the principal store space.) Where alleys abutted these U-shaped office blocks, additional light courts were usually notched out of a rear corner of the block to expand the narrow alleys slightly and bring more light to rear offices, as in the Wainwright, Stock Exchange and Guaranty.

In a similar way, where buildings were closely fitted between other buildings into deep, narrow sites, without adjacent alleys, the notching of light courts into the party walls made fat "Ts" of the building block, as in the projected Portland and the Bayard. In the Schiller, long narrow courting of the party walls resulted in a near "I." Of a total of twenty designs, only one reveals its light court to the street, the Union Trust (see fig. 84). The Union Trust Building in St. Louis opens the light court for the upper floors to the front of the building over a two-story base. The Union Trust still stands in downtown St. Louis in line with the Wainwright three blocks away. Its light court, opening south to the front of the building, looks across the intervening blocks of low buildings directly into the Wainwright light court opening to the rear of the building. In the reciprocity of these practical arrangements, one especially senses the importance of light in these buildings. Obviously, these courts can be truly claimed as a premise for the exceptionally tall Fraternity Temple Building (see fig. 81) which boldly prefigures both the form and the rationale of the New York setback skyscraper (called up by New York's Heights of Buildings law of 1916).[27] Although this anticipation of the setback in Adler & Sullivan's buildings is spectacularly evident, two other, less obvious prophesies for this later development in their work are also important. One is the stepping of the front of the Schiller Building from nine-story wings, which mark the height of the courts notched into the block from either side, to the seventeen-story tower. The other is the hitherto unpublished scheme for the Michigan Avenue Building (1904),

in which a fifteen-story front at the mouth of a deep, mid-block site conceals a U-court within, the south wing only of which is stepped down toward the rear of the lot, each step containing a skylight. Hence the sun from the south can better angle its way to the windows of the north wall of the court, which rises the full fifteen stories (figs. 73, 74; for the front elevation see fig. 106).

In his article on the interior lighting of office buildings, Adler's advocacy of careful lighting for tall office buildings could hardly have been more emphatic, especially coming from one who is customarily praised for his structural skills:

Those who have taken a serious interest in this subject have devoted themselves almost entirely to the structural difficulties incident to the problem. I must confess that I cannot agree with those who place the matter of structural design as first in importance. I can easily imagine a tall office building most admirable in everything that relates to mere construction, and yet worthless to its owners.

The first requisite to the successful occupation of any premises for use as offices . . . is light and air.

The experience of real-estate agents shows that high rentals can be obtained only for well-lighted offices, and that the most desirable tenants will not occupy inferior or ill-lighted rooms at ever so low a rental. Their experience further shows that tenants of high professional and business standing draw into the building which they occupy others of like character, and that occupation of premises by tenants of inferior standing in the community repels tenants of the higher grade. If, therefore, a given building, no matter how favorably located, how soundly constructed, and how well equipped, has many dark rooms, it cannot be rented at all; or, if rented, its tenants will be undesirable in character and standing, and the rental derived from the investment will be small. But while the rents are small operating expenses will be large . . . as great as though the building were filled with tenants paying the highest rent. The amount expended for artificial light will be much greater than if the building were properly planned; and even the cost of repairs will

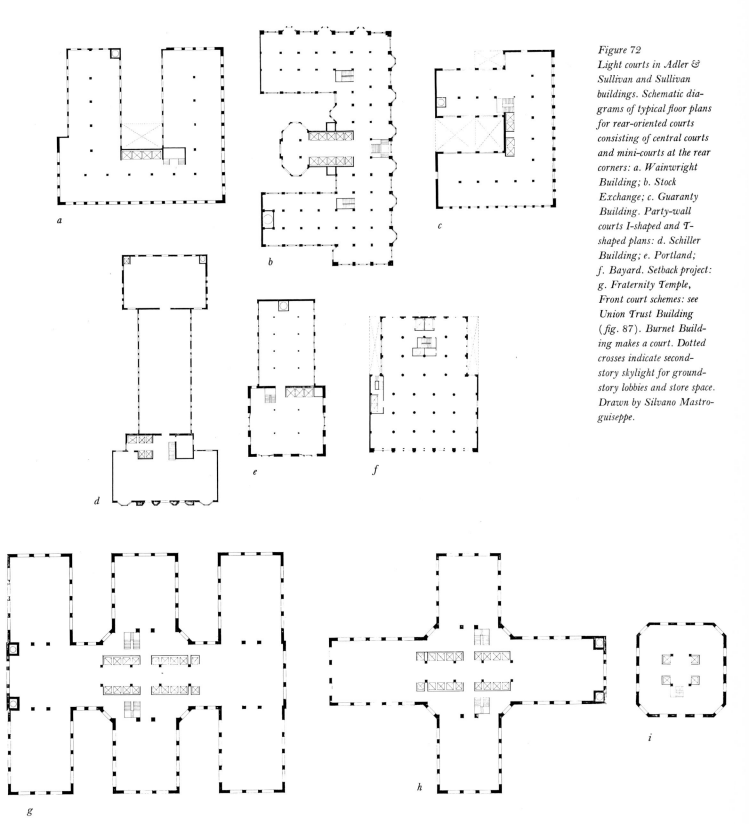

Figure 72
Light courts in Adler &
Sullivan and Sullivan
buildings. Schematic dia-
grams of typical floor plans
for rear-oriented courts
consisting of central courts
and mini-courts at the rear
corners: a. Wainwright
Building; b. Stock
Exchange; c. Guaranty
Building. Party-wall
courts I-shaped and T-
shaped plans: d. Schiller
Building; e. Portland;
f. Bayard. Setback project:
g. Fraternity Temple,
Front court schemes: see
Union Trust Building
(fig. 87). Burnet Build-
ing makes a court. Dotted
crosses indicate second-
story skylight for ground-
story lobbies and store space.
Drawn by Silvano Mastro-
guiseppe.

Figure 73
Louis H. Sullivan, project for 112–116 South Michigan Avenue, Chicago, 1904. Side alley elevation, showing the stepped roof and skylighting of the south wing of the interior light court.

Figure 74
Typical plan for the ninth through twelfth floors. Plans indicate that the stepping occurs only on the south wing of the light court, while the north wing maintains the same floor area throughout. Courtesy Northwest Architectural Archives, University of Minnesota, St. Paul.

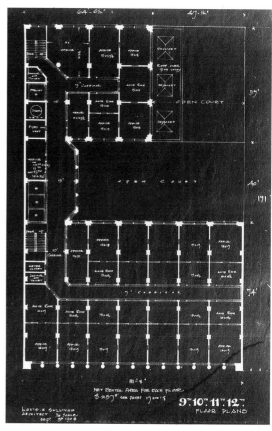

increase, because inferior tenants will not take as good care of their premises as will a better grade.

Another proof of the morality of light and air which will so substantially drive the modern movement! Expectedly for an architect of tall buildings, Adler went on to deplore the calls which were beginning to come for legislation to control the heights of buildings. Temporary restrictive legislation in Chicago was, in fact, partially responsible for frustrating the realization of the thirty-six story Fraternity tower. So Adler's conclusion was heartfelt that the free enterprise system, with cooperation from adjacent owners, could better handle the problem. And in the article he used unidentified Adler & Sullivan buildings as examples to prove his point.[28]

That such an important, and even venturesome, aspect of the function of the office building should be subordinated to the blocklike countenance which these buildings habitually present reaffirms the compulsion of the block in Sullivan's thinking, despite his work with Adler on the scheme for the setback Fraternity Temple. The "four square" aspect of the vast majority of Sullivan's buildings, like that of Richardson's Wholesale Store itself, is a pretense.

In "The Tall Building Artistically Considered," Sullivan lamely justified his neglect of light courts as desiderata for the "artistic expression of the building":

As to the necessary arrangements for light courts, these are not germane to the problem, and . . . need

*not be considered here. These things, and such others
as the arrangement of elevators, for example, have
to do strictly with the economics of the building, and
I assume them to have been fully considered and
disposed of to the satisfaction of purely utilitarian
and pecuniary demands. Only in rare instances does
the plan or floor arrangement of the tall office
building take on an aesthetic value, and this usually
when the lighting court is external or becomes an
internal feature of great importance.*[29]

Sullivan would have been exceptional indeed to have radically broken with the blocky shape for the office building which was then (and even now) so thoroughly established and expected. But for so ardent a self-proclaimed functionalist, his attitude toward light in "The Tall Office Building Artistically Considered" was remarkably cavalier.

Ironically, during the restoration of the Wainwright, in the late 1970s by Hastings & Chivetta, its lighting court was completely transformed into an impressive interior court rising the full height of the building, and making it a major interior feature. Offices around the light court were replaced by corridors, windows knocked out to make a gaping sort of tiered arcade around the well, with the stained glass lobby ceiling floating at the bottom, pretty but without any other function. This new arrangement probably delights most visitors, as the dramatic "ruin" which restoration too frequently brings. Others will be dismayed that the restoration could not have been more thoroughgoing, however grateful they may be for what is left. In effect, Sullivan's Wainwright is somewhat disembodied, reduced to its two exterior walls,[30] its shape, and ornamental fragments inside.

If the sense of the block so forcefully present in the Wainwright was specifically conditioned by Richardson's example, and more generally by predilections for the big block in Chicago office design around 1890, it doubtless owes quite as much to the nascent classicism which was then being viewed as a counter to the "restlessness" of Victorian picturesque composition. Sullivan may have appreciated that the severity of Richardson's

ordering of his Wholesale Store by the simple geometry of its openings was rather more "Renaissance" than "Romanesque." In the Wainwright especially, Sullivan makes Richardson's adumbration of a Renaissance palace (the Strozzi, for example) more specifically "classical." Sullivan himself makes a favorable allusion to the "base-shaft-capital" metaphor as an analogy for the organization of the tall office building, then immediately dismisses this, and other trinitarian analogues for the store base/office shaft/cornice capital, as superficial compositional formulae for what results "naturally, spontaneously, unwittingly [as] a three-part division not from any theory, symbol, or fancy logic."[31] Still, if the classical analogy is to be applied to any of Sullivan's designs, it is best applied to the Wainwright. He decisively separated the granite "base" from the "shaft" of vertical piers above by a projecting, shelflike, decorated molding (although significantly fused with the broad corner piers). The "fluting" of the verticals is appropriately hard and linear, hurrying the eye up the elevation. Incongruously for the metaphor, but underscoring the classical inspiration of the design, each of the "flutes" has its individual "capital" in the form of an ornamented panel immediately under the cornice (thereby doubling as a "pilaster"). And of course the building-as-column is lushly capped by swirls of acanthuslike leaves reminiscent of the Corinthian order. Moreover, apart from the specifics of the base-shaft-capital analogy, the classicism of the Wainwright can be extended to the decisive legibility of all the parts within the compositional whole. The precision with which the parts are articulated, and the hierarchy of plain to decorated surfaces ("Greek," Barr Ferree termed it)[32] are also classical in feeling. Indeed, the very physical presence of the building, its "stance," is reminiscently classical.

Writing twenty years after the publication of his monograph, Hugh Morrison stated that the only substantial change he would make in his assessment of Sullivan's work, were he to redo the book, would be to emphasize how very classical the Wainwright is.[33] It seems to have been Sullivan's discovery of a classical sensibility inspired in part by his brief, but intense, experience at the Ecole des Beaux-Arts in Paris (1874–1875) that permitted him both to call on Richardson's Wholesale Store, and to break decisively with it. Up to the Wainwright, he had been using the geometry of Richardson's openings as complicating variations on a theme. Suddenly, with the Wainwright, he could produce a parallel to Richardson's large statement, but in accord with a new mode of building and sensibility, looking to the future of the large office building, as Richardson could be said to summarize the past.

Here, Sullivan would seem to say, is the *modern* Marshall Field, which is simultaneously the *modern* Renaissance palace. Just how modern is readily apparent in the comparable elision from the Marshall Field to the Renaissance palace effected only slightly earlier by McKim, Mead & White in their New York Insurance Building (see fig. 75) in Omaha, duplicated, as illustrated by Hugh Morrison, for the same company in Kansas City at the same time. In effect, McKim, Mead & White's building represented the stage which the *St. Louis Globe-Democrat* called the starting point for Sullivan's design. The radicalism of the Wainwright erupts from what was, by 1890, the double conservatism of Richardson's block and the palaces which had begun to characterize the emerging "American Renaissance." Yet the Wainwright holds onto this conservatism too.

The Wainwright is generally viewed as the antithesis of overt allusions to the classical past with which eastern architects would create an "American Renaissance" in the 1890s, a point of view reinforced by Sullivan's later strictures against the way this Renaissance engulfed the Columbian Exposition ("The damage wrought by the World's Fair will last for half a century from its date, if not longer").[34] In fact, however, the Wainwright could also be included among its cardinal monuments.

So the blockiness of the Wainwright speaks to the Chicago commercial block and among them,

specifically to the Marshall Field Wholesale Store, to Sullivan's feeling for the classical, and . . . anything else? From beginning to end, the block is there. It was present in his variations on Richardson's theme, and quintessentially present in the three tombs, two of them especially, that cluster around the time of the Wainwright design. For all that his commercial design of the 1890s centers in the expression of skeletal framing, this sense of the box continues throughout—containing the embellished elevations, holding them in. It is even true of the very skeletal Carson Pirie Scott Store (see fig. 107); and spectacularly so of the little Van Allen store (see fig. 119), where the Chicago windows become virtual ribbons of glass. One might expect the ribboning and openness to overwhelm the blocklike compactness of the building; but they do not. And when the commercial commissions fell away after 1904, instinctively Sullivan returned to the box, quite literally. The tombs became banks, strongboxes both.

It is the essence of Sullivan's expressive message that energies held fast are released, and the essence of its drama that both the stage of constriction and that of freedom—the lock and the escape—appear simultaneously. For Sullivan it became the metaphor for creativity itself. In *A System of Architectural Ornament According with a Philosophy of Man's Powers*, drawn just before his death and posthumously published in 1924, his starting point was the husk of the seed being broken to send out the first tiny leaves. And he goes on to speak of the block of inert matter, which is divided geometrically, then further manipulated by the initial forays into the organic, until suddenly it explodes into life (fig. 76a, b, c). It was this process that led to the Wainwright. Sullivan sensed the stirrings within Richardson's block. In a series of designs dependent on the Marshall Field Wholesale Store, he manipulated the block geometrically in Richardson's terms, so that the placement, shape, and scale of the openings in themselves essentially determined the "architecture." Even in this determination of openings, however, Sullivan's inclination for the ornamental asserted itself in his abstraction and manipulation of Richardson's example for the variety of compositional motifs it could provide. Overt ornament appears shyly, but staunchly, in the Walker Warehouse in the impost blocks from which the biggest arches rise, like a mountain flower breaking from the rock (fig. 77). In the Getty Tomb it is more insistent (fig. 78). Is the wide arc inscribed in the block around the door architectural or ornamental? Does it inscribe the voussoirs of an arch; or a segmented, semicircular field containing interior arcs of incised ornament? They radiate outward in widening intervals and narrowing bands, with the effect of widening and dying ripples from a rock dropped in water. The alternate readings are so vividly present precisely because the voussoirs or "ornamental fields" barely disturb the geometrical containment of the block. In the Wainwright Tomb (fig. 79), the interlocking geometry of the openings in the Walker Warehouse becomes more explicitly ornamental: the block becomes two tightly interlocked fields defining the door and the windows, all accomplished by means of sumptuous bands of ornament and the slightest differentiation in plane, which barely disturbs the steadfastness of the block. In the Getty and Wainwright Tombs the block is immediately present, and quite literally made "architecture" by ornamental manipulation. The seed pod bursts into life. Death becomes resurrection.[35] The symbolism is nowhere overt or external; it is integral with the architectural act.

Just at this time the design of the Wainwright Building occurred, "a very sudden volcanic design (made literally in three minutes)": the block opening to new possibilities; the husk exploding with new leaves. But the block remains nevertheless. Coming upon the Wainwright or even the Guaranty Building today amidst the much higher office buildings which now rise around them in downtown St. Louis and Buffalo, the first response of the architectural pilgrim is less likely to be "how tall!" than "how compact, how cubelike!"

So the Wainwright marked the moment of revelation as to what the tall office building should

Figure 75
McKim, Mead & White,
New York Insurance
Building, Omaha,
1887-1890. From The
Architectural Record,
1895, No. 2; Courtesy
Leland M. Roth.

*Figure 76 a, b, c
The seed pod, from the
frontispiece plate of Louis
H. Sullivan*, A System of
Architectural Ornament
According with a Philos-
ophy of Man's Powers,
*1924. b, c: Plates I and IV,
from Louis H. Sullivan*,
A System of Architectural
Ornament According
with a Philosophy of
Man's Powers, *1924.*

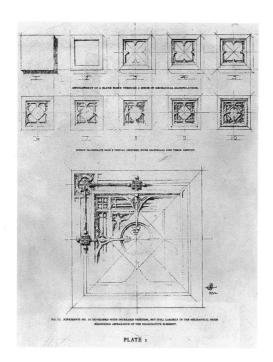

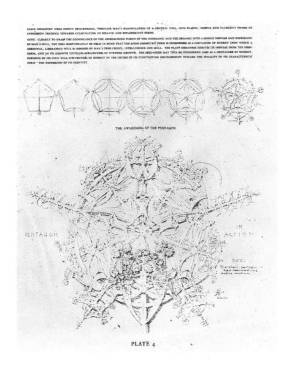

be. Sullivan had only to refine the design, to per-fect it. But of course the story of Sullivan's involve-ment with the tall, metal-framed building is not that simple.

Although he mentioned more, Morrison illus-trated eleven designs by Sullivan for the tall com-mercial building, subsequent to the Wainwright; the Richard Nickel archive contributes nine addi-tional designs (five are published in Twombly). Of these, seventeen are for office buildings, one for a wholesale store (in two versions), and one for a large, twelve-story department store (Schlesinger & Mayer, later Carson Pirie Scott). To these add the late, small, three-story Van Allen Store, for a total of twenty-one examples.[36] These essentially represent Sullivan's contribution to the design of the office and commercial metal-framed building from the Wainwright onward. Slightly more than half are bunched between 1890 and 1893. Four commissions, the Stock Exchange (begun in 1893), the Guaranty, two versions for the unbuilt Chemical National Bank in St. Louis, and the proj-ect for Burnet House in Cincinnati carry Sullivan's commercial style through 1894 and 1895. The Gage, the Bayard, and Carson Pirie Scott Store, plus his project for a building on Michigan Avenue in Chicago extend the story from 1897 through 1904. Then, a blank, until finally, off by itself in 1913 to 1915, the Van Allen Store appears as a diminutive and belated postlude.

Of these twenty-one designs, critics and histo-rians have focused on five: the Wainwright, Guar-anty, Gage, and Bayard Buildings, together with the Carson Pirie Scott Store, although various critics have favored different buildings among this group. But what of the twenty-one designs as a whole? Because many are hybrids of one another, any attempt to classify them typologically is arbi-trary and overlapping to some degree. Yet only in this way can one sense the key ideas in Sullivan's contributions to the design of the tall skeletal office and commercial building (fig. 80).[37]

One grouping stems from the Wainwright, which includes the design for the so-called Trust and Savings, and one version (Nickel refers to it as "B") of a design for an unidentified tall building (all for St. Louis), the Burnet House (Cincinnati), the Guaranty (Buffalo), the Bayard (New York), and a project for a tall building on Michigan Avenue (Chicago). Three of these seven have been among the most praised of Sullivan's works. As a group, they express skeletal framing as a linear opposition of projecting verticals against inset horizontal. Projecting piers run the height of the building as the visible sign of support, across inset horizontals spandrel panels as the visible sign of span—hence the descriptive term for this of "pier-and-spandrel." The projecting verticals may appear to be identical piers (as in the Wainwright) even though only every other pier actually contains a column; or, truer to the facts of the construction, they may alternate with mullions, a larger, squarish pier containing its internal support with a small, nonsupporting cylindrical mullion which serves only to frame adjacent windows (as in the Bayard). Either way, the projecting verticals are closely positioned with only the width of a single standard-sized sash window between, each supported on the decorated parapeting of its spandrel panel. The repetitive verticals tend (except in the Wainwright) to fuse with a richly ornamented cornice, and, more rarely and less decisively, with the base below.

A second group, including one of Sullivan's critically acclaimed buildings, employs the widely spaced structural columns natural to skeletal framing, and expresses the spanned interval between them by a horizontal window. Ideally, in Sullivan's work this occurs as a three-part unit consisting of a central fixed sheet of plate glass flanked by narrow sash windows to control temperature and ventilation. This arrangement came to be called the "Chicago window" because of its assumed invention there, and certainly its popularity in the Loop from roughly 1885 through 1900 and beyond. Less ideally, the space between the columns might contain a pair of normal sash windows, which taken together approximate the "Chicago window." Either way the wall is seen as a reticulated grid infilled with horizontal openings. Whereas

Figure 77
Adler & Sullivan, Walker Warehouse, Chicago, 1888– 1889, detail showing the ornament of the impost blocks. Harold Allen, photographer.

the first group of designs involves a layered treatment of the wall—from the plane of the projecting piers/mullions in to the plane of the spandrel panels, then to the plane of the glass—buildings in the second group emphasize the wall plane as the outer face of the grid, with deeply inset, markedly horizontal openings. There are four examples: two schemes for the unbuilt Chemical National Bank Building in St. Louis, the Meyer Wholesale Store as built (because a preliminary design seems to belong to another group) and the Carson Pirie Scott Store, both in Chicago.

The third group which has two examples and again contains one of the critically acclaimed buildings, crosses bands of horizontal Chicago windows and their parapeting with two or three widely-spaced, stemlike columns, projecting from the wall surface, and flowering into a burst of foliated ornament against the cornice frieze. The Gage Building (Chicago) and Van Allen Store (Clinton, Iowa) exemplify this type.

To these buildings in the first three groups we must return. They represent Sullivan's most creative solutions for exteriors expressive of the nature of the tall skeletal office and commercial building. All of which leaves nine additional designs for consideration. Some are not so much less successful as less complete solutions for the problem which Sullivan set for himself. Overall they reveal the

Figure 78
Louis H. Sullivan, Carrie
Eliza Getty Tomb, Grace-
land Cemetery, Chicago,
1890. Cervin Robinson,
photographer.

Figure 79
Louis H. Sullivan, Char-
lotte Dickson Wainwright
Tomb, Bellefontaine Ceme-
tery, St. Louis, 1892.
Richard Nickel, photog-
rapher. Courtesy Richard
Nickel Committee.

I *a*   *b*   *c*

Figure 80
Skeletal office and commercial buildings by Sullivan grouped according to various design approaches. The first three groups comprise the more radical designs.

more conservative, or less integrated, side of his designs. Two examples even border on confusion. Yet Sullivan's more conservative works include such exceptional designs as those for the Fraternity Temple tower, the Schiller Building, the neglected initial design for the Meyer Wholesale Store, and the Stock Exchange.

The Fraternity Temple tower (1891) and the preliminary project for the Meyer Wholesale Store (1893), both in Chicago, comprise the fourth in our schematic grouping of Sullivan's designs for tall office and commercial buildings (figs. 82 and 83). They continue to explore the Wainwright motif of a densely gridded crossing of piers over spandrels strongly enframed by planes of wall. Whereas the Guaranty and Bayard buildings further articulate the skeletal theme implicit in the Wainwright's interlocked grid, the projects for the Fraternity Temple and the Meyer Store stay with the articulated cube. Bold as it is as a concept for the tall building—boldest of all, in fact—we have already observed that a pyramid of Wainwright buildings comprises the lower stages of the Fraternity Temple tower. In the freestanding nature of this stepped composition, the corner piers become even more

evident than they are in the Wainwright. Insistently framed and stacked, the fields of pier-and-spandrel openings take on a somewhat panelled effect as isolated elevational screens, and especially at the level of the second setbacks. There the cornice is lifted away from the field of piers below, so as to enframe it, immure it, within the wall. The cornice floats above the range of piers as another discrete compositional element. And above this level, all sense of skeletal construction is lost. The tower retreats to a masonry aesthetic. The pier-and-spandrel rationale as the generating impulse for the Wainwright gives way to the sheer wall plane traditionally punched with openings for standard sash windows.

The same framing of the pier-and-spandrel screen occurs in the initial scheme for the Meyer Store. How different the more utilitarian version that was eventually built! The built version justifiably won the plaudits of modernists as a pioneer expression of the kind of horizontal window treatment which became popular by the late 1920s, and for its stripped-down quality as well. But the original version for a much more resplendent effect deserves far more notice than it has received.

d

e

Had it been realized it would have ranked among Sullivan's handsomest buildings. The gridded pier-and-spandrel wall becomes a range of five-story stacks of paired windows, each strongly framed as panels. As in the Wainwright Tomb, bands of ornament edge the panels, like picture frames, in a crinkle of light and shadow. Similarly, the loggia-like run of the windows under the cornice (which again floats as an isolated entity on the plane of the wall, and the long void for the show windows subdivided by columns, close the elevations top and bottom in a panelled effect. So the entire building appears as an interplay of wall and openings organized as frame and panels.

The next group of buildings—the fifth in our schema (or is it a subset of the other?)—reveals a similar conservatism, except that the point of departure is the arching of the Marshall Field Wholesale Store rather than the pier-and-spandrel grid of the Wainwright. Simultaneously to his design of the Wainwright, in fact, Sullivan was also working on the Dooly Block (see fig. 64). The Schiller Building (1891–1892) and the Union Trust Building (1892–1893) represent the extension of the Dooly from the block to the tall building (figs 83 and 84).

Of all his towers, the Auditorium and the Schiller are his finest: the first, a forceful block extracted from the gargantuan block below; the second, more deliberately conceived as a tower, and rising out of his fine theater, the Schiller (later the Garrick).[38] As a composition, the Schiller tower is simplicity itself; the Wainwright redone in arches, with the proportions of the tower determined by the architect rather than the site, so that the arches really do seem (in Sullivan's adjective) "tall." But the plane of the wall rather than the pier-and-spandrel grid predominates, partly because the corner piers are dominant in the narrow elevations, and partly because its sheer surface spreads over the tops of the arches, and contains them. Again, the decorated cornice is isolated from the piers. The narrow arches, cleanly cut into the wall, close-packed but not pinched, and all very severe, are capped by the usual decorated cornice with the much repeated Sullivanian trademarks of mock loggia and projecting slab. In the restraint of the tower rising from the decorated theater front to the decorated cornice, proportions and the incisive refinement of plane and shape carry the day.

Group I: a. Wainwright, James Marchael, photographer; b. unidentified building for St. Louis, scheme "B," Courtesy The Art Institute of Chicago; c. Trust & Savings, Courtesy Chicago Architectural Photo Co.; d. Burnet, Courtesy The Art Institute of Chicago; e. Guaranty, Courtesy Chicago Architectural Photo Co.; f. Bayard, Courtesy Museum of the City of New York; g. project for a building on Michigan Avenue, Courtesy Northwest Architectural Archives.

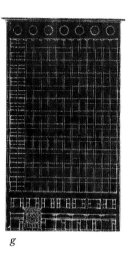

I *f*   *g*   II *h*

The Schiller and its magnificent theater are gone. Its larger variant, the Union Trust (with Ramsey again as the local collaborator), remains in St. Louis, at least above the first two stories. The arches are now two windows wide, with roundels (like those in the Bayard) at their turning; the piers are narrower. So the skeletal sense is greater than in the Schiller although the wall plane still predominates. The well-proportioned austerity of the arches is here somewhat compromised by the less integrated aspects of the design. One of these is the stack of bay windows tucked away at the back of the exposed light court as an axial feature for the elevation (not visible in the photograph). However delightful this puff of space may be inside, it becomes a cramped excrescence on the elevation. More conspicuously, the top two full office floors above the arches are not convincingly disguised as a columned loggia, nor do they terminate the composition with the compactness and decisiveness of Sullivan's equivalent for the Schiller. Here the cornice floats above the enframed loggia in the way that similar effects occur in the Fraternity Temple and Meyer Store. Although decidedly stated as a distinct entity, the cornice does flare in a curve

from the wall in a manner that anticipates the fusion of parts which Sullivan eventually brings to this detail in the Guaranty and Bayard. But essentially, all these buildings which exhibit Sullivan's conservative side reveal an isolation and compartmentalization of architectural parts as discrete entities within the composition, in the manner of contemporary firms committed to Renaissance forms, like McKim, Mead & White.

The Wainwright was a watershed in more than one respect. If it represented both to Sullivan himself and to historians the moment when he found an appropriate solution for the tall office building, it was a moment of some uncertainty, too. Which way to go? Toward a compositionalism akin to that of the Renaissance revival, but using a nontraditional vocabulary of forms? Or toward an even more original manner, which still in the early nineties, the Wainwright notwithstanding, he only dimly discerned?

In his more conservative (yet still creative) vein, the Wainwright ingredients of window lattice, corner piers, and slab-topped cornice could be explored in terms of traditional composition. The result: designs for Fraternity Temple and the

i

j

k

initial version of the Meyer Store both offering promise for future development. Or, simultaneously, the same themes could be exposed to the pervasive afterglow of Richardsonian Romanesque. The style persisted into the nineties in the Midwest, and nowhere more strongly than in Chicago, at a time when it was already passé in the East where it had originated. Could one continue the Romanesque to more radical, more abstract, more modern effect? The result: the impressive Schiller and Union Trust Buildings among Sullivan's office designs, in addition to his Transportation Building.

If there were to be a long future for Richardsonian Romanesque beyond the career of its so early deceased creator—as it soon turned out there was not—the Eastern architectural critic Montgomery Schuyler, for one, suggested in a series of articles in the early nineties that the very abundance of examples in the Midwest, and the excellence of designers like Root in this manner, indicated that the prairie cities might show the way. But, as Schuyler noted in 1891, any continuation of Richardson's style could not expect to retain the massive ruggedness of his own work,

especially as masonry construction for large building was giving way to metal skeletal construction.

As the besetting tendency of Gothic is to tenuity and complication and unrest, so the besetting tendency of Romanesque is to clumsiness and crudity and rudeness. Where mass and weight and power are to be expressed it leaves nothing to be desired, but we can scarcely point either in the original or thus far in the revived Romanesque, to a design that can fairly be called "elegant." Yet elegance is a quality as suitable for architectural expression as force, and no style can be accounted complete until . it is adequate to every expression. It is in this direction that modern architects may develop Romanesque into the elegance of later Gothic, without direct resort to Gothic precedents, and without losing the vigor and massiveness of Romanesque as we know it, where these qualities are required.[39]

To be rugged *and* elegant, these were the twin requirements of a style adequate for the modern office building. And this was exactly what Sullivan was attempting in the Schiller and Union Trust.

How appropriate that the Wainwright and the

III *l*   *m*

he conceives to be the central forces creating the modern America of his day. Knowing *only* the Union Trust—as he too, at that time knew his work only up to the Union Trust—we would sense merely that he means to disrupt whatever is expected in his progressive development of Richardsonian Romanesque with something extraordinary. And what is extraordinary appears here as impatient, even incongruous thrusts.

For example, the Union Trust is the most animalistic of Sullivan's designs. Animal images are frequent in Richardson's work, as might be expected in his lusty embrace of Romanesque with its wealth of animal fantasy. In Sullivan's work, lions especially, along with other catlike creatures appear throughout his buildings. They have either

Group III. l. Gage, Courtesy Chicago Historical Society ICHi–00985; m. Van Allen Store, courtesy Museum of Modern Art, New York.

Union Trust stand within sight of one another in St. Louis![40] Which way to go? Should it be in one of two conservative directions, out of the Marshall Field Wholesale Store, or out of some classically composed deployment of the elements of the Wainwright? Both ways promised original possibilities for future development. But was there perhaps *even more radical potential* in the Wainwright? Not surprisingly, the relatively conservative approaches momentarily predominated in the first years of the 1890s. The more radical way was harder to find.

However, even within the limits of Sullivan's relatively conservative approaches to the design of tall office buildings concurrent with the Wainwright, the unexpected, unusual, even disconcerting appears as an indication of his restless casting about for "new" solutions, which he felt to be there, but could not yet quite locate. Thus, if the Union Trust is the more conservative of the two buildings in St. Louis, it also contains probes toward the "new"—or at least the "different"—which show Sullivan already groping impatiently for something *beyond* the Wainwright. With knowledge of what is to come, we can see that Sullivan is seeking ways to represent the energies which he feels to be latent in office and commercial buildings as the monumental embodiment of what

IV *n*

been passed over in embarrassed silence, or noted without comment. In the Union Trust, a row of placid lions' heads appears in the spandrel panels within the two-story loggia at the top of the building. Just below them, snarling bobcats, pumas, or perhaps female lions provide lively gargoyles off the corners of the building. At the second-story level, seated and winged lions (or griffins?) with escutcheons, a full floor in height, originally sat on heavy brackets, marking the corners of the building and flanking its two-story Romanesque entrance (fig. 85). These seated lions have been lost to the mediocre renovation of the base of the building, together with the band of embowered, circular windows over which they once presided. (Even the round openings have been squared, except for a range of them hidden away in a side alley, cut into plain walls, with tiny lion's heads at their bottoms as the sole remnant of the original decorative program.) The round windows and foliage seem to have evolved from the Wainwright cornice, its oculi enlarged for the Union Trust, its leafage more sedately contained within banded fields. The oculi and their placement may also owe something to the Transportation Building, which is roughly contemporaneous with Union Trust. For the exterior of the Transportation Building (see fig. 67)

Sullivan used the massing format of a Roman or medieval basilica, with roofed side aisle stepped up to a high central nave. Rows of arched openings appear at the lower level and up in the clerestory. Between the two, concealed by the slope of the skylighted aisle roof on the exterior, but very conspicuous from the inside, a row of circular openings is particularly evident in construction views (fig. 86). The motif may owe something to the similar intervention of rose windows within the nave of the Cathedral of Notre Dame in Paris[41] with which Sullivan could have been familiar from his studies abroad. (Were they intended as luminous invocations of wheels in the Transportation Building?) In any event, the circular theme, which intervenes so abruptly and strangely within the window system of the Transportation Building, has the same unsettling effect in the original base of the Union Trust.

The whole of this second-story embellishment is extraordinary, and proof that there is bound to be something experimental in a Sullivan building even when conceived as a relatively conservative composition overall. Too excessive in its flamboyance? Too unarchitectural as a base for the severity above, in its mixture of outsized lions, distended circles, and crinkled foliation? Undoubt-

Skeletal office and commercial building by Sullivan grouped according to various design approaches. The last four groups comprise the more conservative designs.

Group IV: n. Fraternity Temple, Courtesy Chicago Historical Society; o. preliminary design for the Meyer Wholesale Store, from Inland Architect, 1892.

Group V: p. Schiller, courtesy Chicago Historical Society; q. Union Trust, Courtesy Missouri Historical Society. Group VI: r. unidentified building for St. Louis, scheme "A," Courtesy The Art Institute of Chicago.

o

V *p*

q

VI *r*

Miscellaneous: s. Stock Exchange, Courtesy Chicago Historical Society ICHi–19456; t. Mercantile Club, Courtesy The Art Institute of Chicago; u. Portland, Courtesy Richard Nickel Committee.

edly: but Sullivan here seems to be attempting an ornamental and rhetorical equivalent to the opposition of the compressive (bearing) function of the vertical columns in skeletal frame construction against the tensile (spanning) function of the horizontal beams which bridge the intervals between supports. So the supporting properties within the building are visibly gathered into the beasts which sit at crucial corners of the building, those that affirm the block as a whole and the entrance. The expansive stretch of the butting oculi celebrate its spanning properties. Unhappily, both the circularity of the openings and their enframement obscure the sense of the columns coming to the ground. The seated beasts are incongruously emphatic. One might suspect that the client demanded them as some sort of identifying sign for his business, and that they appear against the architect's better judgment. But such seated beasts occur, with as much unexpectedness, in other Sullivan buildings; so the client may be exonerated. In any event, the total effect of this strange combination of elements seems unarchitectural, which substantially accounts for our discomfort. Hyperbole, in both his ornament and especially in his writing, was Sullivan's besetting sin. But, paradoxically, his intent here to make visible in a monumental way the forces acting within the build-

ing is also evident. Similar analogies to forces operating within the architecture appear in the lower stories of later buildings, in different visual terms. That this slightly preposterous, but vigorous array of mismatched forms should have been lost to "modernization" is not surprising, but is a pity nonetheless. Were it in place, it would help to reveal this St. Louis moment of mixed achievement, promise, and bafflement.

But to return to our classifying, a single building may be relegated to a sixth category, to mark yet another conservative approach in the morphology of Sullivan's design during the years immediately after 1890. This is one of two designs for an unknown office building in St. Louis (ca. 1892) — scheme "A" in Nickel's designation (fig. 87).[42] The paired windows are simply punched into the plane of the wall, taking their cue from the reticulated grid natural to the metal skeletal frame beneath. Their pairing gives the tiers of windows across the elevation a somewhat horizontal effect, anticipating a similar, but more marked horizontality in the later two schemes for the Chemical Building, and culminating in the Carson Pirie Scott Store (see figs. 110, 111 and 112). So perhaps this project should be included with the other group. But there are conservative aspects about this scheme which could separate it from the

s

t

u

Figure 81
*Adler & Sullivan, project
for Fraternity Temple,
Chicago, 1891. Courtesy
Chicago Historical Society.*

*Figure 82
Adler & Sullivan, preliminary design for the Meyer Wholesale Store, Chicago, 1893. From Inland Architect, 1892.*

sequence of which it was probably a part. Although one hesitates to judge from this none too clear perspective what the ultimate effect of the building would have been, the horizontal impulse for the tiers of office windows in the unidentified building is not emphasized as it seems to be in the Chemical Bank schemes. There is here a relative equivalence of walling around each window which neutralizes the sense of the horizontal. In the Chemical Bank schemes, and decidedly in the Carson Pirie Scott Store, the horizontal aspects of the wall under and over the windows are markedly broader than the vertical aspects of the wall between the windows. Hence the effect of the horizontal "banding" of the wall by its windows is emphasized in the later buildings. In them, too, the relationship of the horizontal and reticulated treatment of the base and cornice of the buildings is more appropriate and substantially better integrated with the pattern of office windows between than is the case with the unidentified building. The discreteness of its high

cornice, wreathed in foliated ornament with a vertical emphasis, together with the vertical proportions of the base with its awkward mixture of tall arched and rectangular openings, makes it apparent that Sullivan had not yet seriously thought through the horizontal alternative to his more prevalent verticalized expressions for the tall skeletal building. So give this unnamed building a pigeonhole of its own.

Finally, the classifier is, as usual, pushed to the despair of a "miscellaneous" category; in this instance, to account for three more buildings. The most important is the Stock Exchange (1893–1894) in Chicago (fig. 88). In its burly mass it might be said to recall the Marshall Field Wholesale Store one last time. The extensive half-block site and the augustness of the institution may have encouraged Sullivan to take a final look back, but only from the corner of his eye. He clearly meant to depart radically from Richardson's example.

The base of the building decisively distinguishes itself from the offices above, almost as a separate entity. Its grandly decorated entrance arch interlocks with a range of two-storied arching which rides on the low shop fronts at street level. The exterior arching celebrates the two-storied exchange within; ambiguously, however, because it occupies space only to the left of the entrance as one enters the building.[43] Above the base, in the office floors, the repetitive verticals of the projecting bays are piled against the alternating horizontality of the Chicago windows set into the plane of the wall. The cross of a wall of windows by stacks of vertical bays was fairly common in Chicago in the early nineties, and Sullivan doubtless drew on this ubiquitous tradition for his Stock Exchange.[44] John Wellborn Root's masterful Monadnock Building (1889–1891) was closest in spirit. There a single deepset sash window of standard size in the wall plane alternates with a bay of four closely packed windows which undulates out from the wall toward the light and returns. The effect is very sculptural, the bays integral with the wall. One thinks of breathing, as the wall gently expands and contracts. Root's rhythmic integration of the bay with the wall was unmatched by any other office building in the Loop. The only alternative which in any way approached this integration was the banding of repetitive bays to the plane of the wall by horizontal moldings at the top and bottom of the parapeting as in Holabird & Roche's Tacoma Building (see fig. 57), where the sense of a wall wholly disappears and the bays are bound to the poles which the structural columns have become. Sullivan's bay windows in the Stock Exchange show no such integration, nor is the contrast between regular-sized windows for the bays alternating with horizontal Chicago windows comfortable. This alternation, however, is the most original aspect of the Stock Exchange, because no other Chicago office building of consequence shows it. If Sullivan were attempting to redo the Monadnock in a different, more modern way in his Stock Exchange, he seems to do so by opening it up, by employing the two boldest methods of the period of bringing light into the interior—bays *and* Chicago windows. Moreover, the combination set a strong vertical component (the bay) against a strong horizontal component (the Chicago window), for an opposition of rhythms "up" and "across" which recur in Sullivan's work. Here both impulses are echoed in the range of the two-story arches. The elevation is closed at the top by a continuous band of very deepset windows with a row of columns in the slot, again invoking a loggia. This is, in turn, capped by a beetling cornice of ornament, which echoes the ornamentation of the embellished block of the spaciously telescoped arching of the entrance below. For this Sullivan reconsidered his Golden Portal of the Transportation Building.

That this important building by Adler & Sullivan should have been demolished as late as 1978 is especially reprehensible. Its demolition took the life of Richard Nickel, the photographer and dedicated preservationist of Sullivan's buildings, who was recording its demise and gathering fragments of ornament when he was buried beneath its rubble. The Stock Exchange room, reconstructed by John Vinci, is ironically enshrined in the Chicago Art

Figure 83
Adler & Sullivan, Schiller Building, 1891–1892. Courtesy Chicago Historical Society.

Institute, only a few blocks from where the original once existed. The decorated entrance portal stands as a disembodied triumphal arch outside the Institute. Both, in a sense, memorialize Nickel's dedication.

Two lesser designs complete the miscellany. In the projected design for the tower of the Mercantile Club (1891) in St. Louis, the loggia and balconies ludicrously, if somewhat engagingly, overwhelm the office tower (fig. 90). It is as though a highly decorated house had taken on an office building and won. There could be possibilities in an ornamental treatment which capped a plain office tower with a kind of medieval helmet,

its tooled surfaces even extending down to the visorlike grilles over the tenth and eleventh stories; but only if the ornament frankly asserted itself as a mask. It was not, however, in Sullivan's nature to have developed any such superficial or jocose approach to ornament. It is also interesting as an experiment in the use of ornament to set off the luxury of the club against the workaday plainness of the offices within a single building, while attempting some fusion of the two, and an echoing, if more restrained, embellishment at the base around the entrance and shop fronts. (He realized a comparable effect in the slightly later commission for the St. Nicholas Hotel in St. Louis.) On the whole, however, aside from the gusto and inventiveness of the design for the Mercantile Club Building, it hardly seems worthy of him. For one credited with giving form to the skyscraper, moreover, it is revelatory of Sullivan's surprising ineptness with towers. They appear frequently in his designs—for hotels, apartment houses, a provincial opera house, and this one which is in some ways a wilder version of that for the Odd Fellow's Fraternity Temple. One hardly knows what to deplore most in their design, whether the awkwardness of their conical shapes or that of their outsized loggia. His towers for the Auditorium and Schiller Building are exceptions that prove the rule. Both can also be viewed as elongated blocks.

As for the final design in the roster, his project for the Portland Building in St. Louis (1892) (fig. 91), it might be grouped with the Schiller Building and Fraternity Temple because it, too, displays lingering traces of the Marshall Field Wholesale Store. No other elevation by Sullivan, however, reveals a more varied window treatment in swatchlike uncertainty. On the front elevation alone, the store fronts at street level give way to two floors of paired windows cut as discrete rectangles into a smooth-faced wall; above this, seven-story rectangular slots, filled with wide inset bay windows, flank a center stack of conventional windows; then close-packed, two-story arches, before a beetling cornice cap brings the stack of this and that to a finale.

The preceding schematic morphology of the office and commercial buildings, concluding with the Portland, shows that Sullivan was not following a sense of clear "direction" to be pursued by progressive refinement, but making instead a series of thrusts in various directions. Whatever the degree of conviction revealed in particular buildings, a sense of continuous quest predominates.

His attitude toward the Wainwright seems to have been ambiguous. He justifiably congratulated himself on the clarity and directness with which it expressed the tallness of the office building, and the balance with which design considerations for this difficult building type had been acknowledged. But he seems to have questioned what was traditional in its composition. His ornamental approach to architecture encouraged this alternate vision. A period of uncertainty ensued, even thrashing about it would seem, in which all of the motifs and formulae he will use in his tall buildings appear (except perhaps for the pier as stem and efflorescence which he uses in the Bayard). They appear, however, as a curious mixture in which a more turbulent, fluid and responsive plasticity changes traditional compositional schemes. He is most successful during this period where he is more conservative—in the Schiller, Stock Exchange, the initial scheme for the Meyer Wholesale Store and, a little less so, in the audacious Fraternity Temple. All of these look back to the Wainwright and to Richardson, with less of the restless questing for the plastic architecture which wells up in his other designs of the early nineties.

The true break occurs, not with the Wainwright, but with its offspring, the Guaranty. From the Guaranty onward, during the few years in which he continued to receive commissions for the tall office building, his tall buildings manifest in different ways his vision of architecture.

Even those buildings during the early 1890s which reveal certain diffuseness, incongruity and exaggeration of parts, (reminding us of similar qualities in his writings) reveal qualities of design which seem paradoxically at odds with uncertainty, inso-far as these can be ascertained from the drawings. What saves them, in part at least, depends on his taut, incisive temperament in both personality and design. To those who knew him or worked with him, these qualities gave him a haughtiness and arrogance of manner. Wright recalled that his stride was longer than the easy span of his legs, which gave him something of a strut.[45] One feels this incisive side of his personality, its precision and decisiveness, which characterized a part of his creative impulse and against which tendencies toward prolixity, elaboration, and luxuriance warred—those Victorian preferences which Ruskin called "abundance." Repeatedly, those who observed him at work commented on this incisiveness. There is Wright's admiration, for example, at the height of Sullivan's career, for the fullblown appearance of the Wainwright design at the lift of a single drawing from the drafting board. And there is the observation of the president for the People's Savings and Loan Association Bank in Sidney, Ohio, who recalled toward the end of his career Sullivan sitting on the curb across the street from the site for two days once he had the commission, smoking endless cigarettes and meditating on the problem, until he had figured out the full design in his head. He then met with the building committee with a rapid sketch of the result which turned out to be pretty much as built.[46] Some have attributed this incisiveness in design to his training at the Ecole des Beaux-Arts, with its familiar emphasis on the *esquisse*. This involved a quick preliminary sketch on the assigned problem, done without consultation within a very limited period of time. When done, it had to be retained as the basis for weeks or months of elaboration, without substantial deviation from the original sketch. Although Sullivan may have profited by his brief stay at the Ecole from this mode of inculcating a swift grasp of the essentials of a problem, he was as likely to have been attracted to the method because of the predispositions of his temperament. The gifted draftsman who took Wright's place in Sullivan's office, George Elmslie, recalled his manner:

Figure 84
Adler & Sullivan, with
Charles K. Ramsey. Union
Trust Building, St. Louis
1892–1893, before alter-
ations to the base. Courtesy
Missouri Historical Society.

Very punctilious in his ways, Sullivan answered all letters the first day of arrival or next. There was no such idea as first things first, all was one continuous movement, drawing, dictating letters or specifications talking to various and sundry, looking us over. Highly concentrated yet at all times perfectly poised.[47]

These personal qualities of tautness, incisiveness, and elegance extend to his design. Summarizing what he saw as the nature of Sullivan's success in his designs, Montgomery Schuyler wrote in part in the first extensive critical study of him in 1896 that

I have already protested against the narrowness of the appreciation which finds in Mr. Sullivan only the first of our decorators, though that he so clearly is. This limitation ignores the structural instinct, or the reasoned engineering knowledge of mechanical relations, whichever you please, which presides over the placing, the magnitude and the forms of his masses. I should be at a loss to name any other American architect whose perception of these things is more unerring. And surely it is this perception of the importance of the masses, this appreciation of the essential facts of structure that makes the architect in contradistinction to the architectural decorator.[48]

Even when his designs for the tall office building seem confused or incomplete in part, there is always evidence of these qualities that Schuyler saw in Sullivan's work, and always the sense of a passionate quest to break through to his vision of what architecture should be.

To know him at his best (or at least, most innovative) it is to the "classics" that we must return. Among his tall office and commercial buildings, five enjoy special renown. Three are variants on the same idea: the Wainwright, Guaranty, and Bayard. The Carson Pirie Scott Store differs radically from these as a commission and as a design. The Gage is something of an intermediary, but also represents another in the three expressive ideas which are at the heart of Sullivan's contribution to the design of the tall metal-framed office and commercial building.

Restored under the supervision of Cannon Design,[49] the Guaranty Building, (subsequently the Prudential and now returned to its original name) (1894–1895) is, first of all, the pier-and-spandrel treatment of the Wainwright combined with the tall, slender arches of the Schiller; both the radical and conservative strains from Sullivan's groping around 1890 here hybridized. More significantly, the Guaranty is the Wainwright redone in terra-cotta (fig. 92). Instead of the granite base, and brick piers, with terra-cotta reserved for ornamental panels only, the Guaranty is completely sheathed in baked clay. It was only slightly anticipated by Charles Atwood's extension and revamping of the Reliance Building for the Burnham organization (after Root's death), from a four-story to a fifteen-story building (fig. 93). According to the *Architectural Record* of the time, this was the first building of its size and importance to have been completely clad in terra-cotta.[50] Up to that time, the material had visibly appeared in buildings for minor embellishment and invisibly as a fireproof coating to protect metal-framed structures buried under plaster and masonry finishes, or in such other non-resplendent roles as lightweight, fireproof arching to support floors and ceilings. The ductility of the material before its firing permitted the repetitive stamping of Gothicized ornament all over the pearl-gray surfaces of the Reliance. The possibility of using a material which permitted the embellishment of all surfaces surely captivated Sullivan. In his design for the Guaranty, Sullivan may even have been consciously competing with Atwood.

Later, Sullivan wrote a panegyric on terra-cotta, rather surprisingly, in the beautiful rental brochure for his Bayard Building. The anonymous description of the building and its advantages is quite conventional for the most part, making its pitch to the prospective renter much as any real estate brochure might. Its concluding sec-

tion, however, focuses on "the façade" and the material with which it is faced. The language is unmistakably Sullivan's:

The material, terra-cotta or baked clay, is older than civilization yet very new in its modern application. It has been chosen for this front because of its great fire-resisting capacity, its peculiar timely adaptability to the scientific steel-frame method of construction. It is the most plastic of materials in its raw state, suffering itself to be shaped, with marvelous readiness, into every conceivable delicacy and variety of form and movement, yet, when once fired, these forms and delicacies become everlasting; these movements and rhythms of the ornamentation preserve with the persistence of bronze every poetic and airy nothing that the creative imagination has imparted to them.[51]

As Frank Lloyd Wright remarked of his Lieber Meister, "all materials were only one material to him in which to weave the stuff of his dreams. Terra cotta was that one material. Terra cotta was *his* material, the one he loved most and served best."[52] An edge of condescension shows in Wright's remark, because the impressionable ductility of terra-cotta before firing was decidedly antipathetic to his hard-edged, geometric, more severely (and, as he certainly felt), more "responsibly" architectonic approach to ornament. But terra-cotta was ideal as the medium in which to impress the evanescent fluidity of Sullivan's ornament. After the rather heavy, Romanesque-inspired ornament in the terra-cotta spandrel panels and cornice of the Wainwright, the Guaranty shimmered from sidewalk to cornice, with every bit of its terra-cotta raiment embellished—terra-cotta both in its material and in its color.

"Sister" indeed, as Sullivan termed it,[53] compared to the more brotherly burliness of the Wainwright. The taller, more slender aspect of the piers, the graceful continuity and fusion of the piers into the trumpet-curve flare of the cornice (which may have owed something to Root's Monadnock Building), the small oculi of the Wainwright cornice now wide-eyed: all these qualities suggest a nervous finesse and elegance, a scintillant sparkle, which had made its initial appearance in some of the ornament of the Auditorium interiors. For this ornament, Paul Sprague notes that Sullivan's earlier mode of delineation radically changed from a continuous linear profiling of form, often in the spikey, angular shapes of High Victorian ornament, to a more febrile, broken, markedly curvilinear and fluid line, pricked with dots of shadow.[54] Spikes and angles had already largely disappeared on the exterior ornament of the Wainwright Building, to be replaced by curves. These increase its dynamics, as is especially evident in the roll of tendrils around the oculi in the cornice. Still a certain heaviness persists in the Wainwright ornament as though Sullivan had not yet wholly escaped from the influence of Richardson's Romanesque embellishment, and could not yet quite bring himself to use the light touch found in some of the interior ornament of the Auditorium for the greater monumentality required outside.[55] Before he designed the Guaranty, however, this timidity had disappeared. The Guaranty fully displays the characteristics of Sullivan's mature ornament, in its greater intricacy and its wiry, more evanescent line, with light dancing on pitted stippled surfaces (figs. 94 and 95).

The Wainwright may indeed represent the single episode of most aesthetic consequence in the shift from the tall office building in masonry to its skeletal predecessor; yet not only does the masonry tradition persist in the Wainwright, ornament also assumes a traditional, even if exceptionally conspicuous, role in its design. Hence one feels comfortable in "explaining" it. The conventional hierarchy in classical and Renaissance architecture which emphasizes the *geometrical* and *structural* aspects of the building over its ornamental aspect is still reassuringly present in the Wainwright. The Guaranty radically reassesses this priority, making ornament the dominant aspect of the building. It is not merely that ornament covers all the surfaces of the Guaranty, because the nature of terra-cotta encouraged other architects to similar

Figure 90
Adler & Sullivan, project for the Mercantile Club, St. Louis, 1891. Courtesy The Art Institute of Chicago.

prodigality at the time. It is rather that Sullivan sees ornament as more than mere embellishment. It is, in fact, the very means by which his design occurs, and this in two stages. There is, first, the division of the block or field into an ornamental geometry, meeting the program and the need for openings, to be sure, but also providing the armature on which the design can be generated as an ornamental entity; then (although the process is not necessarily sequential), the union of the ornament to this decorative compartmentalization. Sullivan perfected the first stage in the sequence of designs which he cribbed from Richardson. The second occurred decisively with the Getty and Wainwright Tombs.

But before proceeding further, consider Sullivan's own statement, unusually clear, unusually laconic, on his sense of the integral union of geometrical composition with ornament, the one an armature for the other. The occasion was a letter of October 16, 1893 from Daniel Burnham, as director of planning and architecture for the Columbian Exposition, requesting what Sullivan referred to in his response as "a short sketch of our ideas and motives in planning the Transportation Building." If Burnham expected an account as to how Sullivan's design responded to the theme of "transportation," as well he might, he was to be disappointed, for Sullivan replied on November 11 without any mention of the theme for the building whatsoever.

The thought we sought to express in the Transportation Building was this: An architectural exhibit. This thought subdivided itself as follows:
1. A natural, not historical, exhibit.
2. To be expressed by elementary masses carrying elaborate decoration.
3. All architectural masses and subdivisions to be bounded by straight lines or semi-circles, or both in combination, to illustrate the possibilities of very simple elements when in effective combination.
[Up to this point, he asserted that he rejected a historical style for his building in favor of a "natural" manner which originated in simple

Figure 92
Adler & Sullivan, Guaranty Building, Buffalo, New York, 1894–1896.
Cervin Robinson, photographer.

Figure 93
Burnham & Root/D.H.
Burnham & Co.; John
Wellborn Root/Charles
Atwood, designers. Reli-
ance Building, Chicago,
1890/1894–1895. Old
photograph showing the
store base by Root, with
later terra-cotta sheathing
above applied at the time
that Atwood added floors
to the building. Courtesy
Chicago Historical Society
ICHi–1066.

geometry. He did not go on, as would most architects, to describe this geometry as "arches," but in
a manner implying more abstract and ornamental
concerns, as "straight lines" and "semi-circles."]
4. The decorations to be of a very elaborate nature
and chiefly in color.
5. The combination of 3 and 4 to show how easily
and quietly large simple masses carry elaborately
and minutely worked out "ornamentation."
[In other words, although the geometrical composition may retain its pristine state, in an ornamental situation it provides support for the
embellishment.]
6. The chief object of 4 being to show that the
farther the process of systematic subdivision be
carried the quieter and more dignified becomes the
structure as a whole.
7. The use of colored decorations to show the possibility of sequence combination, and repetition when
a great many colors are used:—hence the true nature
of polychrome.
[This approach in ornament is more akin to a
Moorish or Saracenic than to a western approach,
both in its emphasis on polychromy and in the
"systematic subdivision" of the embellishment.
Although the Guaranty is not polychromatic, it
does display all-over surface ornament which is so
systematically and extensively subdivided as to
suggest infinitude. Its effect is "quiet and dignity"
for the building "as a whole"—a repose in which
the rhythms of the ornament partake of the total
shape (or better, shaping) of the building, and
intensify the shape by providing the pulsing
rhythms which suffuse it.]
8. The use of a symbolical human figure in color to
to show its great value in architectural decoration.
[A point to be considered shortly.]
9. A long series of minor considerations, entering
too minutely into detail to be here enumerated.
10. The summarizing thought, that all this should
be done in a natural and easy way,—as willing to
teach while searching for beauty.
[Throughout, Sullivan conceives of the building
as a demonstration, an educational tool. While the
Transportation Building housed exhibits designed

to instruct its audience about the advertised theme, the building *would teach them about architecture. It was a gloriously idealistic and arrogant finale from one architect to another who had inquired as to the meaning of his work. Indeed, throughout his ten points Sullivan maintains that the architecture of the building* is *its most essential meaning.*][56]

As with the decorated skin of the Transportation Building, so the all-over ornamentation of the terra-cotta clad Guaranty suggests the influence of Saracenic ornament. While Sullivan worked through the stylistic shift from Romanesque to Renaissance which characterized a momentous shift in the American architectural sensibility of his day, he also turned to an architectural style in which ornament was dominant in the architectural design. In the same article of 1896 in which Schuyler praised Sullivan for being more than a mere decorator, and proclaimed him as an architect who warranted the designation for his sureness in disposing and proportioning masses, together with his appreciation for structure, he went on to criticize a certain "Oriental" aspect to his work.

There is an intermediate process, the functional modelling of parts to express more forcibly and more minutely the structural relations. It is in this that Mr. Sullivan seems to me to have been upon the whole less successful than in the disposition of his masses at the beginning of his work or in the adjustment and the design of his ornament at the end. Now it is precisely this in which the Asiatic builders have been less successful than the European builders, so that . . . Amiens and Cologne are worthier of study and of admiration than the Mosque of Cordova or the Taj Mehal. It is this difference, I think, much more than any specific resemblance of form that gives so much of Mr. Sullivan's work its Oriental air. It is true that he never shows that lack of sense of the mechanical basis of architecture that is so often met with in Saracenic building. It is true also that his decoration has architectural significance, which is so often lacking to the Saracenic decoration. . . . But in

stopping short of a complete architectural development modes of building so widely different in time and place and purpose find a point of resemblance.[57]

In short, Schuyler faulted Sullivan from the western perspective of classical and Renaissance design which held that ornament should be subordinated to a hierarchical modelling of parts. At this moment of the resurgence of Renaissance ideas, indeed Schuyler may even have feared that Sullivan's embrace of exuberant naturalistic ornament marked a partial regression to something akin to the Victorian appetite for ostentation. Ornament, too often overblown, had been a cardinal means by which Victorian architects convinced themselves that they elevated "building" into "architecture." To Ruskin, for example, ornament, especially naturalistic ornament, was "something added," by which the architect kindled the first of the seven lamps (that of Sacrifice) through the extra effort and thought presumably required for embellished components over what was needed for pared-down equivalents. At a time when the idea of Renaissance "decorum" was in the ascendant with its demands that a culturally sanctioned canon of ornament be applied to the "right" places in the building, Sullivan's extravagant, naturalistic and individualistic approach to ornament was especially suspect. (Reservations about this aspect of his work continue today.) To him, however, ornament as a major element in architectural design was not something added but something integral, providing animation and expressive properties to the building. Hence the "Oriental" flavor of his work, as he instinctively turned for cues to a tradition in which ornament reigned supreme. This source of inspiration surely contributed to the dynamic linearism and geometrical abstraction which came to undergird his luxuriant naturalism, although other kinds of ornament (Celtic, for example[58]) may also have informed the "Saracenic" aspects of his work. Even if bits of Saracenic exoticism can be discerned in his early work (as in much Victorian design), only with the Getty and Wainwright tombs and the Transportation Build-

ing did he really begin to grasp how such ornament might be used to further his particular architectural vision. The raiment of the Guaranty represents its complete absorption into Sullivan's manner, so that whatever is Saracenic is thoroughly mingled with other ornamental influences, and is no longer handled as literally as in the ornament of the Transportation Building.

Although it may seem that the division of the elevation of the Guaranty is in every way analogous to that for the Wainwright, this is not quite true. Throughout Sullivan has taken the Wainwright format and adjusted it, however subtly, more toward the ornamental. Consider the most

obvious adjustment at the cornice where the piers fuse with it (fig. 96). Whereas the cornice ornamentation is confined in the Wainwright to its own decorative field and seemingly supported by piers which appear to be self-contained pilasters, in the Guaranty the arching from pier to pier creates a scalloped elision with the luxuriance above. Consider also the manner in which the generous circle of the cornice oculi relate to the semicircular arches immediately below and, especially noticeable at the corners, to the quarter circle of the flaring curve which unites the entablature of the cornice to the incisive termination of its projecting cap. Although the vine motifs at the corners of the building, climbing the cornice with tendrils curling around the edge of the capping, have been criticized for a literalism which is allegedly unarchitectural, they nonetheless underscore the assertiveness of Sullivan's ornamental aims in the Guaranty. They also suggest that the entire elevation can be imagined as a flattened Corinthian column, horizontally stretched.

In the Wainwright, there is a sense of "windows" fitted between the piers, partly because of the heavier framing and more normative proportions of the openings, mostly because of a "lintel" worked into the ornament over each window and still below the individual assertion of the parapet under each window, which the change of ornament from floor to floor accentuates. In the Guaranty, the relation of void to solid is more abstract. Framing around the window is minimized. Window proportions are slightly forced down toward the horizontal. Each parapet ornament is identical. Although the foliated clumps on each of the spandrel panels derive from a foliated lintel bursting with a foliated keystone at the center, they are so placed as to be alternately read at the top of one window or the bottom of another as the eye scans the elevation. Taken together, these qualities intensify the effect of the pier-and-spandrel wall of the Guaranty as an all-over pattern, or decorative lattice. The fluctuating quality of solid and void gives a stunning porosity to the cubic quality of the building over all.

The same qualities of abstractness and porosity characterize the shop window base of the Guaranty. The contrast between the square section of the bounding piers at the building and portal corners and the cylindrical columns separating the shop windows; the ambiguity as to whether the shop windows are to be aggrandized as one expansive, subdivided opening, or three separate, modest ones; the pop of the encrusted column capitals from "inside" to "outside" the shop windows through the fold in the plate glass at the transom level—these aspects, too, are essentially ornamental in spirit.

Hence the geometrical organization of the Guaranty betrays Sullivan's ornamental sensibility—

the underpinning, so to speak, of the overt ornamentalism which animates the surfaces throughout. This surface ornament has, of course, received most attention. Contrast it again with the Wainwright. There the heavier, more Richardsonian decorative motifs seem fitted to the panels. To be sure, the eye scans the building and makes a band of them—a "weave" of the crossing of plain pier over submerged ornament which came to mean so much to Frank Lloyd Wright, and which he would develop. But the eye is repeatedly caught by the individual motifs, by their framing, by their change from floor to floor, by their subordination to the dominant piers. The more conventionally architectonic approach of the Wainwright has its virtues; but the ornament of the Guaranty is a different matter. All spandrel panels are identically decorated with a gauzy gridded pattern which skims the surface. A raised square of foliated ornament erupts on each panel, centered and toward its bottom. As the sun moves around the building these cubic clumps burst into light or sink into shadow, each window given its brooch. One can so immerse oneself in the architectural textile that the windows lose their identity as such, as the glass participates in the glitter and sparkle of the whole. Clots of matted foliage mount the piers creating a pulsating movement along their length until absorbed by the tangled swirls of foliage caught up in the circular movements of the cornice.

At the base of the building (fig. 97)[59] clusters of diamond shapes become arrows, seemingly sprung in opposite directions from the centers of the elongated panels resulting from the vertical and horizontal surfaces made by the frame. They appear to stretch the surfaces in their opposition. They impinge as arrows, threatening the loci where the vertical and horizontal aspects of the frame meet pod-shaped forms, the lower half bursting into foliage, the upper left plain, as an untouched surface of the terra-cotta. Sullivan frequently used such untouched surfaces in his ornament as a kind of eye of calm in the ornamental storm—an affirmation of the plane, an allusion to the primal stuff in which the infinitude of the "idea" is born. The arrows threaten this eye (seed pod, egg), bombarding it from all directions. The tough nodule of stuff simultaneously holds out against the onslaught and releases new life.

The portal indicates the sort of Orientalism that Schuyler found disturbing. Although derived from quattrocento prototypes, the flanking pilaster panels which visually "support" the semicircular (segmental) cornice are wedded to the surface of the building, while the projecting pediment floats somewhat independently and abstractly above them. The capitals, which break through the folded show windows, show non-western influence too: they have a cushion shape rather than the typical inverted bell shape of Corinthian capitals; hence

more distended by the superimposed weight upon them than tightly supporting. Their surfaces are richly encrusted, as though the decorative aspects of western capitals were fragmented, and the pieces returned to the cushion as a rich brocade. The horizontal ribboning of the shaft also opposes their more structural treatment in western architecture as smooth or vertically fluted cylinders. Such details permit the enlargement of Schuyler's characterization of the non-classical influences on Sullivan's work: not merely Oriental (or Saracenic), but also Byzantine and Romanesque.[60] Perhaps instinctively Sullivan adjusted the Renaissance aspects of the Guaranty to greater archaism of shape, fusion of members and exoticism of aspect as a means to establish a degree of distance from the classical and Renaissance prototypes which marked the norm of Western European precedent. Significantly, in this respect, Richardson, Sullivan, and Wright followed similar courses.

Ornament here clearly, if diffusely, animates in a visible way those forces assumed to coexist in architecture—partly mechanical, partly kinesthetic, partly allegorical, partly the lyrical excess and exuberance born of the momentum of giving way to the other interrelated energies. Critics (myself included)[61] have complained of incongruities in Sullivan's designs. Is the treatment of the base congruent with what occurs above? Are the stylized recalls of quattrocento doorways appropriate to their context? Is the patterning of the spandrel panels and piers too disparate? Is the transformation from the pulsating piers to the matted cornice completely resolved? Or (again) is the stranglehold of the climbing vines on the projecting capping slab of the roof at the corners of the building too naturalistic? All possible flaws, and the critical diddler is vexed that they were not "fixed" to make the "explanation" for the Guaranty as neat, say, as that for the Wainwright. Whether or not the Guaranty might have been better for the fixing, in the actual experience of Sullivan's building such caveats tend to be set aside. One tends even to admire the perversities, for the same reason that Sullivan admired Whitman.

Do I contradict myself?
Very well, then, I contradict myself,
I am large—I contain multitudes.

Indeed, there is a sense in the Guaranty that each member of the composition pulses with its own life. As Schuyler noted, each reveals, in its particular ornamental rhythms, its role structurally and expressively within the elevation. The skin or ornamentation unites these disparate rhythms into an architectural tapestry. In Sullivan's quaint phrase, the "systematic subdivision" of the terra-cotta raiment of the Guaranty takes its form and gives form to the compelling rectangular solid of the building, with its trumpet flare at the cornice and the crisscross of the earth-red lattice against the sparkle of the inset glass.

Critics and historians have always admired the Wainwright and the Guaranty. Even when Sullivan's star was dimmest—from around 1910 to the early 1930s—his role in suggesting an alternate approach to the skyscraper in these buildings was duly recognized. It was then the heyday for the skyscraper, when the erroneous cliché that the skyscraper was America's only, or at least greatest, contribution to the history of architecture was generally accepted. Hence, pioneering ventures in its design, like Sullivan's, were bound to be noticed, even if, as noted in the phrase of a popular survey of American architecture of 1927, his originality was a "lost cause."[62]

By contrast with the continuous recognition accorded to the Wainwright and Guaranty, another of Sullivan's tall office buildings which has become a key work in his achievement, the Bayard in New York (1897–1898), has been less consistently appreciated (fig. 98). According to Frank Lloyd Wright, it was Sullivan's favorite building.[63] In 1898 and 1899, shortly after its completion, two of the leading New York architectural critics of the time, Russell Sturgis and Montgomery Schuyler, praised it. It existed from then on in a submerged life as a fantastically overdressed lady for its use as loft space on narrow Bleeker Street in downtown New York, amidst the lumbering darkness of neighboring factory and warehouse buildings, with trucks rather than limousines at its door. Recently, like the Wainwright and the Guaranty, it has undergone restoration, along with many other buildings in the adjacent Soho area. And in the refurbishment, sadly, the manufacturing and shop enterprises for which its loft space was designed, have been driven off. Architects, designers and publishers have gentrified the building, although it would seem that the highly decorated exterior has been waiting all these years for just this sort of clientele.

Fortunately for its visibility, it almost fronts on alleylike Crosby Street where it terminates at Bleeker. Backing down Crosby, and squeezing as tightly as possible to its east side, the elevation of the Bayard (frustratingly, but with appropriate drama) edges *almost* into full view, so that it can be comfortably seen in its tight surroundings. Fortunately, too, it faces south and, in contrast with the dark, hulking buildings which frame it, bursts on the spectator in the sense that Sullivan intended. For surely this patch of purple prose in the rental brochure for the Bayard can only be Sullivan's:

Rising thus—cream-white, maidenlike and slender, luxuriant in life and joyous as the dawn of wistful spring, this poem of the modern will ever daily hail the sun on high and the plodder below with its ceaseless song of hope, of joy, of the noble labor of man's hands, of the vast dignity and power of man's soul—a song of true democracy and its goal.[64]

Making allowances for the overwriting, (which must have surprised the how-much-for-how-many-square-feet mentality of the average renter of loft space to whom the brochure was addressed) Sullivan's effusion approximates the experience the Bayard brings to us. Both Sturgis and Schuyler praised this "poem of the modern" on its completion as an especially appropriate expression for the terra-cotta clad, metal-framed, tall office building.

stop against which to butt interior partitioning in the much compartmented office building.

The Bayard arrangement had a long preparation in three previous projects done between ca. 1892 and 1894. Although the precise order of their design is still uncertain, the essence of an evolving solution to the design of the tall building is clear from the sequence. In one of two projects (scheme "B") for an unidentified office building for St. Louis (fig. 100), Sullivan couples the windows within tall narrow arches as he couples them within a planar grid in an alternate version (see fig. 87). Their scalloping of the lower edge of the cornice is echoed in the "Romanesque" arching at the base, which is now so flamboyantly distended as to seem absolutely impatient with any medieval precedent. The leaping quality of the arches provides a fitting frame for some of Sullivan's most extravagant fountains of foliage, from which seated figures seem to emerge to either side of escutcheons. For the Trust & Savings project, the anachronistic base of the unidentified building has been replaced by the more sober, modern approach with vaguely Renaissance overtones which Sullivan will use in both the Guaranty and the Bayard (fig. 99). The figural elements of the preceding composition have been moved to the cornice, as more sedate standing and winged figures at each of the corners of the building. Finally, in the projected east wing renovation of Cincinnati's leading hotel of the period, the Burnet House—of which Schuyler makes much in his article, without illustrating it—Sullivan fully develops the formula for the window wall which he will use in the Bayard (fig. 101). Within each of the tall arches between the structural piers of the Burnet House, double interior arching occurs with an oculus and, most importantly, the major piers alternate with cylindrical mullions. The uninterrupted cylindrical piers replace the broken, story-by-story mullions in the previous projects. So the scheme for Burnet House combines the revelation of major and minor structural rhythms within the window wall with a sense of the vertical continuity of major membering from base to cornice. The base itself, which had been

And so it is; more so than the Wainwright and Guaranty. In the Bayard, Sullivan replaced the identical cross-section of the piers in his earlier buildings by an alternating system of square piers and cylindrical mullions. This arrangement proclaimed that only every other vertical contained a structural column, thanks to the widely spaced supports possible in metal skeletal framing, and that the intervening vertical played a subordinate structural role by merely dividing the window spaces between structural columns with two windows instead of one. It also served as a convenient

Figure 97
Adler & Sullivan, Guar-
anty Building, detail of the
base. Cervin Robinson,
photographer.

*Figure 98
Louis H. Sullivan, with
Lyndon P. Smith, Bayard
Building, New York,
1897–1898. Courtesy
Museum of the City of
New York.*

nominally Romanesque in the unidentified building, and modern with classicizing overtones in the
Trust & Savings project, becomes overtly Renaissance in the scheme for Burnet House. There could
be no clearer evidence of Sullivan's casting about
among the possible "styles" of the day, weighing
what was waning in the fashionable adaptation of
past styles for current use against what was
"coming in," while conjecturing as to what might
be "modern." The Guaranty interferes with the
development, implicit in these three projects,
carrying parts of it forward, but essentially returning to the format of the Wainwright. Not until
the Bayard does Sullivan consummate his restless
investigation of a more direct expression of the tall
metal skeletal frame in an executed building.

If both Sturgis and Schuyler were enthusiastic
about the Bayard as an indicator as to what the
future of the tall metal framed building should be,
both also had reservations:

*Were it not for the most unfortunate treatment of
each great opening between the uprights in an arch
and a seeming system of tracery in the head, this
front might be pointed to as completely realistic in
design . . . if the reader will eliminate by mental
process these five great arches with their subordinate
arches and the oculi which fill their heads, he will
have the architectural treatment of the metal
building of our cities in the future.*[65]

Writing less than a year later, Schuyler took much
the same tack: "This is the thing in itself. . . .
There is no attempt to simulate the breadth and
massiveness appropriate to masonry in a frame of
metal that is merely wrapped in masonry for its
own protection." Then a caveat, the same that
Sturgis had earlier raised about the skeletal expression of some of the most progressive tall office
buildings in Chicago. "Not that the gauntness and
attenuation of the resulting architecture are in this
case altogether agreeable to an eye accustomed to
the factitious massiveness of the conventional
treatment." Despite ornament "which is of a quality that no other designer could have commanded,"

the Bayard reminded Schuyler of "Rufus Choate's famous toast to the Chief Justice; 'We look upon him as the East Indian upon his wooden idol. We know that he is ugly, but we feel that he is great!' . . . The Bayard Building is the nearest approach yet made, in New York at least, to solving the problem of the skyscraper."[66]

So these progressive critics praised the Bayard for the directness with which it exhibited the "facts" of skeletal framing and terra-cotta sheathing, although Sturgis criticized it for being overly ornamental, while Schuyler faulted its emaciated membering. Thereafter, the Bayard largely disappeared from public notice. Morrison's book of 1935

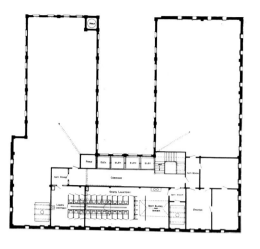

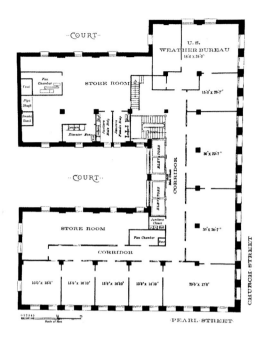

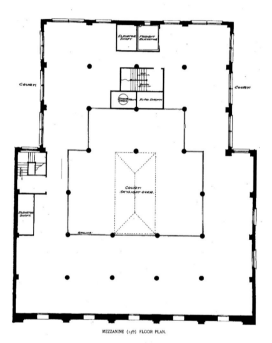

scarcely changed matters. Like Sturgis, he praised the logic of the building, and deplored the ornament (as could be expected of a modernist historian in the mid 1930s), then went on to cite Sturgis and Schuyler. Not until Scully made the Bayard a key work in Sullivan's *oeuvre* did it begin to re-emerge in public consciousness. Scully saw the Bayard as the most decisive example of Sullivan's use of composition and ornament for empathetic effect, at a time when theories of empathy were pervasive. Jordy and Menocal elaborated.[67]

The Bayard continues the expressive verticality of the Wainwright and Guaranty Buildings, which is here visually accelerated, so to speak, by the terra-cotta cladding of the piers. But the broad arching of the Bayard elevation, reinforced by the mini-arching within, tends to carry the eye in a rolling motion, up, and around, and down the adjacent pier. Sullivan himself spoke on several occasions of the circulatory systems of the tall building, of forces felt as rising and falling within it. For example, to Montgomery Schuyler he specifically indicated that the revelation of the circulatory system accounted in part for the Bayard elevation.[68] To Sullivan, the cornice functioned not only as a cap, but also as the locus of reciprocating movement. The piers were at once the agents of visible ascent in the elevation, making the building "tall"; they were also the agents of mechanical descent, conveying loads to the ground. The sensibility is remarkably Gothic, where the piers of the great cathedrals are simultaneously experienced in this double way. Sullivan also felt these circulatory forces in the mechanical systems of the building: in the rise and fall of its elevators, and in the currents in plumbing and heating pipes, with their machinery in the basement responding to more machinery and water tanks at the roof.

At least allusively and tentatively in his musings on the tall building, Sullivan was perceptive enough to think of such interior systems of energy as a dimension of the architectural program, and worthy of consideration for architectural expression—an attitude that only became widespread in the 1960s with Louis Kahn's "served and servant spaces" and Reyner Banham's historical analysis of the significance (and too often the visible insignificance) of mechanical systems in modern architectural design.[69] Sullivan's rhapsody of the topmost story as the climax of the circulatory systems within the modern office building provided additional justification for his wrapping the top story within his lavishly embellished cornices, in addition to its compositional role as the proud terminus of the building. In actual fact, of course, the heroic role of the top story in the "life" of the average tall office building is more mundane than Sullivan would have had it, unless corporate board rooms or other special purpose functions occupy the floor. However, commissions for corporate headquarters never came his way. Plans for the Wainwright, Guaranty, and Bayard buildings show how prosaic the usual rooftop floor was in speculative office buildings (fig. 102). Aside from the expected spaces allocated to storage, janitorial, and mechanical functions (the last being substantial for hydraulic elevators), the Wainwright originally consolidated most of its restroom facilities

Figure 103
Observation deck on the roof of the Auditorium.

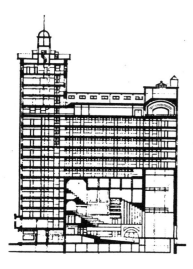

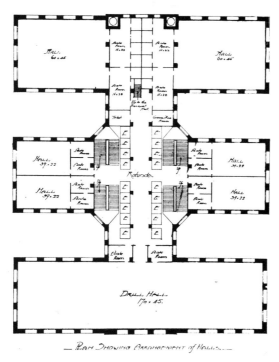

*Figure 104 a, b, c
Club floor plans in two of
Sullivan's tall buildings.
a, b. Schiller Building.
Cross section and plan of
thirteenth floor. Courtesy
The Art Institute of Chi-
cago. c. Fraternity Temple
Building. Odd Fellows
clubrooms on tenth floor.
Prospectus "To the Odd-
Fellows of Chicago and the
State of Illinois," Chicago
n.d., but presumably 1891.*

at the top of the building, along with a bootblack
and barber shop. Among the top-floor tenants of
the Guaranty, only the allocation of one cubicle on
the floor to a United States Weather Station may
have risen slightly above the prosaic. Signals (flags
by day, lights by night) from a tower on the roof
could be seen by mariners on Lake Erie.[70] Func-
tionally, if not rhetorically, his handling of the top
floor of the Bayard seems most appropriate. The
embellished cornice floor with its circular windows
served as a deep mezzanine around a skylighted
well for a two-story work space which subsequent
alteration has filled in.

Yet Sullivan obviously envisioned a grander
destiny for the rooftop story. Given the commissions available to him, Sullivan had two possibilities for uses consonant with the importance he
accorded to the crown of the tall office building: an
observation tower or clubrooms. Both were important parts of his life. As occupant of the loggia in
the Auditorium tower, he surveyed Chicago from
a conspicuous height; he was also an ardent member of the rooftop Cliff Dwellers Club.

Above all, the loggia and oculi which repeatedly
top his tall buildings call up the idea of an outlook.
There was, in fact, a cupola on the roof of the
Auditorium tower which sheltered a stair to a rooftop observation platform (fig. 103) and another
atop the Schiller. His most spectacular observation
platform occurred just below the conical pinnacle of
his project for the Fraternity Temple (see fig. 81),
with awkward, but symbolically vivid, balconies
projected in four directions. Failing this use, could
he perhaps have imaged it as a prospective relo-
cation for a floor of his office, so that he could
continue to place himself at the top of the local
profession? He also briefly considered an observation deck for the Carson Pirie Scott Store.[71]

Of the two functions for aggrandizing the significance of the topmost floor, clubrooms offered a
more promising alternative, especially at a time
when the new cosmopolitanism of the American
metropolis encouraged their proliferation. Sullivan's design for the three-story Mercantile Club,
its top floor framed by an observation loggia,

Figure 105
Louis H. Sullivan, Bayard
Building, detail of the base
as it appeared in the early
1980s.

represented his most overt celebration of the club-house climax to the office building (see figs. 90 and 104). So overt, indeed, it seemed as though a lavish nineteenth-century boathouse might have been deposited by cresting flood waters on a submerged office building, and snagged there once the flood receded. Aside from their own quarters at the top of the building, the Mercantile Club intended to rent less splendid space below to other clubs or for offices. None of his other buildings, however, had clubs on the top floor. In their project for the thirty-six story Fraternity Temple, the Odd Fellows meant to outdo Burnham & Root's Women's Temple and Masonic Buildings (both 1891–1892), in combining boastful visibility for lodges with business acumen (figs. 81 and 104). (At the time, the

Masonic Temple, with eighteen stories—twenty-two counting the dormers in its gabled attic—peaked as the tallest building in the world). In the Fraternity Temple the symbolic role of the club rooms seems to have been reversed from the pinnacle to the base out of which the tower rose. Above the first two stories devoted to stores and walk-up businesses, floors three through six were assigned to rented club rooms. On the tenth floor, behind the decorated cornice at the first setback, the Odd Fellows had their lodge, with a drill hall completely occupying one of the three wings. The very scale of their operation doubtless forced them to one of the lower floors. Unhappily, neither of these combined club and office buildings was built. Only in the Schiller Building did Sullivan realize a

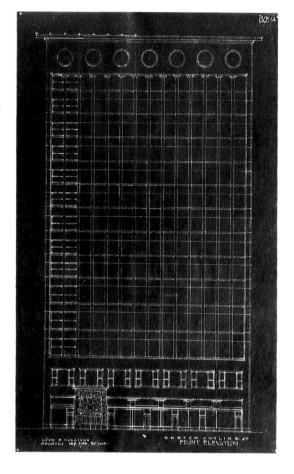

club room in one of his office buildings (see figs. 83 and 104). A German social artistic club had its function rooms, restaurant, and another small theatre on the thirteenth floor. As the cross-section of this complex building indicates, the club rooms existed just below the roof of the stem of the T, to provide for the increased heights of the one or two club rooms and the assembly hall. An ornate, cupolaed belvedere poked through the roof to shelter a spiral stair which gave access to a rooftop observation and recreation deck. With a theater at the base of the building, club rooms above and an observation deck at the top, it was the most cosmopolitan statement of use that Sulli- van realized in his tall buildings, even if the three

functions were scattered within the building. To the hauteur of the dandified clubman, height was congenial. To the dreamer of large diffuse visions, the sweep of the panorama and the dissolve of precision toward infinitude were exhilarating. No wonder, then, that the cornice which sees, which looks out, should have been an obsession through- out his tall buildings.

Although the average clubman under the cornice and the average tourist on the observation deck might have felt themselves in the privileged posi- tion which altitude always suggests, they could hardly have been expected to appreciate the addi- tional privilege of their position at the pinnacle of Sullivan's "circulatory system"—oblivious as they would have been to the poetic implications of the submerged structural and mechanical systems within the tall office building. But for him, the metaphoric implications of the circulatory system went even deeper. He also associated this rising and falling of forces with opposed, but interre- lated, energies toward life and death, the ultimate cycle of nature. In "The Tall Building Artistically Considered" he shifted from the prosaic to the rhapsodic reaches of "form follows function." "Unceasingly," he wrote, "the essence of things is taking shape, and this unspeakable process we call birth and growth. Awhile the spirit and the matter fade away together, and it is this that we call decadence, death."[72] (On either side of the Auditorium, murals by Albert Fleury utilized themes from Sullivan's essay "Inspiration": on one wall, a springtime scene with the legend, "O soft melodious springtime, firstborn of life and love"; opposite, its autumnal counterpart, "A great life has passed into the tomb and there awaits the requiem of winter's snows.")[73] In his buildings, Sullivan meant to make palpable the simultaneous sense of rise and support—sensations upward and downward, or what he termed growth and deca- dence—which are inherent to architecture.

None of his buildings more successfully em- bodies this sense of a circuit of forces working within the elevation than the Bayard, although it is also felt in the Guaranty, and alluded to in the

Wainwright. Nor is it only the Gothic linearism of the modeled piers, speeding the eye up and around the arching inscribed within arching, with the swirl of foliated energy at the turning, that gives this effect. Scully has argued that the cylindrical mullions can be alternately viewed as rising colonettes or as stretched cables suspended against their decorated weights, which have dropped like suspended sash weights in the slot between the piers to the top of the second story.[74] Whether or not Sullivan explicitly thought in this ingenious way about the mullions, energies shifting from "up" to "down" and back again are diffusely felt in the elevation. On the other hand, one means of achieving this effect of which Sullivan was surely conscious was his fusion of the "base" and "capital" of the elevation with its "shaft" of office space, in contrast to the demarcation of all three elements in the Wainwright, and of base and shaft in the Guaranty. The fusion at the top of the Bayard is self-evident, but fusion at the base is equally important to his effect (fig. 105). Even as the horizontal windows of the second floor of the Bayard, capped by their decorative frieze, make its base, the piers of its shaft break into the base. Whereas the piers remain aloof from the base in the Guaranty, here they descend into immediate rapport with the cylindrical columns of the ground floor, even as they rise to the arching of the cornice. As squat, compact cylinders at the base of such a tall building, incarcerated by the framing of the square piers at the corners and entrance to the building, the one-story columns provide a sense of sturdy support.

The columns can be compared in their lush exoticism to precedents in the Guaranty. Again the quattrocento entrance is definitely deflected toward Saracenic prototypes in the polygonal flanking columns decorated with panelled ornament. So is the floating quality of the segmented pediment, set on a narrow ledge, as though thrust out from the columns on a projecting tray.

Against these movements felt in the larger elements, the clumps of ornament climb the plain surfaces of the elevation. Above the show windows of the ground floor, the compact clumps of foliage fan out horizontally to make a frieze for the base of the building; in the spandrel panels of the office floors, they spread slightly to either side and flare up at the centers (a more constricted variant of a similar effect in the panels of the Guaranty). Like jets slightly flaring and bursting in gaslights, they flicker their way, through another row of lions' heads garnished with leaves, up to the matted climax. Their leitmotif of upwardness acts to counter forces of decadence within the larger members. The very differences in the treatment of the subordinate elements of the ornamentation of the pier-and-spandrel window walls in the Wainwright, Guaranty and Bayard Buildings indicates something of Sullivan's inventiveness as an ornamentalist: first, the containment within panels; then, the veil of the whole surface in a kind of pointillist shimmer; here, the staccato bursts of an all-over pattern of separated units.

In the cornice, winged female figures extend the upward movement of the piers. As we have observed, they make their first prominent appearance between each of the big arches surrounding the lower level of the Transportation Building at the Columbian Exposition (1893). There each muse holds a plaque commemorating a major contributor to the history of transportation. They also appear in nearly contemporaneous preliminary designs for the Victoria Hotel in Chicago (1893), and in the project for the Trust & Savings Bank Building of St. Louis (1893) (see fig. 99). The design haunted Sullivan; he returned to it, improving on it for the Bayard. He improved it most specifically in replacing the broken mullions between the paired office windows of the Trust & Savings with the continuous vertical cylinders of the flanking towers of the Burnet Building (fig. 101).

Sullivan's critics have generally deplored the winged figures. Only Menocal has been sympathetic.[75] But even granting their relative limpness as both sculpture and sentiment, they do play a significant role in the Bayard decorative scheme, and in his decorative system, as he indicated to Burnham in ticking off the contributing factors to the meaning of the decorative scheme of the Trans-

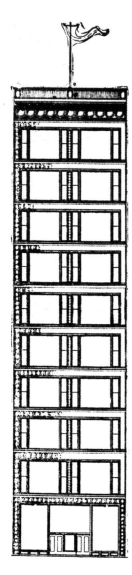

Figure 107
Louis H. Sullivan, Schlesinger & Mayer (later Carson Pirie Scott) Department Store, Chicago, projected elevation for Wabash Street entrance, published in the Chicago Tribune, *July 5, 1896.*

portation Building, however succinct and delphic his statement:

8. *The use of a symbolical human figure in color to show its great value in architectural decoration.*

Sullivan seems to have taken much the same position as John Ruskin with respect to the hierarchy of abstraction appropriate for the use of geometry, plants, animals, and human figures in ornamentation.[76] Whereas ornament originated in geometry, abstraction was progressively subdued as one rose in the scale of living things. Insofar as Sullivan does make sparse use of animals and human figures, they display the progressive naturalism which Ruskin advocated. At the pinnacle of the evolutionary heap, the human being is most realistically portrayed, although in an idealized manner.

The formal function of the human figures in the Bayard is self-evident. Their stance atop the piers sustains the verticality against the tendency of the eye to circle the arches and move down the adjacent pier. Whereas the narrow arching of the Guaranty makes a nicked, dogtooth sort of edging to the bottom of the cornice, the larger scoops of the Bayard arching require some stabilizing vertical. And what better choice than the winged female figures? The spreading wings reinforce the opposed branching of the arches. They also provide a visual bracket for the projecting cornice slab.

Such formal considerations, however, were only a small part of Sullivan's repeated attraction to such figures. He constantly strove to make his ornament more than merely ornamental. Muscular forces were an inherent component in the nexus of energies that he meant his ornament to encompass. If geometry and plant life carried the burden of his ornamental message (as they mostly do in architecture), this was no reason to deny other realms of inspiration, and to let them show through, as in the revealing, if awkward, eruption of the seated figures from fountains of foliage in one of his two schemes for an unidentified office building project for St. Louis (see fig. 100).

The winged figures at the cornice of the Bayard recall the guardian angels that sometimes hover in the heights of Gothic cathedrals; or, as Menocal also reminds us, and Van Zanten too,[77] they invoke the trumpeting angels that Sullivan recalled from his youth in Boston, crowning the corners of Richardson's bell tower for the Brattle Square Church (1870–1872). Not really angels, however, these are winged allegories, counterparts to figures particularly evident in murals and monuments of the "American Renaissance." As in those monuments, these secular sisters docilely rise to the spirit of the ceremonial occasion. Precisely because they are a different order of being from the rest of the decoration in the Bayard, they "stand aside" from our involvement with the more abstract or botanical aspects of the ornament, reigning above in an aloof, elevated manner, even as they are also caught up in its rhythms. Thus they function here as vestal virgins whose stance embodies the vertical quality of the piers, the expansive and opposed gestures of the branching arches, the spreading support of the cornice frieze, and the sheltering quality of its lid. Formal properties are translated into kinesthetic sensations, they epitomize and concentrate energies more diffusely operating throughout the elevation. As reigning deities, they also celebrate the forces of "life" and "growth" against those of "death" and "decadence." Surely, too, Sullivan's obsession with these winged figures recalls what might be termed the logo of his career—the seed pod bursting with wings of life.

In his *Autobiography of an Idea*, Sullivan tells us how vastly impressed he was with Michelangelo's Sistine Chapel when, during his period of study in Paris in 1874–1875, he made a brief, three-day excursion to Rome. Only three days in Rome, and he informs us that most of two of them were spent with Michelangelo. It was the sense of heroic figures in heroic motion that captured his imagination. In Chicago, before and after his European trip, a young fellow architect, John Edelmann, conditioned and reinforced his view of Michelangelo. Imbued with a smattering of German transcendental philosophy, which was then pervasive in what was a very German city, Edelmann spoke of the expression of "suppressed functions" as the essence of artistic creativity.[78]

Analogous lessons came to Sullivan through his lifelong study of botany. As a young student in a Boston high school, he tells us of his fascination with botany, under an inspiring teacher, Moses Woolson, and specifically of his study of Asa Gray's *School and Field Book of Botany.* Gray himself occasionally came down from Harvard to take over Woolson's class.[79] Much later, in advising the student of ornament how to proceed in his *A System of Architectural Ornament According with a Philosophy of Man's Powers,* Sullivan recommended the study of Gray's work and Beecher Wilson's *Cell in Development and Inheritance.* George Elmslie, Sullivan's design assistant, recalled:

He was so taken up with Professor Wilson's "on the cell," that the first thing he did after reading his mail, in the mornings, for quite a while was to make drawings from memory, marvelously, of the various stages of the cell's evolution, as then known, and explain the processes to me. He knew the whole book; great retentive powers.[80]

It was not the visible surface of plant life that stirred Sullivan, but its anatomy and growth. So what he came to call the idea of "suppressed functions" is variously manifest in Sullivan's life and career. "Suppressed functions" of the human body, of plant life, of buildings—the theme of suppressed energies for Sullivan was all-embracing while energies from one realm diffusely interact with energies from others. To Sullivan these energies could only be fully embodied in architecture through ornament—ornament conceived, however, with awareness of its most profound possibilities.

The Wainwright, Guaranty, and Bayard Buildings are related to one another as the architectural species within Sullivan's work which most successfully and radically constitute his idea of the tall office building. Taken together, they assert the expressive nature of this new building type in two somewhat contradictory ways. On the one hand,

the office building should assert its primary division as base, shaft and capital—a concept essentially classical. On the other hand, it "must be tall, every inch of it tall"—a concept essentially medieval. Clearly the development within these three buildings inclines from classical to Gothic. Sullivan's classicism appears in his continuous reliance on the column analogy for the overall organization of his elevations; in the four-square containment of the building as a compact entity, bodylike, and frequently stance-like in the tenseness of the verticals which command his pier-and-spandrel elevations; in the prominent cornices; in certain ornamental aspects, such as the quattrocento entrances and cylindrical columns with capitals at the ground floor of the Guaranty and Bayard, and in the Bayard, the antefixes which cap the cornice. Medievalism occurs in the naturalistic bias of the ornament, as a whole, and in specific allusion to medieval precedent in some instances: such as the Romanesque-inspired ornament of the Wainwright; the crisp layering of the skeletal wall from the plane of the piers, to that of the spandrel panels,

Figure 108
Louis H. Sullivan, Schlesinger & Mayer Department Store, Chicago, 1896. Wabash Street entrance to the main store as realized, with pedestrian bridge from the elevated platform of the Loop. Courtesy Chicago Architectural Photo Co.

Figure 109
Louis H. Sullivan, Schles-
inger & Mayer (later Car-
son Pirie Scott) Depart-
ment Store, Chicago.
Preliminary design for
a nine-story building,
1899. From The Archi-
tectural Record, *April–*
June 1899.

to that of the glass; the vertical rise of the piers, especially in their linear modeling in the Bayard; the alternation there of square pier and cylindrical mullion, mimicking the comparable alternation of supports typical of sexpartite vaulting, as well as in the fusion of these differing supports with the triforiumlike arching under the cornice. Pointing especially to the Bayard, Menocal has related this reconciliation of classical and Gothic ideas with pervasive French attitudes toward just such reconciliation, beginning in the eighteenth century and recurring throughout the nineteenth. Van Zanten extends the idea in observing how, from the beginnings of his architectural education, Sullivan simultaneously absorbed nineteenth-century rationalistic ideas from the progressive approaches to design stemming from both the English reform Gothic and the French Néo-Grec movements, which filtered into the United States during the 1870s and 1880s.[81]

In this building sequence, the Wainwright celebrates the moment when the block became what Sullivan believed the tall office building should be: the "modern poem," but still incarcerated within the cuboid confines of its masonry past, analogous perhaps to Michelangelo's slaves. The Guaranty is the Wainwright transformed by the shimmering raiment of its taut terra-cotta skin, expressive in its litheness of the energies of the modern world, the medievalism of the vertical piers of the Wainwright extended by the tall, narrow arching. The Bayard is the Guaranty transformed, the emphasis now placed more on the framing elements than on the surface.

The final design in the group is more schematic in character. In fact, it may have been little more than this. It was not a commission, but Sullivan's effort to obtain a commission. His work on the Schlesinger & Mayer Store was ending in 1904, with no major prospects in sight. Having heard of the availability of two adjacent lots on Michigan Avenue facing on Grant Park, he dangled the opportunity by letter to a number of potential investors. He informed them that he had drawn up a prospective building for the site, complete with

Figure 110
Louis H. Sullivan, Carson
Pirie Scott Department
Store, 1899/1903–1904.
Original recessed loggia for
the top floor and cornice
have been altered. Cervin
Robinson, Photographer.

Figure 111
Adler & Sullivan, project for the Chemical National Bank, scheme "A," St. Louis, ca. 1894. Courtesy The Art Institute of Chicago.

Figure 112
Adler & Sullivan, project for the Chemical National Bank, St. Louis, ca. 1894, project "B." Courtesy Richard Nickel Committee.

plans and even a financing scheme. He invited them to send for copies of it, to no avail (figs. 74 and fig. 106).[82] Ornament in the projected building is sparce, although it might have increased with an actual commission. Its quality principally derives from its proportions and a sensed incisiveness of line and profile. Essentially it is a stripped version of the Guaranty, but the treatment of the cornice and its support by piers with capitals returns to the Wainwright. It was as though Sullivan would generalize on the sequence of radical designs out of the Wainwright, laying bare in a formulaic manner the armature on which the development was premised.

The Carson Pirie Scott Department Store is another species of business building, one might say *the other* species of the downtown skeletal building. The vertical stacking of cubicles for business offices, in the one instance, the horizontal spread of space for display, in the other: it is a measure of Sullivan's achievement as an architect for business that he so thoroughly accepted the premises implicit in both, and created prototypes of great originality for both at a time when they were being defined.

It became Carson Pirie Scott in a change of ownership as early as 1904, the very year in which Sullivan completed his work in two stages, for its original owner Schlesinger & Mayer. The commission resulted from furious competition among the leading State Street merchants during the 1880s and 1890s. With Marshall Field as pacesetter, its immediate competitors on State Street—Schlesinger & Mayer; Siegel, Cooper & Co. (later Leiter); Mandel Brothers; the Boston Store; Rothschild; The Fair; and Carson Pirie Scott—had all expanded out of their original buildings, repeatedly annexing adjacent properties, breaking through party walls to aggrandize space, all the while adding "departments," along with square footage. The phenomenal growth of Schlesinger & Mayer during the 1890s is typical. Between 1891 and 1897, square footage jumped incrementally from 32,000 to 60,000, to 130,000, to 160,000, to

300,000.[83] An early view of the Reliance (see fig. 93) shows how its rival, Carson Pirie Scott burrowed from building to building, diagonally across the street from Schlesinger & Mayer, until it punched into the lowest floor of the Reliance, and virtually exhausted the available store frontage on its State Street block. The new Leiter (1889–1891) (see fig. 59) and Fair (1890–1891) stores were in the process of building when, in 1890, the *Chicago Economist* commented on them as bellwethers for the future scale of the State Street department store. "There is still some doubt as to the extent to which retail business can be carried up to the upper stories of high buildings." Yet, the article went on to say, Field and Schlesinger & Mayer already had important departments as high as the third and fourth floors. Although there were "ladies who seriously object to ascending to these floors by means of elevators," their numbers were dwindling. The *Economist* concluded that "we may now consider the lofty retail building one of the certainties of the future.[84] So, as the big retial stores in Chicago expanded horizontally in the early 1890s, they began to swell vertically too. Clearly, considerations of convenience, safety, and identity demanded the architectural aggrandizement of this hodgepodge growth into what was truly a "department store."

As early as 1890–1891, Schlesinger & Mayer had called on Adler & Sullivan[85] on several occasions. Although there was talk even then of raising to ten stories the agglomeration of building which comprised the store, nothing came of this grandiose scheme. Instead, piecemeal additions lifted portions of the exterior by two stories, while some remodelling occurred inside. The larger scheme was probably doomed, initially, in part, by constant changes of plan with the rapid expansion of the store and, in part, because of economic uncertainty with the general downturn in business which led to the Panic of 1893 and its aftermath. In any event, Schlesinger & Mayer did not recall Sullivan until 1896 (after Adler's departure). The impending completion of the elevated railway on Wabash Avenue, one block away and parallel to State

Street, led Schlesinger & Mayer to acquire property fronting on Wabash in order to obtain a presence as well as an entrance toward the potential customers which the elevated would bring. Originally, the commission was to have involved the enlargement of a single building by two stories, plus complete renovation inside and out, with a connection through this building to the main store. Then the store management had another of its frequent changes of mind. It decided on a wholly new ten-story building for its narrow site on Wabash. An elevation of Sullivan's design for this project appeared in the July 5, 1896 edition of the *Chicago Tribune* (fig. 107). With a one-story show window base, the wall above showed two stacks of Chicago windows, topped by oculi under a parapeted roof, which was to have featured an observation deck.[86] The *Tribune* topped its view of the elevation with the triumphant flutter of an outsized pennant. Well it might, for this is startling in its glassiness and minimal walling. It would seem to have been even bolder in these respects than the final building. At very least this was true for the show windows and the skimpiness of their decorated frame. In these respects it indicated that Sullivan was catching up to the most forthright expressions of metal skeletal framing as extravagantly infilled with glass as possible—his response to buildings like the Reliance (see fig. 93). But crude as the *Tribune* image is, it also hints at the taut surfaces, incisive edging, linear patterning and arresting proportions of the finished building. Aside from his ornament, these were qualities in which Sullivan excelled. Clearly, too, this architectural sliver announced a modular scheme capable of expansion to encompass any degree of success that Schlesinger & Mayer might attain in the future.

Then another change occurred in the store management's plans. The larger ambitions were pared back to renovation after all (fig. 108). Sullivan radically opened the original building to plate glass toward the ground, and encased the masonry above in metal. An exquisite metal and glass bridge at the second-floor level coupled

Figure 113
Louis H. Sullivan, Carson Pirie Scott Store, detail of the show window base of the building in its original state. From The Architectural Record, *July 1904.*

the elevated platform to the newly renovated store. White paint completed the dazzling transformation, in marked contrast to the usual shop front on Wabash Avenue. It was all subsequently demolished.

Another hiatus in building operations ensued, until 1898, when Sullivan was called again. Finally, the management was ready in earnest to start the replacement of their hodgepodge quarters with a new building, although seesaw changes of instruction to the architect continued. For the new building Sullivan designed both a nine- and twelve-story version (figs. 109 and 110). These were subsequently reduced to nine stories, and the store management decided to build no more at that time than the rear three window units on Madison Street (minus the marquee, as a carriage entrance, which was added later). Only a small piece, but at last the building which is now Carson Pirie Scott was underway.

His designs at this time for Schlesinger & Mayer obviously harked back to Sullivan's Meyer Wholesale Store, as built, and his unbuilt schemes for the Chemical National Bank Building in St. Louis (1894–1895) (figs. 80, 111 and 112). There he also used horizontal windows—not the Chicago windows of his schemes for Schlesinger & Mayer, but paired windows to obtain something of the same horizontal effect for each of the openings, and for their cumulative effect across the elevation as a subtle banding of the wall. As in the store, the Chemical project emphasizes the horizontal impulse by making the parapeted part of the wall under each of the windows markedly wider than the narrower intervals between the windows. Anticipatory, too, is the apparent incisiveness of the punch of the windows into the plane of the wall of the Chemical Building, and the suggestion (shortly after the "White City" of the Columbian Exposition had risen in Chicago, in what was then a radically new palette for American architecture) that the building be of white brick. If the multiplication of vertical piers and columns was an appropriate response to the height of the tall office building, so the reticulated grid of the wall implied by the horizontal windows was appropriate as a visible reminder of the invisible structural grid of the skeletal metal frame. It recognized that, in a rectangular grid, the *spread* of the floor beams is just a little more emphatic than the *rise* of the widely spaced supporting columns. Why Sullivan waited so long to again experiment with an aesthetic approach to the tall skeletal building which the Chemical project carries so far is a mystery. Doubtless the poetic appeal of "tallness" was more attractive to Sullivan than the more logical expression of the structural grid. His overt counter of the horizontality of the Chicago windows in the Stock Exchange by the vertical cross of the stacked bays (fig. 88) would seem to underscore the point. If, as is widely maintained, he adopted the horizontal emphasis when the horizontality of the show windows for Schlesinger & Mayer made it particularly appropriate to do so, one wall of the Chemical Building also appeared relatively long, especially in its seven-story version, although less so in a twelve-story variant.

Sullivan may have thought it too long for his preferred vertical treatment, even as he worked on the Guaranty which would be his most verticalized composition. Certainly the increasing use of the Chicago window by other architects in the 1890s made Sullivan more familiar with its potential, and led to his eventual use of the device, but only belatedly, as though he resisted for a while what was irresistible. In any event, for the Schlesinger & Mayer commission the shelved solution for the Chemical Building again looked good.

Not until 1902 did the management recall Sullivan to extend the initial unit, now raised back to twelve stories (with the three topmost floors lower than those below).[87] Construction at this time occurred in two phases. The first included a width of three more windows on Madison Street, the turn of the corner, and a balancing three windows on State Street. This phase, which began in the summer of 1902, was ingeniously managed so that foundation work was completed for the new addition in the basement on a round-the-clock schedule, while normal selling operations continued through Christmas over the jacked-up floors above. After Christmas, demolition of the old corner wedge occurred and the new building rose swiftly during 1903–1904 on the already prepared foundations.[88] Once the corner had been completed, a further phase extended the State Street elevation by four more window units (seven in all). To his great bitterness, when yet another section was added to the State Street elevation in 1906—this time by Carson Pirie Scott—the new management turned to Daniel Burnham, who continued Sullivan's design. Although Sullivan's building is today universally known as the Carson Pirie Scott Store, ironically he never received a commission from its management.[89]

Originally advertised as a marble building with bronze frames for the show windows, its publicity promised "the most magnificent affair of the sort in the world."[90] Budget considerations apparently (fortunately, perhaps) compelled the substitution of off-white terra-cotta and cast iron. (The cast iron ornament was painted green over red under-

Figure 114
Louis H. Sullivan, Carson Pirie Scott Store, detail of a wreath motif over the corner entrance. Courtesy John Waggaman for Sandak.

painting, the second coat lightly rubbed to reveal ruddy flecks in the highlights, to which John Vinci restored it in 1979.[91] The famous circlet of doors at the base of the inset corner cylinder did not occur in the design as originally published. The initial scheme would have organized the show windows into a series of superbays, three show windows to each. One of these bays folded around the corner at State and Madison, so that a climactic polygonal display window, rather than doors, occurred at this point. Five entrances were fitted all around the building into the wedges resulting from the slanting walls of adjacent bays.

The most important alteration from the initial schemes was the continuation of the cylindrical inset as the corner of the building down to the ground, with doors replacing the polygonal display window. George Elmslie claimed this as his suggestion, although it accorded with an earlier arrangement of doors at the corner of the Schlesinger & Mayer Store, as well as with similar signature portals for other department stores,

including the world famous Parisian department store, Au Printemps.[92]

The Carson Pirie Scott Store takes its cue from the show windows: markedly horizontal, projected out from the wall plane of the upper stories toward the passing shopper, and extravagantly framed with the most exuberant ornament in Sullivan's career. Most of it was executed by Elmslie, according to him and other contemporaries who knew the situation, although inspired and supervised by Sullivan.[93]

On the spanning frieze over the show windows (fig. 113), tendrils spin with an energy more mechanical than botanical, tilted subtly at various angles with one another, out from the plane of the relief. Or perhaps they roll as breaking waves, spilling a foam of leaves as they churn, with a surge of leaves swelling over the top of the bounding frame. And above this frieze, another over the second-story window caps the two-story base of the building, with heavier leafage welling to a keystone-shaped cartouche at the center, but in a fountainlike *whoosh*, and tumbling like water to either side. Vegetable, liquid, and mechanical energies all come to mind.

Originally, the vibrancy was enhanced by Luxfer prism glass, filling the transom areas over the show windows, and now blind with metal infill panels. Contemporary accounts of the design called particular attention to the prism glass, then a new material only two years old and another indication of Sullivan's sympathy for the "modern."[94] The windows were designed to throw light through the tile-shaped prisms deep into the space within, substantially lighting the show windows as theatrical spotlighting does today. Their prismatic quality intensified the dance of light over the ornament. Originally, too, Sullivan emphasized the points of crossing for the skeletal frame above the show windows—where supporting and spanning elements meet—by ornamental bursts. Part cartouches, part capitals, part brooches, part giant buttons, these unruly wreaths encircled the interlocked "SM" monogram, and spilled out over the lower corners of the second-story windows. Radically different as Sullivan's treatments are for the bases of the Union Trust, Guaranty, and Carson Pirie Scott (compare with figs. 85 and 97), all depend on the outward indication of the same schema of underlying energies. Signs of spreading and stretching energies appear in the spandrel panels, compressive forces are evident on the face of the supports, and (in the later two buildings) some climactic development occurs at the crossing of span and support in the structural lattice. The cabbagelike swirls of ornament which initially projected from the crossings of the lattice over the show windows of the Carson Pirie Scott were removed a number of years ago when pieces began to fall, threatening passersby. During the years of modernist ascendency, sentiment generally applauded the mutilation. Even now, when ornamented buildings have returned to fashion, many regard these bursts of ornament as too unarchitectural in their exuberance and placement. But the entire frame of the lower two stories is conceived as a decorative skin with eruptive bursts. The bursts above the show windows frame them with "capitals." They contrast with the constricted noddule of untouched surface at the crossings of the skeleton lattice at the second-story level. So the points of crossing can be seen as foci of energy, whether potential or explosive—as seed germ or foliation. These bursts or ornament at the ground floor level also once worked in a syncopated rhythm with the "keystone" bursts at the centers of the spanning friezes over the second-story windows.

And of course they respond to the extravagant ornamental bursts that still remain: the leafy escutcheons on the Madison Street marquee which fronts the first section he built and, most prominently, the semicircle of wreaths above the corner entrances. Again, their theme is the infinitude of potential—raw surface in one instance, glassy void in the other—out of which, and around which, the turbulence of tendrils and leafage spin (fig. 114). The wreaths over the doors are *tours de force* of ornamental contrast. The agitated surface of the foliated frame opposes the limpidity of the pool of

*Figure 116
Louis H. Sullivan, Carson Pirie Scott Store, diagonal view of the upper story windows. Richard Nickel, photographer. Courtesy Richard Nickel Committee.*

recessed glass, shifting from black void to mirrored reflection or blinding light; the physical energy of the leafy masses contrasts with the tenderness of tendrils pulled out over the edges of the pool, and gently veiling it. At either side, below the wreaths, the tendrils are drawn into an interlocked monogram, "LHS," at the springing of the arches, which is appropriate even though Elmslie may have been actually responsible for this splendid decoration. Such bursts of ornament ultimately aggrandize into the quasi-elevational scale of some of the ornament in the later banks.

If this quality of exuberance to the point of excess in Sullivan's ornament has attracted the most criticism, it is also at the heart of what is most fascinating about his design. Through a variety of strategies, he pushes ornament to the brink of its architectural possibilities, sometimes, to be sure, over the edge of propriety. Yet precisely this sense of ornament risking the heroic role, rather than playing the accessory bit part, is what makes Sullivan's design so exceptional.

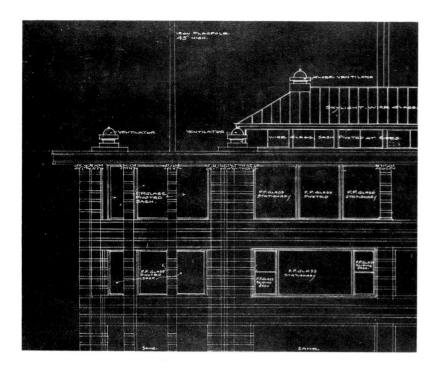

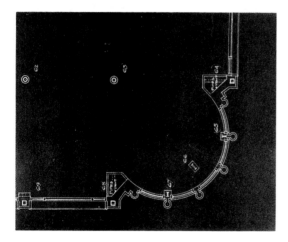

*Figure 117 a, b
Louis H. Sullivan, Carson
Pirie Scott Store plan and
elevation of the corner
entrances. Courtesy Chicago
Historical Society.*

In Carson Pirie Scott, the point of contrast which most strikes the observer is, of course, that between the fantasy embellishment of the show-windowed base of the building and the business-like severity of the taut white terra-cotta surface stretched over the upper floors (fig. 115). As a straightforward expression of the true nature of the skeletal steel frame with architectural significance, it has never been surpassed. For this reason, it seemed to be the climax in Sullivan's work, to adherents of International Style modernism. Sigfried Giedion, in his enormously influential *Space, Time and Architecture* ignored what seemed to him the regrettable (or, to an ardent modernist, at least irrelevant) base of the building to praise its upper stories as though they *were* the building.[95] To be sure, Sullivan's inset Chicago windows emphasize the structural lattice, whereas the canons of the International Style would have dictated that the glass be pushed to the outer plane of the wall to celebrate the thinness of the protective surface lightly stretched around the volume of interior space. It is a question of which "reality" one chooses to celebrate: the structure which supports the building, or the space made by the walls enclosing it. Will it be the physicality of the skeleton (always the emphasis in the late nineteenth-century Chicago commercial style), or the ethereality of space? Yet, to the modernist's awe, there it was: the upper floors of the Carson Pirie Scott are nothing but a linear grid infilled with glass. In the blur of the hasty glance or of Giedion's illustration, it could be viewed as modernist reductionism of the severest sort.

Actual experience of the building reveals it differently. Each of the horizontal windows is edged in a narrow, scooped molding, projecting slightly beyond the surface stretched over the frame. This sets off the rectangle. Delicate ornament within the molding band makes the edge vibrate in the light. The framed rectangles are aligned between equally narrow moldings, running the length of the elevation, also crinkled with light, but imbedded. So one molding subtly isolates the individual rectangles; the other subtly weds them *en masse* to the overall pattern of the elevation, bringing their horizontality into accord with the "run" of the wall. This, in turn, accords with the "run" of the show windows below. The narrow bands occurring within the alternating courses of wide-narrow-wide-narrow tiling inscribe horizontality into the surface itself. The neutral crossing of the lattice, across and up; the self-containment of the sharply defined rectangles; the insistent horizontality overall; the smooth planes of the tiles against the slight shimmer of the linear decorative bands: these aspects work together to create the total composition of the wall, and work separately to set up shifting tensions within it. It is exquisite in its refinement, yet so incisively articulated as to be extraordinarily vivid. If in the Wainwright, Sullivan brought the lavish interior ornament of the Auditorium outside, so, in the upper stories of the Carson Pirie Scott it is tempting to imagine that he might have shifted the deluxe light court of the period from its concealed position within the block to the elevations. The white ceramic walls with their elegant inset moldings not only appear in his Guaranty court (fig. 71), but earlier, and a bit more spectacularly, in the light court of Burnham & Root's Rookery Building (1885–1886). Light courts like that of the Rookery may have inspired the white brick walls contemplated in schemes for the Chemical Bank, and eventually brought to Carson Pirie Scott.

Even the severest aspects of the wall indicate an ornamental sensibility. And viewed obliquely (fig. 116)—as is, of course, the way that one sees it passing by, and precisely what Giedion refused to acknowledge—the whole elevation blossoms with the richness of the ornamental borders concealed in the surfaces of the inset of the window within the frame (its reveal). Shy efflorescence, coming from the crannies of a technology which makes "crannies" obsolete, the effect overall narrows the alleged discrepancy in treatment between the upper floors and the store front base.

The walls rise to the reduced height of the three topmost floors which here doubtless occurred either to minimize the discrepancy between the

nine stories of the initial increment, or for economic reasons. The wiry ornamented quality of these stretched surfaces may be the most "Saracenic" of all his wall treatments, but utterly underivative. Sullivan, however, must have welcomed the way in which the diminution of the top stories of the Carson Pirie Scott prepared for the simulated loggia, with its striping and roof slab. Fortunately, he terminated the elevation with an economy of means which, had he stuck to his initial corniced scheme, would have been embellished (see fig. 109). Although a tentative design only, the corniced version seems to show a series of foliated brackets positioned to mark the tops of the columns, a derivative of the slightly earlier Gage motif (discussed below). Had the first scheme

been realized, the ornamental character of the base would also have occurred in a much more restrained manner at the top of the building, and the validity of the Giedion sort of modernist interpretation of the Carson Pirie Scott would have been further confounded.

The inset prow of the corner entrance emphasizes the two street elevations as planes. It prevents their union as a volume, marking another distinction from canonical International Style buildings, especially in conjunction with Carson Pirie Scott's parade of the structure throughout.

In the latticed elevations running along State and Madison Streets, the structural columns are concealed within the tight skin of the gridded wall. A beautifully designed reveal effects an angled transition back to the recessed portal with its circlet of projecting cylinders (fig. 117). Hence the structural columns, imbedded within the lattices, abruptly appear at the corner, like the interior layers of a flayed anatomical figure, even though the exposed vertical columns are, like much of Mies van der Rohe's structural display, surrogates for what actually occurs. The plan of the corner

shows how the actual structure—two I-beams and a free-standing column inside—does the work, while the exposed columns receive the glory.

Carson Pirie Scott unites the two basic expressions for skeletal framing in the same building: first, projecting vertical piers; second the gridded frame. In a way, so does the Gage Building, but so uniquely as to constitute a third mode which Sullivan used in his most successful expressions of the metal-framed commercial building. Whereas the other two are "standard" approaches to the problem, his Gage Building is an exceptional solution, with few imitations or parallels. The commission came to him just after his completion of the preliminary schemes for Schlesinger & Mayer, and just prior to their decision to begin the project with the initial piece on Madison Street. So the two buildings developed for a while in tandem, although work on subsequent phases of the department store extended substantially longer.

In a sense, of course, the Gage is no more than widely spaced piers projected out in front of an

Figure 120
Louis H. Sullivan, John D. Van Allen & Son Store, Clinton, Iowa, 1913–1915, ornamental details. Cervin Robinson, photographer.

infill of stacks of Chicago windows, as the treatment of two adjacent buildings by Holabird & Roche makes clear. This eminently sensible firm, whose motto (more appropriately than Sullivan's) could have been "form follows function," are notable for their straightforward treatment of the metal-framed building, as here. In this instance, their commission called for three adjacent buildings on Michigan Avenue—six, seven, and eight stories, respectively—for three millinery establishments which combined retail sales in the lower floors with workshops above. The firm with the eight-story building, Gage Brothers, called on Sullivan to provide a custom-designed front (which Holabird & Roche later enlarged by four more stories, keeping to Sullivan's design).

Sullivan accepted the elements of the Holabird & Roche elevations as his starting point: a frame around the ground floor shop windows; Chicago windows above; two projecting piers; an enclosing frame for the elevation as a whole. The frame of the shop windows for the Gage Building provided Sullivan (via Elmslie again) with another excuse for saracenic cast iron surface ornament.[96] A splendid ornament, it was stupidly and ruthlessly junked for "modernization" as late as the 1960s. Above this, Sullivan altered Holabird & Roche's red brick and terra-cotta coating with white terra-cotta tiles. He intensified the frame around the building, capping it in an incisive way by a strongly projecting roof slab. Again he strongly emphasized the block, even in so skeletal an elevation. He reproportioned the Chicago windows of the neighboring buildings, and gave them transoms filled with Luxfer prisms, as a preliminary to their slightly later use in Carson Pirie Scott.[97] It was a sensible arrangement in order to direct daylight as deeply into the sewing rooms as possible, while simultaneously reducing the glare that full plate glass windows would bring. He divided the horizontal window area into bands of four windows, decorating their parapets with the same sort of isolated, rhythmic ornamental bursts as he had used in the Bayard. He adjusted the pier profile to give it a thinner look and more vertical impetus.

In the most radical transformation of all, he topped each of the piers with a gush of foliated ornament, set against the otherwise plain surface of the cornice frieze. This foliated gush visually disengages the columns from the stack of horizontal spandrel, window, and transom bands it crosses. The columns appear somewhat like trees (palms, perhaps), standing a little in front of the elevation to which they are attached. Foliated analogs to the winged figures of the Bayard Building, this leafage also serves the dual function of upward and outward spread, with tremulous support as visual bracketing for a projecting roof slab. The motif appears with reticent elegance in the capitals which float off the pipestem column of the Wabash Street bridge from the elevated platform into the Schlesinger & Mayer Store. It seems to be perpetuated in the cornice of the preliminary perspectives for the store. It continues, transformed, in the leafy cartouches which button the upper corners of the show windows of Carson Pirie Scott and perhaps in the more disparate gush and roll of the foliage in the friezes over the second-story windows (see figs. 108, 109, and 113).

These geysers of ornament can be deplored as images of "suppressed energy" which are both too literal and too unsuppressed. So can the abruptness with which the plainness of the shaped pier spouts its foliage like a pipe disgorging liquid. As a tree analogy, this would be more complete if their trunks came to the ground (along with the bounding frame of the building as well) and did not appear to have been cut off by the frame of the show windows, behind which they disappear. Alternatively, their trunks should seem to originate from the shelving which tops the show window base of the building.[98] Neither condition prevails. Hence these heavy forms so confidently rising seem also disturbingly cut through and floating. The whole decorative scheme of the Gage seems more fragmented than comparable schemes for the Wainwright, Guaranty, and Bayard. Yet once more, Sullivan has found an original solution for the expression of the skeletal metal frame which discloses the sense of energies inherent to it.

Figure 121
Adler & Sullivan, Guaranty Building, Buffalo, 1894–1896, lobby interiors. Patricia Layman Bazelon, photographer.

The need to embellish Holabird & Roche's laconically functional elevations brought Sullivan back to the straightforward problem of the piered commercial building of modest height, radically infilled with glass, which, years before, he had confronted in the Troescher Building (see fig. 60). In a general way, the Troescher foretells the Gage in the piers crossing over the long window bridgings they support, although what is *ad hoc* in the earlier building becomes self-evidently aesthetic in the later. More specifically, the Troescher anticipates the Gage in the rigid stems which sprout tight, bristling lotus blossoms at the cornice. So the theme for the later building seems to hark back to the beginnings of Sullivan's ornament in such late-Victorian motifs as this. But what a transformation! In the Troescher, the ornament is a mere decorative plume to the workaday hat. In the Gage Building, the realms are interactive. Ornament makes the elevation; the elevation makes the ornament. In both buildings the weak point remains the precise relationship which should exist between the street level shop front and what is above.

Finally, the modest Van Allen Store in Clinton, Iowa (1913–1915) (fig. 119) is something of a reprise of the Gage. Here greatly reduced tree or plant forms are truly outrigging to the block, crossing the extravagant ribbons. (One thinks of Mies van der Rohe's sawed-off I-beams clinging to the building as though magnetized, but entirely different in character.) The bracketed rooting of Sullivan's mini-trees clearly support them off the wall planes, and eliminate the ambiguity of whether or not their counterparts in the Gage elevation are properly supported. The floating quality of the Van Allen ornaments is further enhanced by the attenuation of the verticals, and by the counterpointed way in which these rodlike elements alternate with the solid look of the square piers. The ambiguous readings really work here. Do the laid-back piers frame the windows, or the out-front decorated rods? Are we dealing with one long window, subdivided across the entire elevation with minor openings flanking them, or six win-

dows? That each of the modified Chicago windows should have a single sash window for ventilation, set close to the decorated verticals, further complicates the ways in which the windows are alternatively viewed. In several of Sullivan's later buildings one senses that he is especially interested in animating his design by introducing possibilities for alternative readings of the same architectural components. It is true for the lattice of the Carson Pirie Scott Store; it may explain the uncertainty of any definitive reading of the Gage Building, where, however, shifting perceptions of Sullivan's intent do not lock into crisp alternatives, but slide into perplexity. Again, this approach to design reveals the ornamentalist.

As an expression of the skeletal commercial building, the Van Allen Store is extraordinarily original, and deserves far more attention than its obscurity and modesty warrant. There is a degree of poignancy, too, in the way the economy of this building bares Sullivan's approach to design. Here, to begin, is the simple box once more, fiercely asserted, and especially so as the centerpiece in the business district of this small midwestern town. Sullivan's fine sense of proportion and surface maintain the compactness of the block despite the alternating ribbons which boldly cut across it: ribbons of ruddy tapestried brick, their edges flickering with bands of imbedded ornament in reddish terra-cotta, alternating with extravagant ribbons of glass. Then he transforms the box by laying his three batons of ornament across the ribbons.

Is there an even closer reverberation here of such Victorian foliated stems as the lotus spikes which decorated the cornices of Sullivan's very early Rothschild Store (1880–1881) (see fig. 4) and Troescher Building? Possibly, but he needed to look no further for inspiration than the congealed flowers of Art Nouveau decoration as these became rigid, geometrical, and condensed with the shift in taste by the late nineties away from exotic curvature toward Arts and Crafts stolidity. Such flowering stems appear in a more purely decorative way in some of the late banks, especially in the Home Building Association Bank (1914) in

Newark, Ohio, in the Farmers' and Merchants' Bank (1919) in Columbus, Wisconsin (see figs. 146 and 152), and in Sullivan's final building, his two-story Krause's Music Store (1922) in Chicago.

In the mini-trees of the Van Allen Store the old fusion and fluidity of his ornament have broken down into a combination of isolated parts—leaf separated from leaf, and leaves from stems. An increased naturalism, with a della Robbia distinction in color, intensifies the separateness of the pieces. Green leaves and brown stems are set off against the white and blue conventionalized flat ornament which fixes the tree to the cornice; its bright colors are, in turn, set against the russet brick. There is an emblematic, harvestlike quality to the embellishment. By earlier standards, these are modest ornamental offerings, pinched back from the exuberance of earlier efforts, substantially for reasons of budget no doubt, in part perhaps from some decline in ability. But how appropriate this reprise is! The more so because its modesty makes the process so evident, without dispelling the magic. In Sullivan's efforts to give form to the skeletal office and commercial building, it was his final attempt.

THE LOSS OF SULLIVAN'S, OR OF ADLER & Sullivan's, buildings is appalling. By some fluke of fate, however, the most important of his office and commercial work remains—those, that is, comprising the group from which one would select the irreducible core of what was most exceptional in Sullivan's achievement. The Wainwright, Guaranty, Gage and Bayard Buildings, together with the Carson Pirie Scott Store still stand. Moreover, almost all of these have undergone restoration,[99] and all continue to serve the kinds of uses for which they were built. Add to these the preservation of the Auditorium as his most substantial public work, the three tombs, and every one of his very personal later designs of any consequence for small bank buildings in midwestern agricultural towns. There is reason for some satisfaction.

Yet, among his commercial and office buildings, immediately leading up to the Wainwright and Demolition of the Walker Warehouse and Dooly Block (fig. 63 and 64) has eliminated Sullivan's most austere, most purely geometrical buildings. Only the Ryerson Tomb (fig. 41) is left to demonstrate how much the architectural power of the ornament depends upon the forceful layout of the primal block or elevation, on the distribution and shaping of openings, and on the modulation of the principal parts. While celebrating Sullivan as an ornamentalist, the recall of the severity of these designs is salutary. Sullivan himself admonished that the plain building was to be preferred to ill-considered ornamentation.[100] Schuyler long ago said as much in lauding Sullivan as not only "the first of our decorators, though that he so clearly is," but also observed his "perception of the importance of the masses" and his "appreciation of the essential facts of structure that makes the architect in contra-distinction to the architectural decorator."[101]

Kin to the extremely severe Walker Warehouse and Dooly Block, the demolition of the Schiller and the Stock Exchange (figs. 83 and 88) have not only eliminated two of his finest buildings, but also those that most compellingly mediate between the severe and ornamental aspects of his architectural sensibility. In both, the directness of his handling of the office floors on the elevation is countered by the sumptuous ornament on cornices and around entrances (extending to the entire base of the Schiller). In conjunction with the loss of the Walker and Dooly, their destruction means that the more conservative strain in Sullivan's commercial and business design has wholly disappeared, except for the Union Trust (fig. 84). Although less coherent as a design than the other four buildings, the happenstance of its survival makes more urgent its continued preservation, and all the more because of its immediate proximity to the Wainwright.

The most important of Sullivan's plain or substantially plain office and commercial buildings occurred around 1890 (from the exterior of the Auditorium of around 1886 to the completion of the Meyer building and the Stock Exchange in 1893 and 1894). Although occasional commissions for the plain sort of building continued to come to him, they were for relatively modest buildings. Clients who wanted a major office building done in the severe manner of what *Industrial Chicago* boasted as the "Chicago commercial style" characteristic of the Loop office building of the 1890s,[102] would not look to Sullivan. On the contrary, his clients typically wanted something that would be viewed as clearly "special."

We still know very little about the clients of the principal commercial and business buildings for whom Chicago architects designed during the 1880s and 1890s. Up to now, the best known clients for first-class office buildings in the plain "Chicago commercial style" have been Peter and Shepherd Brooks of Boston. Heavy investors in Chicago real estate, they financed an astonishing number of the outstanding buildings in the severe "Chicago commercial style." Burnham & Root's Montauk (1881–1882), a pioneer building in establishing the trend, Rookery (1885–1886) and Monadnock (1884–1891), an addition to the Monadnock by Holabird & Roche (1893) and, by the same architects, the Marquette (1893–1894): all major buildings in the severe style, they were financed by the Brooks brothers through their Chicago real estate manager, Owen F. Aldis. Peter Brooks stated his preferences with his first commission in Chicago. "I prefer to have a plain structure of face brick . . ." he wrote in part to Aldis on March 25, 1881, "with flat roof to be as massive as the architect chooses. . . . The building throughout is to be for use and not for ornament. . . . Its beauty will be in its all-adaptation to its use."[103]

Investors like the Brooks brothers did not patronize Sullivan. Nor did another type of inves-

tor in business buildings of the period, less clearly defined, but who may be generally characterized as the corporate executive. A growing group, the wave of the future for top business management, as it turned out, their inclinations in architecture increasingly influenced what even the speculative investor would come to want for the highest grade of office accommodations. These investors sought the cachet of prestige and sense of continuity which the creative adaptation of historical styles could bring. They presumably looked to firms like McKim, Mead & White or Daniel Burnham, following his thorough conversion to Renaissance forms, for the image they sought. Again, none of this breed of investor came to Sullivan's door.

From what little we know of Sullivan's clients, they were local entrepreneurs of marked, apparently somewhat parochial, individuality, who had made it big and wanted to celebrate the fact with a sound investment which would also make a splash. Ellis Wainwright was the second generation owner of a local brewery who combined his resources with some from his mother to order up the most beautiful office building in St. Louis. Something of his attitude toward the kind of splendor which Sullivan could supply touchingly appears in the obituary to his young wife, bringing another call to Sullivan for her tomb.

The friends of Ellis Wainwright were startled yesterday morning by the announcement of the death of his lovely young wife, who passed away in the full flush of youth and beauty, surrounded by all that life could offer in happiness. Scarcely any one was aware that Mrs. Wainwright was ill, and her untimely end was the theme of many tongues yesterday in the city of her birth, where she has so long reigned as the very crown and flower of St. Louis beauty. Mrs. Wainwright appeared in a box party Friday night at the Grand Opera House, looking radiant and full of health, and after three days of illness she died of peritonitis. As Miss Lottie Dickson, daughter of Alanson Dickson of this city, Mrs. Wainwright was admired and sought after, and during her happy married life

she has been one of the prominent society leaders.
Always gracious and easy of access and a true and
devoted friend, Mrs. Wainwright leaves many
to mourn her loss.

Mrs. Wainwright's portrait appeared in
Frank Leslie's Illustrated Newspaper *a year ago*
among the belles of America. She was described as
being the most beautiful woman in St. Louis, and
as one of the social lights. As her husband is very
rich, he enhanced her loveliness by exquisite French
costumes and by jewels of every description. She
was rather tall, with a queenly carriage and some-
what haughty manners. A small nose, straight and
perfectly chiseled, complexion a delicate pink and
white, deeply fringed hazel eyes, shining beneath
finely marked eyebrows, and hair almost matching
the color of her eyes—she was strikingly handsome.
She and her husband formed part of a gay coterie
of young married people, who were seen at all the
most modish entertainments. Last spring Mr. and
Mrs. Wainwright took possession of their new and
elegant house on Delmar avenue, in one of the most
fashionable parts of the city. The house is built in
the Early English style of architecture, of rough
hewn brown stone and granite. Here the couple enter-
tained friends in regal style, amid rich surround-
ings, the home being adorned with fine paintings
and rare and costly decorations.[104]

A gilded bird in a gilded cage. Does one sense
in this pathos of beauty smothered in all the beauty
that money could buy some sensibility for quality
which also led Wainwright to his choice of architect? That Wainwright collected paintings by the
Barbizon painters, and apparently travelled in
France, may account for his attraction to an architect of Sullivan's quality. Or for Wainwright would
any architectural extravagance have done nearly
as well for his celebration of the good life? His
good life came first from proceeds from beer;
later, from traction franchises, until charges of
fraud drove him to Europe. He eventually returned
to St. Louis, but with his reputation and apparently
at least some of his prosperity eroded.[105]

In Buffalo, it was the even more mysterious
carriage maker, Hascal L. Taylor, from a nearby
farming village, who struck it rich in Pennsylvania
oil and dreamed of erecting the finest, most beautiful office tower for the local metropolis to be
known as the Taylor Building. He died, however,
during the very month in which Sullivan completed
his drawings, and immortality passed to Taylor's
contractor, the Guaranty Construction Company,
which decided to proceed with the enterprise.[106]
Similarly, the Gage brothers decided to outdo the
adjacent competition in Michigan Avenue's most
fashionable milliner's row by adding to the workaday elevations of the others a flourish of architectural plumage.[107] While their new store was being
built, Schlesinger & Mayer repeatedly boasted in
the Chicago press that they sought the most beautiful department store *in the world*[108]—a boast
which, as it turned out, has proved to be close to
the mark, at least for the exteriors.

These individualistic businessmen, somewhat
provincial, but perhaps cultured in some degree,
appear to have been roughly the same type who
patronized Wright, except that many of Wright's
clients had gone through the chastening, and possibly civilizing, experience of the widespread Arts
and Crafts interlude, as eventually so did Sullivan's
patrons for his late banks. The clients for Sullivan's
office buildings seem rather to have represented
the end-phase of the most ambitious and venturesome Victorian clients who sought a certain con-
spicuousness in what they commissioned. Sullivan's rhetorical design would have been just right
for them. Showy, popular, extraordinary, modern,
high-flown in sentiment; these qualities in his
design would seem to have struck a responsive
chord in his business patrons.

More late Victorian than "modern," too, was
Sullivan's quest for a "new" ornament based upon
naturalistic (especially botanical) inspiration
rather than upon historical motifs. Indeed, his exaggerated regard for naturalistic ornament in the
first place was essentially Victorian. On the other
hand, there was an urbanity about Sullivan's
design, an abstractness, and a tense litheness in
its refinement which proclaimed a post-Victorian

sensibility. So did the suave ghosts of academic historicism which only became omnipresent in the 1890s and, somewhat unassimilated, uncomfortably haunt Sullivan's office buildings—the allusions to quattrocento portals, classical columns, and heavy Renaissance cornices, as well as borrowings from the interior walling of medieval cathedrals brought outdoors. If these were signs of Sullivan's having passed beyond the late Victorianism of much of his early work, so of course was his engagement with the "modern" problem of the proper expression for the tall office building, which had already begun to take on the scale and impersonality of the bureaucracies it housed.

There are those—most extensively and convincingly, David S. Andrew—who have questioned whether the lavish praise of Sullivan as the architect who "gave form to the skyscraper" is the exaggeration of modernist misconception and sentimentality.[109] Andrew argues in part that modernist criticism has condoned as worthwhile the boastfulness of the narrowest sort of business entrepreneur, bent on self-advertisement at any cost. It has also accepted Sullivan's inappropriately ornate and individualistic approach to the design of the tall office building as though it were a proper expression. It has compounded the error by accepting Sullivan's tall buildings, along with his incoherent and vainglorious pronouncements in justification of them, as profound and prophetic for the future of architecture, when, in fact, their example has been deleterious. The charges have some justification, but some exaggeration too, which we can here examine in a general way only.

By comparison with Sullivan's misplaced rhetoric for the office building, was it not sounder to have pursued either of the two alternatives for design of the tall office building favored by other architects of his day, along with their clients? Thus, those who viewed the office building primarily as a tool for maximizing return on capital would keep it plain and simple, at least on the exterior.[110] Alternatively, those who viewed it primarily as an institutional monument to the prestige of corporate business would extend the

continuity and grandeur of past institutions by adapting their architectural trappings. During the 1890s both of these alternative views as to how to approach the design of the offce building prevailed over that held by Sullivan and his clientele. It seems to have been the principal reason for the eventual failure of his career (personal reasons apparently being less cause than effect).[111] By 1900, his way of designing seemed entirely too idiosyncratic, especially for office buildings, which had become his specialty. The clientele for his kind of design had withered away in the big cities. It persisted, for a while, in small towns, where attitudes lingered which favored the Sullivanian mixture of individualism and naturalism. Having specialized in the dominant business commission for the city, Sullivan was demoted to the dominant business commission for the small town. Office buildings gave way to banks. Then, eventually, the void.

At this late date it seems inappropriate, however, to take sides for any of these three approaches, whether the plain mode, or the revivalist mode, or the individualistic mode. The situation at the time called up all three possibilities. All could be justified. All resulted in some buildings of high merit. As a participant in the competition, with strong convictions as to the proper course to follow and a personal stake in the outcome which involved his very being, Sullivan was understandably biased.

Despite his achievement in other types of buildings—in theaters, tombs, and banks especially—the high visibility of his tall buildings, their number, their occurrence in his career when he was at the peak of his powers, and the importance which he himself accorded them, taken together mark them as the pinnacle of his achievement. Moreover, his own stature has surely been magnified by its identification with a building type which physically, institutionally, and symbolically dominates the American city; one which also has been traditionally considered the most distinctive American contribution to the typology of architecture. Seeing the current effect of the gargantuan skyscraper on American cities from one end of the country to the other, however, the thoughtful observer may be inclined to denigrate earlier euphoria as to their value. A building type which so swaggeringly proclaims its arrogant domination of other buildings, and so conspicuously asserts profit-making and the booster spirit over all other virtues, has surely been over celebrated. In Sullivan's case, does an architectural career as committed to the tall office building as his possess sufficient range or scope of social commitment and expression to justify his exalted stature in the history of modern architecture? Was the cause worthy of the exegesis and the ornament he expended on it? Variations of these questions could of course be asked of all architects whose work has substantially embraced the skyscraper; but Sullivan's special (one could say, mythical) role in its early development makes him particularly vulnerable to the criticism.

Sullivan saw the problem of the tall skeletal building as the single most intractable "modern" problem for architects of his time and place. (He was wrong: for example, humane housing and community design, then and now, are surely more worthy of solution.) Yet tall buildings were at the very heart of what was architecturally new and challenging around 1890, and especially in the Midwest. One cannot read such midwestern architectural journals of the time as the *Inland Architect and News Record* (Chicago) or the *Northwestern Architect* (Minneapolis and Chicago) without being caught up in the fervor of comment on the tall office building, seemingly much more intense in these magazines than in their eastern counterparts. Even at this time, it was viewed as a peculiarly American building type to which western inventiveness had made major contributions. Much of the technological innovation of the period was especially relevant to these buildings, whether in foundations, structure, fireproofing, mechanical equipment, construction techniques, or new products. Likewise for much of the aesthetic speculation of the period, which fretted over the ideal solution to such qualities of tall buildings as their excessive height, attenuated structure, monotonous elevations and extravagant glazing. All were

substantially at odds with customary Victorian approaches to high-style design, and the more daunting for their simultaneous appearance as problems inherent to the tall office building. The tall office building also drew attention for its symbolic qualities, as a conspicuous monument to business energy and prestige at a time when business was thought to embody (not incorrectly) the economic and human forces which would propel American society to world power and leadership. It was an aspect of the naive imperialism of the day. None of the leading architects of the "American Renaissance" emerging from the "Gilded Age" wholly escaped the blighting hubris of the moment, even as the hubris also accounted for much of what was distinguished in its building.

Confronting this "new" problem, Sullivan dared to approach it in a "modern" spirit. Like all those who are especially identified with modernism (here referring to a broad outlook toward work and life rather than to whatever may be defined as the specific movement or style of "modern architecture"), Sullivan was modern in the first instance because he asserted himself as such; then because he found expressive means to make his assertion plausible; finally, because he had the conviction and courage to live out his life as a "modern" spirit regardless of personal consequence. He is the first American architect to have convincingly committed himself to what can be termed a self-consciously, heroic modern point of view in some sense of what this would come to mean in the twentieth century. (Only his adored Whitman in nineteenth-century American culture approaches Sullivan in this respect.) He is also among the threshold figures of those world wide whose buildings and attitudes compel consideration of their achievement in any large account of modern architecture in the twentieth century. Evidence for the modernism in his work is augmented by his writing, in which he specifically depicts himself as a modern architect, however wearying its incoherence, and nineteenth century its florid style. Especially during the late nineties, toward the end of the high period of his work on the tall skeletal building, he briefly epitomized the modern spirit for a group of eager young architects concentrated in the Midwest.[112] He became Lieber Meister to Frank Lloyd Wright, who could be said really to have been less specifically committed to a modern position than he.[113]

So his sense of the modern first deserves recognition. Even at the present time, when the ideals of recent "modernism" have become suspect to many, one admires the drive, courage and vision with which he confronted the architectural type and its problems where what was then modern seemed most especially to reside. To his further credit, the solutions he arrived at have persistently haunted subsequent developments in the tall skeletal building, and this despite decades, early in the twentieth century, during which they were eclipsed, but never quite forgotten.

If the tall office building provided the most visible arena for Sullivan's modern outlook, could he make a worthy modern monument of this recalcitrant problem—worthy of the institution it served and which he excessively admired, worthy of its prominence, and worthy through some sort of grandness of treatment to take its place beside past grandeur while also asserting the modernity especially appropriate to this building type? His rhetorical demands on the building required something more than the plain "Chicago commercial style." Setting aside his more industrial commissions, Sullivan's most severe commercial buildings, the Walker and Dooly blocks (see figs. 63 and 64) occurred in the shadow of Richardson's example, and probably with client insistence. As soon as the tall skeletal design office building occurred in Sullivan's work with the Wainwright Building, however, it was elaborately ornamented. So were all such commissions. Only the severe Meyer Wholesale Store as built and the Michigan Avenue project can be considered exceptions (figs. 82 and 106). Yet the first was a reduction of something originally intended for lavish embellishment. The second, at the end of the line, was essentially a schematic proposal. Even in its diagrammatic form, it exhibited some ornament, which Sullivan

would surely have elaborated had a potential client been willing. So he clearly considered that there was a nobility in tall buildings, however exaggerated his regard for them might be, which called for ornamentation.

In seeking ornament for this explicitly modern building type, this period offered two broad avenues of choice: either fashion some fresh amalgam from the design dictionaries of the time, or turn to nature. Inspiration from nature was the Victorian alternative for those who sought "original" ornament beyond the styles, as the very format of Owen Jones's much used *Grammar of Ornament* implies. Having piled up thousands of snippets of ornament from the historic past, Jones finally appended a brief section on the great alternative— just ten plates in all—after ninety devoted to historic ornament.[114] The very division between the bulk of the compendium of historic ornament and the slight sheaf of line drawings of basic leaf and flower forms added at the end makes its own proclamation: design from the infinite abundance of precedent as nineteenth-century encyclopedism had opened up this precedent, and/or design from the infinite abundance of naturalistic principle which has repeatedly informed ornament in the past and stands open to the continuous invention of new ornamental forms in the future. Given these choices, between one which was essentially prescriptive and the other essentially suggestive, there is no doubt as to which the ornamentalist with modern ambitions would favor. Especially was this the case for Sullivan, who had been inherently attracted to nature from the beginning, from his mother's interest in flower painting, through the numerous episodes in which his kinship with nature is recorded in *The Autobiography of an Idea*. In fact, Transcendentalism seems to have enjoyed its sunset phase in the Midwest, well after it had faded in the East.[115] Moreover, as Van Zanten elaborates, Sullivan's predispositions toward naturalistic ornament found sympathetic reinforcement in the most progressive late-Victorian theory of ornamental design.[116]

Is naturalistic ornament, however, inherently

appropriate for buildings as insistently reticulated, planar, and sharp-edged as the tall metal-framed building? More to the point, is Sullivan's particular kind of naturalistic ornament, which never wholly freed itself of the eruptive, florid, assertive naturalism of late-Victorian design, too flamboyant for its function? Even the most favorable critics of his work have questioned incidents of ornamental excess in his design. In fact, however, in his mature ornament Sullivan adapts his naturalism to the reticulated austerity of the metal frame in several ways. The first is by the proportioning of the grid itself, which already gives it an ornamental aspect, as is baldly evident in his Michigan Avenue project (fig. 106). Much of his ornament employs all-over geometrical surface patterning (for example, figs. 55 and 97), sometimes as the sole means of decorating a portion of the building; sometimes as the geometrical foil from which crescendoes of more naturalistic ornament swell. These, the most three-dimensional aspect of his ornament (and generally the most censured), are themselves generated from basic geometrical shapes. As already observed, they are also abstracted away from allusion to particular species, and appear as generalized leaves, stems, pods, buds, berries, thorns, and tendrils, consonant with Sullivan's belief that original ornament derived from nature should not imitate the surface appearance of specific plants, but their inherent shapes and underlying anatomy.[117] He also endowed them with a lithe, linear energy of stem, and with a surge and pulsation of leafy climax suggesting mechanical rather than vegetable impetus. So the qualities of the ornament are inflected toward the qualities of the support.

Yet there is also a conscious dichotomy between the two realms, a sense in which the ornament resists complete absorption into the architectural fabric (even in the Wainwright, where its subordination is most evident) [see figs. 70 and 95]. Rather Sullivan seems to intend a dialogue between technology and nature, akin to that of his memory from childhood in his *Autobiography of an Idea*, which records his fright and bewilderment on suddenly coming across the looming gauntness of a metal-framed railroad bridge amidst a lush landscape—his fear of the alien presence mingled with his awe of the engineer's power to counter nature by his huge contrivance, with which he became reconciled, and eventually exhilarated.[118] His ornament also sets up a degree of contrast between the technology of the building and its resplendence. The ornament emerges from the structure, taking its principal cues from it, but also asserts a degree of independence. It records the structure which sustains it, and glorifies it; but, like a blossom, also transcends it, until, in our visual delight with the flower, the plant seems almost to exist solely in its bloom, even though we remain peripherally aware of what sustains it. Ornament plays a transcending role.

Transcendence is a cardinal function of ornament, possibly its ultimate role. It is even more cardinally a function of music. Sullivan was devoted to Wagner, another indication of his affinity for modernity in the 1880s and 1890s, when "Wagnerism" was the controversial movement in music.[119] Sullivan's ornament, in fact, came out of the concert hall and onto the building, out of the Auditorium and onto the Wainwright.

Nor is his excess limited to the ornament. It also appears in his desire to include clubhouses and outlooks in his office buildings. Not that they were inappropriate to the tall business building; their inclusion in first-class office structures was part of a widespread movement for the establishment of urban clubs at the time. It is rather the exaggeration of their presence in many of Sullivan's office building designs, whether as functioning entities, or merely as the wish for their presence, as in the lavish surrogate loggias at the cornice without more than a symbolic presence. They indicate his eagerness to push his tall building into something grander than it inherently was. In the same way, his tangential remarks on the mystique of its circulatory system, however provocative, even more revealingly proclaimed his weakness for the overtly rhetorical.[120]

Transcendence and rhetorical aggrandizement suggest a sensibility for the sublime. The sublime aspires to infinity. Sullivan repeatedly called up the infinite in his writing.[121] To him as a late-Victorian ornamentalist, Near Eastern design, together with its principles, was especially available to invoke the sensation of infinity through its use of melding color, its extensive subdivision of field, and intricate surface pattern. Fully a third of the plates in Jones's *Grammar* lopsidedly reported the results of fresh investigations (his own included) into Moorish and Saracenic ornament, and spread out the results for designers. So again, Sullivan may have been attracted to the prospect of what was "new" in late-Victorian design, as well as the luxuriousness which this ornament promised.

His use of color on the exteriors of his office buildings in the 1890s is, surprisingly, quite conservative. But a similar conservatism revealed itself in the movement of ornament from his theater interiors (beginning with the Auditorium) to the exteriors of his office buildings (beginning with the Wainwright, with the all-over quality of the ornament of the Auditorium interior only appearing in the Guaranty). There is a comparable delay before color as a major ingredient in his elevations appears in his banks at the end of his career. Two preserved interiors from his office buildings, however, especially permit the experience of Sullivan's use of melding color to create an enveloping sumptuousness. The astonishing restoration of the exchange room from the Stock Exchange, as preserved in The Art Institute of Chicago, and the only slightly denatured restoration of the lobby area of the Guaranty in Buffalo (figs. 55 and 121) show how an iridescent palette of dusky, sensuous color, laced with gilt in a mix of mosaic, terracotta, bronze and painted iron can transport the observer toward the sensation of infinity which Sullivan first realized ornamentally in his theaters.

Insofar as Saracenic inspiration helped to bring the same qualities to the exteriors of his tall skeletal buildings of the 1890s, it was not through color, but from the infinite subdivision and intricate patterning of ornamented surfaces. In his report on the Transportation Building to Burnham, he had described it as "the process of systematic subdivision."[122] In his work, Saracenic infinity continuously opposed Renaissance measure.

The longing in Sullivan to push toward the infinite also doubtless encouraged his repeated modification of Renaissance compositional schema with Gothic allusion, as it evolved from Romanesque arching stretched to accommodate the tall building. It was as though he were naturally inclined toward the deeper sensitivity within the western tradition for the expression of the infinite which Gothic forms provided. Neither Renaissance nor Gothic, however, let alone Saracenic, was essentially more than a guide to possibilities for his design. But then, it is also true that evidence of his eclectic borrowing remains never wholly subsumed into his own manner (as, say, Wright managed to do, using Sullivanian elements as one of his influences). They recall again a certain persistent hold from the past, which makes Sullivan's quest for the new a lifelong struggle, never wholly resolved. Is it an inherent weakness of an approach to design in which the phenomenon of transcendence comes so immediately to mind? Transcendence implies a movement out of something else, with some residue of what was transcended perhaps left behind, incompletely assimilated.

If Saracenic inspiration was one means of providing Sullivan's ornament with a sense of the infinite, the example of nature was more important. Infinity has always characterized nature. To Victorians, parallels readily occurred between the state of nineteenth-century society in the western world and the combined guises in which the awareness of nature's infinitude came to them: from its diversity as this was vastly enlarged by the enthusiasm for scientific collecting and classification; from the certainty of its inexhaustibility as a resource; from the unprecedented abundance implicit in its exploitation; from a moral view of nature in which the very plenitude of its manifestations betokened some Infinite Source from which the bounty flowed. Sullivan was caught up by this euphoria for the infinitude of nature, part secular, part sacred, in the late-Victorian world. The very qualities which he sought in his natural ornament—its lavishness, its generalization, its inspiration from primal botanical elements, and its energy—called up the other contexts from which it derived its larger meanings.

These mutually reinforcing means by which Sullivan invoked a sense of infinity in the embellishment of his tall buildings also provide a cluster of symbolic meanings more directly applicable to the buildings. Infinity was appropriate hyperbole for the scale and repetitiousness of the tall office building, especially as the normative scale of what he built aspired to the truly skyscraper magnitude of his vision for the Fraternity Temple. It was appropriate, too, for the energies he felt in American business, as his buildings epitomized this dynamism. It was appropriate, ultimately, for the larger energies of the American people, as he imagined these embodied in the tall office building as the consummate monumental expression of the popular will of its time and place. Allusion to all these meanings for infinity float through his writings.

Ornament which was infinitely natural, abundant, energetic and buoyant fittingly expressed an idealized view of the nature of the American people, or alternatively (to use his own phrase) of American democracy. No wonder he was attracted to Walt Whitman's *Leaves of Grass*, when, in 1887, he stumbled across a copy "searching among the shelves of a book store," as he wrote to Whitman. "I was attracted by the curious title: Leaves of Grass, opened the book at random, and my eyes met the lines of Elemental Drifts. You then and there entered my soul, have not departed, and never will depart."[123] He wrote as poet to poet, enclosing a copy of his own overwrought "Inspiration" for Whitman's scrutiny. Like Whitman's grass, his ornament also possessed qualities which could plausibly make it expressive for Sullivan's idealized view of American democracy.

Although his curvilinear plant forms are often assimilated into European Art Nouveau, his approach to ornament and its expressive qualities was different.[124] Art Nouveau ornament typically sought out exotic flora, or exoticized what was common: rose buds, Japanese iris, lilies, orchids. He stayed with commonplace leafage, berries, pods, thorns. Art Nouveau tended toward attenuated, highly stylized, uniquely shaped forms, with implications of erotic sinuosity. His forms were full-bodied and intensely dynamic; they were mostly normative in proportion, even when exploded or stretched. Art Nouveau focused hypnotically on the exceptional motif. His ornament fused into matted superimposition. Art Nouveau plant forms took over the architectural frame, bending it to their undulations. His mostly stayed within the reticulated fields decreed by the frame, however much the energies might challenge their confinement. Art Nouveau ornament flirted with preciosity, strangeness, and evil. His possessed a sense of vigorous optimism and generosity. Certain tendencies in Sullivan's early ornament, which was overtly late Victorian in the angular manner of Frank Furness, indicate how he, too, might have developed aggressive flower motifs and rigid violence of shape in leaf and stem into something more akin to Art Nouveau. But by the time of the tall buildings, Sullivan's ornament instead "sang the song Democratic." "Poet" was, to him, the highest title to which any artist could aspire.[125] Like Whitman, he would be the Super Poet Leading the People. Nietzsche was another in his personal pantheon of super heroes, which also included Richardson, Michelangelo, Wagner—all heroes in the grand manner.

The theatrical grandiloquence of this dandyish, reclusive architect cannot be denied. His thinking jumped from an idealization of the creative self to an idealized abstraction of society. The void in Sullivan's reasoning reflected both his personal solitude and a persistent lack in American culture. There was no sense of community in between. Again Schuyler's criticism of the tall buildings comes to mind: ornamentation on the one hand (the mark of the individual genius); the effect of the whole on the other (the sign of collective afflatus); something missing in between.[126]

Surely a case can be made against hyperbole which is sublimely out of touch with the prosaic task at hand: spectacle masking the truth it pretends to celebrate. To have devoted this celebrational effort to public buildings, to churches, to cultural institutions, even to the embellishment of sumptuous residences, would have been more appropriate, although Sullivan himself never seems to have bemoaned his lack of monumental commissions. In fact, it was the magnification of the mundane in the tall office building, together with its novelty and its importance in the American city, which comprised its attraction for him as the vehicle for an architecture that was plausibly at once "monumental," "new," and "democratic." Sullivan's fallacy, then, could be that of confusing the challenge of what was new and most expressive of power in his society as an indication of popular energy or will, and hence deserving a rhetorical treatment which was really undeserved. In somewhat different terms, such ideas are central to Andrew's case against Sullivan.

Is this, then, the "last word" on what is typically considered to have been the central episode in Sullivan's career? But with respect to the tall office building, there are also the issues that he addressed in his work, and the compelling manner in which these issues are forced upon us because of what he did and the way he did it. Summing up, there is his confrontation with the new and the conviction that newness demands fresh expression. There is his quest for the expression of this newness as an emanation of the creative self working between the pragmatics of the functional solution and current architectural conventions and styles. There is the felt equilibrium among structure, program, and expression which is intensely experienced in these buildings. There is the effort to redefine the expressive role of ornament, to elevate it from its traditional role as subordinate embellishment and, cognizant of the symbolist and empathetic currents of his day, to make it a medium by which the whole building is plastically animated. There is the variety in his approaches to this end. Finally, there is his attempt to project a larger social or public meaning for his buildings, worthwhile despite its hyperbole. One does not need to concur with the whole of his program to recognize that these are serious issues of continuing concern. One does not have to deny the degree to which some of what he did fell short of his intentions, or even perhaps that some of it was misguided, without recognizing its worth. One does not have to espouse the worst excrescences of what the skyscraper may have become to appreciate that the tall office building provided a convenient choice for his architectural endeavor, given the time in which he worked and his own personal need for the kind of dramatic demonstration which it then seemed to offer.

Then too, let us not forget the buildings. Retracing the circuit of his most significant tall office and commercial buildings—St. Louis (where there are two examples), Chicago (again two), Buffalo and New York—one is surprised anew at the energy of the ornament and the way it animates the whole building, the sure sense of proportions and, in the best of them, the anatomical feel to the architectural components in their litheness, relatedness, their clarity (even under the ornamental skin) and density. It is a pleasure to see them returned to a substantial portion of their former glory, and a pleasure, too, to learn how many who work in them take special pride in the fact. Sullivan's tall buildings do not anticipate the ruck of surrounding run-of-the-mill skyscrapers. They rebuke them, and—without the advantage of the urbanistic dress-up of trees, or plazas, or atria—they nevertheless become monuments in their cities for what they themselves are.

*I should especially like to express my gratitude for the use of the Richard Nichel Archive in the preparation of this essay. Nickel was an outstanding architectural photographer who devoted much of his too brief life to photographing Sullivan's work and championing his cause. Nickel planned a "complete works" of Sullivan, which is being carried forward by others. When completed, this volume will contain detailed documentation on all buildings. Catherine Roy Cummings and John Vinci have been especially kind both in granting me access to the Archive and in facilitating my use of it in practical and knowledgeable ways. And of course I am grateful, too, to my colleagues in this endeavor, whose insights and enthusiasm have contributed to this essay, most especially Wim de Wit's labors on my behalf in Chicago photo archives.

As this manuscript was going to the editors, I was fortunate enough to see an advance copy of Robert C. Twombly's *Louis Sullivan: His Life and Work* (New York: Elisabeth Sifton Books and Viking, 1986). Wherever his work effected last-minute alterations in my manuscript, I have noted the fact. Three works on Sullivan will always be valuable for their general coverage of his buildings: Hugh Morrison, *Louis Sullivan, Prophet of Modern Architecture* (New York: Museum of Modern Art and Norton, 1935), Narciso G. Menocal, *Architecture as Nature: The Transcendentalist Idea of Louis Sullivan* (Madison: University of Wisconsin, 1981) and Twombly's volume. Carl Condit, *The Chicago School of Architecture* (University of Chicago Press, 1964) places Sullivan's buildings in the context of contemporary tall commercial buildings by other major architects in the city.

The excerpts introducing the essay are taken from the following: Sullivan letter soliciting a client for his project for a building on Michigan Avenue, 1904 (see n. 81); Frank Lloyd Wright, *Genius and the Mobocracy* (New York: Horizon, 1949), p. 59.

1. Minimal piers with two and three windows supported on metal bridging in between were common in masonry construction; see, for example, Sullivan's Troescher Building (fig. 60). Building height, however, was limited with support from masonry piers without interior metal structural columns, and especially if walls were to be minimized to maximize fenestration.

2. The interior structure was a mixture of iron and wooden columns supporting heavy wooden floors: iron columns fireproofed with a terra-cotta sheathing for the first through third floors; wood columns from the fourth through seventh floors. The interior was, moreover, partitioned into three parts by fire walls, which may also have performed a supporting function. James O'Gorman, "Marshall Field Wholesale Store: Materials Toward a Monograph," *Journal of Society of Architectural Historians* 37 (October 1973): 182f.

3. I give partial account of the widespread influence of the Marshall Field Wholesale Store on Chicago architects shortly after its completion in *American Buildings and Their Architects: Progressive and Academic Ideals at the Turn of the Twentieth Century* (New York: Doubleday/Anchor, 1976), pp. 30–52. See also Condit, *Chicago School*.

4. Illustrated in Morrison, *Sullivan*, plates 12 and 13, p. 328; also Twombly pp. 166, 167.

5. Frank Lloyd Wright, *Genius and the Mobocracy* (New York: Horizon, 1949), pp. 48–54, for example, considered that Sullivan was overly impressed by Richardson's work. See David Van Zanten's essay in this volume for the conditioning in Sullivan's background which accounted for his attraction to Richardson's Wholesale Store.

6. Morrison, *Sullivan*, pp. 88ff.

7. Louis Sullivan, *Kindergarten Chats and Other Writings* (New York: Wittenborn, 1947), pp. 28–30.

8. Claude Bragdon, *More Lives Than One* (New York: Knopf, 1938), p. 157. Bragdon published an article on Sullivan, "An American Architect, Being an Appreciation of Louis Henry Sullivan," *House and Garden* 7 (January 1905): 47–55. He later edited Sullivan's *Kindergarten Chats* and *Education and Democracy*. He wrote a preface for *The Autobiography of an Idea*.

9. The newspaper item appears on p. 5. A copy is in the Nickel Archive.

10. See n. 8. "The Tulip" is installment 22 in the *Kindergarten Chats*. Twombly, *Sullivan*, pp. 284f., discusses the tulip metaphor.

11. Louis Sullivan, *Autobiography of an Idea* (New York: Dover, 1956), p. 298.

12. See especially, Winston Weisman, "Philadelphia Functionalism and Sullivan." *Journal of Society of Architectural Historians* 20 (March 1961): 3–19.

13. Barr Ferree, "The High Building and Its Art," *Scribner's* 15 (March 1894): 297–318. Montgomery Schuyler, "Architecture in Chicago: Adler & Sullivan," *Architectural Record*, "Great American Architects Series,"

no. 2 (published separately, December 1895); conveniently available (with minor exceptions) in Montgomery Schuyler, *American Architecture and Other Writings* 2, William H. Jordy and Ralph Coe, eds. (Cambridge: Harvard University Press, 1961), pp. 377–404. Donald Hoffmann, *The Architecture of John Wellborn Root* (Baltimore and London: Johns Hopkins University Press, 1973), pp. 162f. and his "John Root's Monadnock Building," *Journal of Society of Architectural Historians* 26 (December 1967): 273, maintains that the design of the Monadnock Building which slightly preceded that of the Wainwright, is the first thorough-going expressive success for the tall office building, but not for the tall *skeletal* office building, since the Monadnock was supported on masonry bearing walls. It is skeletal metal framing which characterizes subsequent structure for the tall building and its skyscraper successors. Moreover, the Wainwright directly expresses skeletal framing in its window treatment, as the Monadnock does not. So the Wainwright would seem to retain its historic position.

14. Published in *Lippincott's* 57 (March 1896): 403–409. The article is conveniently available in Sullivan, *Kindergarten Chats*, p. 203.

15. Ibid., p. 206.

16. Ferree, "The High Building," p. 314.

17. Idem.

18. Schuyler, "Adler & Sullivan," *American Architecture and Other Writings* 2, p. 390. Morrison, *Sullivan*, pp. 152ff.

19. See n. 27 for discussion.

20. Sullivan, *Kindergarten Chats*, "Tall Office Building," p. 203.

21. See discussion, pp. 78f.

22. The first three quotations above are most conveniently available in Bessie Pierce, ed., *As Others See Chicago* (University of Chicago Press, 1933), pp. 396f., 409f., 383f. They come from George W. Steevens, *The Land of the Dollar* (New York: Dodd Mead, 1897), William Archer, *America To-Day* (New York: Scribner's, 1899) and Paul Bourget, *Outre-Mer, notes sur l'Amerique* (Paris/New York: Lemerre, 1895). The final citation comes from Montgomery Schuyler, "Adler & Sullivan" in *American Architecture and Other Writings* 2, p. 381.

23. *Industrial Chicago*, *The Building Interests* 1 (Chicago: Goodspeed, 1891), pp. 168f. See also Wichit Charenbhak, *Chicago School of Architects and their Critics* (Ann Arbor, MI: UMI Research Press, 1981); and Robert Prestiano, *The Inland Architect: Chicago's Major Architectural Journal, 1883–1908* (Ann Arbor, MI: UMI Research Press, 1981).

24. O'Gorman, "Marshall Field," p. 175 and *passim*, emphasizes this aspect of the building.

25. Rental brochure, *The Wainwright Building* (St. Louis, n.d.), unnumbered. Copy in Nickel Archive.

26. *Buffalo Daily Courier* (July 9, 1895), p. 5. The headlines read: "Spare No Expense / Progress of the Work on the Guaranty Building / The Courts to be Faced with Enameled Brick which Cost 24 Times as Much as the Ordinary Kind." Copy in Nickel Archive. *Industrial Chicago* 1, pp. 377f., notes that most glazed brick was imported at the beginning of the 1890s, and that the first American brick makers to manufacture such brick had only recently opened operations in Massachusetts shortly before 1890.

27. Sullivan, "The High-Building Question," *The Graphic* 5 (December 19, 1891): 405. The article is reproduced and discussed by Donald Hoffmann, "The Setback Skyscraper City of 1891: An Unknown Essay by Louis H. Sullivan," *Journal of Society of Architectural Historians* 29 (May 1970): 181–87. The Fraternity Temple is presented in a brochure issued at the time of the launching of the project, which specifically summarizes the advantages of its massing, *To the Odd-Fellows of Chicago and The State of Illinois* (Chicago, n.d.): "The bold breaks and deep recesses of the long facades serve at once to admit light and shade, to admit external light and air to the interior of the building and to give an interesting diversity of outline and an effective play of light and shade to the long street fronts. The discontinuance of the terminal bays above the tenth story prevents the casting of light-destroying shadows into the lower offices, and develops the second element of the progressive recessions from base to pinnacle, which constitute an important feature of the design. Structurally these terminal features serve as buttresses for the long arms of the cross, which is the typical characteristic of the plan, and from the center of which, buttressed in every direction, rises the noble tower which is the culminating feature of the structure." Copy in the Nickel Archive.

28. Dankmar Adler, "Light in Tall Office Buildings," *Engineering Magazine* 4 (September 1892): 171–86. Citations from pp. 171ff.

29. Sullivan, *Kindergarten Chats*, "Tall Office Building," p. 203.

30. The restoration of the Wainwright is best covered in George McCue, "Spirit From St. Louis; Wainwright State Office Complex," *Progressive Architecture* 62 (November 1981): 102–107. It is linked to and extended by a fine addition by Mitchell Giurgola in association with Hastings & Chiretta.

31. Sullivan, *Kindergarten Chats*, "Tall Office Building," p. 208.

32. See above, n. 16.

33. Hugh Morrison, "Louis Sullivan Today," *Journal of American Institute of Architects* 26 (September 1956): 98–100.

34. Louis Sullivan, *The Autobiography of an Idea* (New York: American Institute of Architects Press, 1924), p. 325.

35. I discuss the tombs further in *American Buildings: Progressive and Academic Ideals*, pp. 111–18.

36. The four projects not published by Twombly are for the taller variant version of the Chemical National Bank Building, an unidentified St. Louis building, Burnet House, and the Michigan Avenue building.

I eliminate from consideration two tall apartment buildings and Sullivan's hotel projects, except that for the Burnet House because of its importance for the Bayard Building. They present different considerations from the office and commercial buildings, and do not, in any event, significantly change the account of Sullivan's contributions to the design of the tall skeletal building. The apartment houses are perhaps more relevant than the hotels. One of them, the Eliel Apartments (1894) for Chicago, exists in a quick elevational sketch only. It is published in Paul Sprague, *The Drawings of Louis Henri Sullivan* (Princeton University Press, 1979), pl. 79. A perspective for what appears to be a twelve-story apartment house, also for Chicago, exists in the Nickel Archive, where it is dated ca. 1894–1895. The ground floor, devoted to stores, shows an elaborately ornamented frame around show windows with a pair of cylindrical columns to either side of a entrance. Above, the window wall is framed by two vertical bays with individual windows punched into the plane of the wall between. The top three stories are incorporated in a loggia-like arching, and the whole is capped by a hipped roof. In short, it is a rather undigested combination of compositional motifs found elsewhere in Sullivan's work. It is reminiscent of his approach to the Portland Building.

37. I have devised a similar grouping for Sullivan's tall buildings as they appear in Morrison's *Sullivan* (and excluding the additional designs in the Nickel Archive); see Jordy, *American Buildings: Progressive and Academic Ideals*, p. 152. To prove that there is nothing sacrosanct about the present grouping, note that I there placed the Wainwright and Stock Exchange differently from here, with equal validity I believe. The classification scheme adopted here is not meant to be an irrevocable ordering of Sullivan's design for the tall, skeletal office and commercial building, but merely a means of grasping it in its entirety and of sensing the nature of its variety and development. See also below, n. 42.

38. On the theater, see Van Zanten, pp. 46–51.

39. Schuyler, "The Romanesque Revival in America," *Architectural Record* 1 (October–December 1891): 198. It is conveniently available in Schuyler, *American Architecture and Other Writings* 1, p. 224, which also reproduces extensive excerpts from Schuyler's other writings on Richardsonian Romanesque, including two long articles on the importance of the style in the Midwest in the early 1980s. See also the introduction to this volume, pp. 34–47. *Industrial Chicago* 1, 48, summarizes the eclectic architectural situation around 1890: "Modern styles are usually mixed copies of those of former eras. But the schools of Richardson and Root show a systematic application of ideas, and emergence of certain clear ornate principles from heterogeneous elements that may, in the end, lend superb grandeur to the Chicago commercial style and afford unallayed satisfaction to the people." See also pp. 67ff. for a specific discussion of Romanesque in Chicago.

40. Incidentally, Sullivan's Union Trust is one in a fascinating row of late nineteenth-century commercial and institutional buildings which include Henry Ives Cobb's Chemical National Bank Building (1895), Alfred B. Mullett's Old Post Office (formerly Federal Building and Custom House) [1874–1882], although Mullett's precise role in the design has been questioned because he resigned as supervising architect at the time the building got underway, and most construction drawings are signed by his successor James G. Hill. On the west side of Union Trust, the handsomely gridded building, sheathed in white terracotta, was designed by the local firm of Mauran, Russell & Crowell as the Railway Exchange Building, (now Famous-

Barr) [1912–1913]. Cobb's building recalls the demolished Tacoma Building (see fig. 57), and perhaps provides as good an approximation of this important demolished Chicago building as can be obtained. The entire row should be preserved intact.

41. Demitri Tselos, "The Chicago Fair and the Myth of the 'Lost Cause,'" *Journal Society of Architectural Historians* 26 (December 1967): 263ff., first made this observation; repeated in Narciso G. Menocal, *Architecture as Nature, Transcendental Idea of Louis Sullivan*, pp. 47ff., 53.

42. Here I am especially grateful for insights derived from Twombly, *Sullivan*, pp. 321f. Originally I included the two schemes for the Chemical Building in this grouping. But clearly he is correct in seeing them as precedents for the Carson Pirie Scott Store.

43. A balancing banking space originally occupied the other end of the building behind the arcade, but only one story in height. No photograph of this has been found. Sullivan seems to have had nothing to do with its interior design.

44. Major office and commercial buildings in the Loop with some arrangement of bay windows inserted into a wall of windows for compositional, as well as functional, effect which might have influenced Sullivan's Stock Exchange, include the following: Jenney & Mundie's Manhattan Building (1888–1891), Burnham & Root's Great Northern Hotel (1890–1892), Ashland Block (1891–1892), Majestic Hotel (1892–1893), as well as their Monadnock, Holabird & Roche's Tacoma Building (1887–1889), although it is very different in character from the Stock Exchange, their Caxton Building (1889–1890), and especially their south Addition to the Monadnock (1893). All are illustrated in Condit, *Chicago School*.

45. Wright, *Genius and the Mobocracy*, p. 43

46. Morrison, *Sullivan*, p. 180

47. Letter from George Elmslie to William Purcell, dated October 6, 1944. Copy in Nickel Archive. See also a comparable reminiscence from another member of the office force after Sullivan had left Adler, William L. Steele, in Morrison, *Sullivan*, p. 179.

48. Montgomery Schuyler, "Adler & Sullivan" in *American Architecture and Other Writings* 2, p. 402.

49. The restoration of the Guaranty, and all the forces that went into it, are elaborately discussed in the *Sunday Maga-zine* section of the *Buffalo News* (December 11, 1983); also Scott Melnick, "Public Financing Key to Historic Preservation," *Building Design and Construction* 26 (October 1985): 60–69.

50. Charles E. Jenkins, "A White Enameled Building," *Architectural Record* 4 (January–March 1895): 299–316. Condit, *Chicago School*, p. 100, maintains that the earlier second Rand-McNally Building (1889–1890) by Burnham & Root was the first building completely clad in terra-cotta. If so, the apparent heaviness of the building, which derives indirectly from Richardson's Marshall Field Wholesale Store, is hardly expressive of the material.

51. Rental brochure, *The Bayard Building* (New York: Rost Printing and Publishing, n.d.), unnumbered. Copy in Avery Library, Columbia University.

52. Frank Lloyd Wright, *The Natural House* (New York: Horizon, 1934), p. 24; also *Genius and the Mobocracy*, p. 58.

53. See n. 10.

54. Sprague, *Drawings of Sullivan*, p. 6f., locates the beginnings of Sullivan's mature ornament in 1890, pointing to his ornament in the Auditorium Banquet Hall as the decisive work, evident in drawings 32–34 in Sprague's catalogue of the collection in Avery Library, Columbia University. Sprague places the pinnacle of Sullivan's architectural drawings during the 1890s (drawings 35–114).

55. See Van Zanten, p. 36ff.; also Jordy, *American Buildings: Progressive and Academic Ideals*, p. 128.

56. Letter, Sullivan to Daniel Burnham, Chicago, November 11, 1893. Collection of the Burnham Library, the Art Institute of Chicago.

55. See Jordy, *American Buildings: Progressive and Academic Ideals*, p. 128.

56. Letter, Sullivan to Daniel Burnham, Chicago, November 11, 1893. Collection of the Burnham Library, the Art Institute of Chicago.

57. Schuyler, "Adler & Sullivan," reprinted in Schuyler, *American Architecture and Other Writings* 2, pp. 402f.

58. Vincent Scully, "Louis Sullivan's Architectural Ornament," *Perspecta* 5 (1959): 78ff.

59. Ibid., p. 73ff.

60. Lauren S. Weingarden, *Louis Sullivan's Metaphysics of Architecture* (1835–1901): *Sources and Correspondences with Symbolist Art Theory* (Ph.D. diss., University of Chicago, 1981) pp. 411–41 elaborates on this aspect of Sullivan's work very perceptively.

61. Jordy, *American Buildings: Progressive and Academic Ideals*, pp. 132ff.

62. Thomas Tallmadge, *The Story of Architecture in America* (New York: Norton, ca. 1927), the heading for chapter 8 is "Louis Sullivan and the 'Lost Cause.'"

63. Frank Lloyd Wright, *Saturday Review of Literature* 13 (December 14, 1935): 6.

64. Rental brochure, *The Bayard Building*.

65. Russell Sturgis, "Good Things in Modern Architecture," *Architectural Record* 8 (July–September 1898): 101.

66. Montgomery Schuyler, "The Skyscraper Up-to-Date," *Architectural Record* 8 (January–March 1899): 255–58 *passim*; reprinted in Schuyler, *American Architecture and Other Writings* 2, pp. 438–41 *passim*.

67. See Van Zanten, also Narciso G. Menocal, "The Bayard Building: French Paradox and American Synthesis," *Sites* 13 (New York, 1985): 4–23. Jordy, *American Buildings: Progressive and Academic Ideals*, pp. 156ff.

68. Schuyler, "Skyscraper Up-to-Date," Sullivan, "Kindergarten Chats," *Kindergarten Chats*, p. 121, also p. 208.

69. Reyner Banham, *The Architecture of the Well Tempered Environment* (University of Chicago Press, 1969; 2nd revised ed. 1984).

70. *Buffalo Courier*, January 1, 1886. The Richard Nickel Archives.

71. Twombly, *Sullivan*, p. 336.

72. Sullivan, "Tall Office Building," reprinted in *Kindergarten Chats*, p. 208.

73. Sherman Paul, *Louis Sullivan, An Architect in American Thought* (Englewood, NJ: Prentice-Hall, 1962), pp. 143–46, reproduces Sullivan's own description of the murals from "Ornamentation of the Auditorium," *Industrial Chicago* 2, pp. 490ff. He illustrates one of the lunettes (spring) and the proscenium arch.

74. Scully, "Sullivan's Architectural Ornament," pp. 77ff.

75. Idem. Menocal, *Architecture as Nature*, pp. 50f, 56–58, 68–71; also his "Bayard Building," pp. 4–9, where he also disproves the myth that the six female figures were the idea of Silas Alden Condict, the presumed client, although he only bought the building shortly after its completion. He allegedly intended the angels as symbols of fair dealing during the six business days of the week. This myth of the "House of Angels" came down in the Condict family, and was publicized by Meyer Berger in his column "About New York," *New York Times* (May 15, 1957), p. 51M. Berger was ignorant of the time of Condict's purchase, and of the long history of the winged figure in Sullivan's work. I myself commented negatively on the figures in *American Buildings: Progressive and Academic Ideals*, p. 146.

76. See, for example, John Ruskin, *The Seven Lamps of Architecture*, "The Lamp of Beauty" secs. 33, 40.

77. Menocal, *Architecture as Nature*, pp. 50, 56–58; Menocal, "Bayard Building," p. 15.

78. These are familiar episodes in the *Autobiography*, pp. 165f., 207f., 234.

79. Ibid., pp. 165f.

80. Letter, George Elmslie to William Purcell from Pasadena, October 6, 1944. Copy in Richard Nickel Archive.

81. See Van Zanten references, and Menocal, "Bayard Building," passim.

82. The series of confidential handwritten letters which Sullivan wrote to thirteen potential clients from September 7 to October 15, 1904, are all variations on one another. The tone gradually alters as he realizes the fruitlessness of his quest, from businesslike concentration on the nature of the projected building and its economic feasibility at the start to a more importunate tone at the end in which he draws attention to his worth as an architect. The proposed site was 112–116 South Michigan Avenue. Correspondence file in the Burnham Library, Art Institute of Chicago; copy in the Richard Nickel Archive. (It is a portion of one of these letters which appears at the head of this essay.)

83. *Economist* 15 (Chicago: June 13, 1896): 729. Copy in the Richard Nickel Archive.

84. *Economist* 3 (May 24, 1890): 651. Copy in the Richard Nickel Archive.

85. The complicated building history of Sullivan's involvement with the Schlesinger & Mayer (Carson Pirie Scott) Store is detailed by Menocal, *Architecture as Nature*, appendix B, pp. 168–79, and by Twombly, Sullivan pp. 335f., 344–48.

86. See above, n. 71.

87. The foundations of the first section on Madison Street could not sustain the loads of three additional floors. Hence this section of the store remains nine stories high.

88. For a good account of this phase of the construction, see, "The New Schlesinger and Mayer Building in Chicago," *Brickbuilder* 12 (May 1903): 101–104. There were precedents in Chicago for continued operations on some floors while buildings were being radically rebuilt. The nearby Reliance Building is one example; see Jordy, *American Buildings: Progressive and Academic Ideals*, p. 53, and Hoffmann, *Root*, p. 181.

89. Holabird & Roche subsequently extended the Burnham addition, still in the Sullivan manner, but with some unfortunate compromise.

90. *Economist* 19 (Chicago: May 28, 1898): 612, stated that the store would be in marble and bronze, using the same materials as Ernest Flagg's newly completed Corcoran Gallery in Washington, D.C. (1892–1897). It "shall surpass in beauty of distinction and materials used in construction and embellishment anything that has heretofore been attempted." Mention of marble continued in the *Economist* 20 (November 5, December 3, 1898): 538, 582. The boast occured in the latter article. Copies in the Richard Nickel Archive.

91. Information on the painting of the cast iron is taken from letters by William Gray Purcell to Edith Elmslie from Pasadena, Calif., dated March 4, 1953 and from Purcell to Richard Nickel, dated July 10, 1961. These letters provided the basic information for Vinci's restoration. Copies in Richard Nickel Archive.

92. Menocal, *Transcendentalist Idea of Sullivan*, pp. 69, 77.

93. Both Morrison, *Sullivan*, pp. 200ff., and David Gebhard, "Louis Sullivan and George Grant Elmslie," *Journal of Society of Architectural Historians* 19 (May 1960): 64, maintain that Elmslie was substantially responsible for the design of the ornament around shop windows and the entrance of Carson Pirie Scott.

94. "Daylight as an Investment," *Inland Architect* 32 (January 1899): 58

95. Siegfried Giedion, *Space, Time, and Architecture* (Cambridge, Mass.: Harvard University Press, fifth rev. ed. 1967), pp. 388–90.

96. William Gray Purcell to Edith Elmslie from Pasadena, Calif., dated March 4, 1953: "As to Gage Brothers—I can tell you definitely that George did it all."

97. *Inland Architect* (March 1899): 20, again comments on the novelty of the Luxfer prisms. The prisms were only introduced in 1896, and the Gage Building represents an early and extensive use of them.

98. Interpretations of the composition of the Gage elevation as an exemplification of "suppressed functions" are varied. Scully, "Sullivan's Architectural Ornament," pp. 77ff.; Jordy, *American Buildings: Progressive and Academic Ideals*, p. 157; Menocal, *Architecture as Nature* pp. 68f., 74f., provide a range of possible interpretations for the composition. That there is no agreement on a specific interpretation seems to indicate that Sullivan has created neither the unambiguity of a dominant reading for the elevation, nor the ambiguity of a contrived dual reading in which either of two alternatives is equally valid. Rather he leaves the viewer with a degree of uncomfortable puzzlement. Most significantly, however, all three critics agree as to the empathetic and kinesthetic nature of this elegant and provocative design.

99. On restoration, see citations in ns. 30, 49 and 90.

100. Especially in his "Ornament in Architecture," *Kindergarten Chats*, p. 187, where he urged the young architect to start with buildings "comely in the nude."

101. See n. 48.

102. See n. 23.

103. Condit, *Chicago School*, p. 52. See especially Hoffmann, *Root, passim*, but particularly pp. 19, 27, 156–66. Significantly, Sullivan himself cited Brooks, Aldis and William E. Hale, the client for the Reliance Building, as the men most responsible for the modern office building; Sullivan, "Development of Building—II," *Economist* 56 (Chicago July 1916), p. 40, cited in Hoffmann, *Root*, p. 19. On the skyscraper and attitudes toward it at the time, see Kenneth Turney Gibbs, *Business Architecture: Architectural Imagrey in America* (Ann Arbor, MI: UMI Research Press, 1984).

104. *St. Louis Globe-Democrat*, April 15, 1891; partially cited in David S. Andrew, *Louis Sullivan and the Problemics of Modern Architecture: The Present Against the Past* (Urbana and Chicago: University of Illinois Press, 1985), p. 96.

105. Both Daniel, *Sullivan*, pp. 97f. and Twombly, *Sullivan*, pp. 285f. characterize Ellis Wainwright, the first unsympathetically, the second favorably.

106. "Buffalo Gets Its Treasure Back," *Buffalo News Sunday Magazine*, December 11, 1983, p. 12. Significantly, Taylor originally intended to build an opera house to connect with the Guaranty on an adjacent lot at the corner of Church and Franklin Streets; see *Buffalo News*, Sunday Magazine section, December 11, 1983, p. 18. His vision of a combination office and theatre building may have led him to Adler & Sullivan.

107. See p. 138.

108. See n. 90.

109. Full citation appears in n. 104.

110. It should be added that even Chicago office buildings with plain exteriors frequently boasted ornamental extravagance inside; see Jordy, *American Buildings: Progressive and Academic Ideals*, pp. 73f.

111. Although this seems to be the consensus with respect to recent appraisals of the "failure" of Sullivan's practice, I particularly base this conclusion on the judicious assessment of evidence and previous opinion by Twombly, *Sullivan*, passim, but especially pp. 396–406.

112. On this episode in Sullivan's career, see especially Menocal, *Architecture as Nature*, pp. 82–94 and Twombly, *Sullivan*, pp. 364–68.

113. The "conservative" nature of Wright's position in architecture *vis-à-vis* that of the modernists who tended to appropriate him to their cause as part of the "modern movement" is most perceptively, if with some exaggeration, developed by Norris Kelly Smith, *Frank Lloyd Wright, A Study in Architectural Content* (Englewood Cliffs, NJ: Prentice-Hall, 1966).

114. Owen Jones, *The Grammar of Ornament* (London: Day, 1856); this was republished in a less luxurious edition for designers (London: Quaritch, 1868) when some plates were divided making 112 in all. Sprague, *Drawings of Sullivan*, p. 5, sees Jones' *Grammar* as a foundation for Sullivan's ornament.

115. Menocal, passim, makes this theme a central aspect of his study. See also, Weingarden, *Sullivan's Metaphysics*, passim.

116. Van Zanten, "Early Sullivan."

117. This is especially evident in both comments and drawings in Sullivan, *A System of Architectural Ornament According with a Philosophy of Man's Powers* (New York: American Institute of Architects, 1924).

118. Sullivan, *Autobiography of an Idea*, pp. 81–85.

119. Discussions on Wagner's critical ideas on music in culture occur in Auguste de Gasperini, *La nouvelle allemagne Musicale: Richard Wagner* (Paris: Heugel, 1866) and Adolphe Jullien, *Richard Wagner: His Life and Works*, Florence Percival Hall, trans., 2 vols. (Boston: Knight and Millet, 1900).

120. See p. 122.

121. Sullivan repeatedly uses the phrase "Infinite Creative Spirit" in his writing. Weingarden, *Sullivan's Metaphysics*, discusses the concept extensively and its role in Sullivan's architecture.

122. See n. 56.

123. Sherman Paul, *Louis Sullivan, An Architect in American Thought* (Englewood Cliffs, NJ: Prentice-Hall, 1962), pp. 1ff. For Whitman's influence on Sullivan, see Weingarden, pp. 224–306.

124. Jordy, *American Buildings: Progressive and Academic Ideals*, pp. 147–150.

125. "Poet" repeatedly appears in Sullivan's writings as the highest goals to which the creative artist or architect can aspire. It emphatically suggests that Sullivan's approach to ornament is not decorative, but expressive, with "meaning." The nature of this "meaning" and its relation to symbolist empathetic and certain metaphysical currents of his time are most extensively examined in Weingarden, *Louis Sullivan's Metaphysics of Architecture*.

126. On Schuyler's critique, see n. 57.

The Banks and the Image of Progressive Banking

WIM DE WIT

Louis Henri Sullivan (1856–1924) is one of the hardest figures to place in American architecture, though his distinction and his creativity are indisputable.

—Lewis Mumford, *The Roots of Contemporary American Architecture*

WHEN ON JANUARY 1, 1915, THE NEW BUILDING of the Merchants National Bank in Grinnell, Iowa, was inaugurated, it had already received a great deal of attention[1] (fig. 122). The townspeople who had seen this structure going up during most of the previous year had wondered at its peculiar shape. It did not resemble any building they had seen before, nor did its unconventional blocklike form seem well adapted to its environment. Several months earlier when a rival institution, the Grinnell Savings Bank (fig. 123), had opened its new building—located diagonally across the street from the new site of the Merchants National Bank—there had been no such reaction; at least, the papers did not mention any particular surprise. Although that building too was unlike any other in town, the residents of Grinnell could easily relate to its classical style and limestone façade, with pilasters supporting the cornice. It expressed the stability and strength appropriate to a bank.

The Merchants National Bank, however, possessed none of these qualities; instead, one was confronted by colorful stained glass and a wealth of terra-cotta ornament clustered around the entrance and a circular window, all set against a background of bluish red brick. The two newspapers in town published front page accounts of the opening. Both articles stressed the innovative character of the building, suggesting that it had evolved not out of any past precedent, but out of the architect's imagination alone. According to the *Grinnell Herald*, "It was realized first in the mind of Louis H. Sullivan, of Chicago, its architect.

Sullivan dreamed the building. It is his dream come true."[2] The correspondent for *The Grinnell Register* wrote in a similar vein, "The man who drew the design must have steeped himself in the atmosphere of the Arabian Nights, Arabian Days and the Tales of the Persian Fire Worshippers until it worked like hashees [sic] and the sub-conscious mind took control and saw, in a vision, the complete semblance of the thing that was to be."[3]

However unusual the Grinnell bank appeared to local reporters, it was, in fact, Sullivan's fourth bank building in seven years. The banks in Owatonna (Minnesota), Cedar Rapids, and Algona (both in Iowa) were in equally striking contrast to their environments and, except for the Algona bank, rich in ornamentation. Moreover, while Sullivan was working in Grinnell, he was also building banks in Lafayette, Indiana and Newark, Ohio; a few years later he would build banks in Sidney, Ohio and Columbus, Wisconsin. Sullivan worked also on the alteration of a bank in Manistique, Michigan, and he mentioned several other prospects for bank buildings that never materialized.[4]

Looking at this list, one might imagine that Sullivan was one of the most popular architects of bank buildings in the Midwest. But Sullivan was not the only architect to work successfully in this field. Several Prairie School architects designed banks: Frank Lloyd Wright himself built banks in Dwight, Illinois (1905) and Mason City, Iowa (1909); Purcell and Elmslie were involved in the design and construction of at least eight banks between 1910 and 1916;[5] William Steele and

Parker Berry, both former employees of Sullivan, and George W. Maher all built at least one bank in the 1910s. Architects not allied with this group also were involved in bank design: although Daniel Burnham is best known for his office buildings in large cities (several of which contain banks), he too designed small-town banks in the Midwest: the Sioux Falls Savings Bank in Sioux Falls, South Dakota (1909), the Black Hawk National Bank in Waterloo, Iowa (1910), and the Old Commercial National Bank in Oshkosh, Wisconsin (also from 1910) among them. There were even architecture firms whose specialty was bank design. A. Moorman & Company of St. Paul, for example, specialized in bank design and published a collection of plans called *The Bank Builder*. Thus, by the first decade of this century, bank design—even in small towns—had become sufficiently lucrative that it appealed to large firms as well as small ones.

These facts have a direct bearing on the meaning

of the eight banks which comprise almost all of Sullivan's architectural work realized during the last twenty years of his life. In order to understand them fully, we must consider why so many banks were built by Sullivan and others at this time. Only this context, I will argue, enables us to understand why some bankers chose Sullivan as their architect and to appreciate Sullivan's contribution to bank design. The Merchants National Bank in Grinnell provides a case in point, because we know the facts surrounding its commission. Yet we are still unable to answer the most fundamental questions about the significance of Sullivan's banks.

In the early twentieth century, Grinnell was a small rural town of little more than 5000 inhabitants whose income was principally derived from agriculture or agriculture-related industries. Farmers and other businessmen profited from an economic boom during this period, insuring the prosperity of banks as well. Not surprisingly, both of the largest banks in town decided around 1913 to build new buildings to better serve their clients, and both institutions looked to the city of Chicago to find their architects. The Grinnell Savings Bank hired the firm of Hyland and Green while the Merchants National Bank selected Louis Sullivan.

Sullivan had initially been invited to Grinnell by Benjamin J. Ricker, a Merchants National Bank director who had seen one of Sullivan's earlier bank buildings.[6] In addition to his involvement in the bank, Ricker was also director of a glove manufacturing company. He was married to Mabel Tompkins, from Oak Park, Illinois, who might have sparked his interest in Prairie School architecture.[7] In 1911 Ricker had commissioned Walter Burley Griffin, who had worked as a draftsman for Frank Lloyd Wright, to build a group of five houses in Grinnell, but only Ricker's house was realized.[8] Griffin was unavailable after 1912 when he won the competition for a new capital in Canberra, Australia, where he moved in 1914. Instead, two architects were considered for the Grinnell bank project. Sullivan was asked to apply after Ricker had visited his National Farmers Bank in Owatonna. At the same time, William G. Purcell

presented himself as a candidate after hearing about the job from the director of the Owatonna bank.[9] It is not clear why Sullivan was selected instead of Purcell, but it is evident that during his visit to Grinnell, Sullivan deeply impressed the bank directors; indeed, nine months later when the new building was opened the local newspapers were still talking about his visit and about the time he took to make his first sketch design. "Shutting himself up almost without food, he concentrates every thought upon his work as zealously as a Buddhist priest sinks his identity in the larger thought of the Nirvana. When exhaustian [sic] comes a cup of black coffee quickens the fagged brain."[10] Immediately after Sullivan's proposal was approved by the directors, the design process was initiated and construction soon followed. In late April 1914 the project was awarded to the contractor who had recently built the Grinnell Savings Bank[11] and within eight months the new Merchants National Bank was finished.

Although this sequence of events provides a rather detailed chronology of the building's genesis, it does not reveal why the directors of the Merchants National Bank were willing to risk hiring an architect whose idiosyncratic ornament might scare away clients. More important, it does not explain the unique character of Sullivan's contribution to bank architecture.

Sullivan's banks were built over a fourteen-year period, almost equal in length to Sullivan's partnership with Dankmar Adler. Yet, despite the attention the late works have recently received, our understanding of them is inadequate.[12] The meaning of Louis Sullivan's banks can only be located in the context of bank architecture generally and in the context of Sullivan's career.

At the turn of the century important changes were taking place in the field of banking as a consequence of both economic and social developments during the previous two decades. One of these changes involved the bankers' re-evaluation of their profession, and the establishment of standards for developing this profession into a specialized vocation. They also established their own profession organizations, whose purposes were to provide bankers with forums where they could meet, discuss their common problems, and develop strategies to solve them. One of the most pressing issues in the 1890s was the fact that the banker had lost the respect of the public. They were perceived as crooks who made large sums of money at the expense of their clients. The anger of a farmer from Texas is typical: "The banking business is an evil. Bankers are leeches on the business body. When bankers prosper the people mourn. Banking destroys more wealth than other business. . . . Millions of dollars are furnished by the people to the banks, in the way of deposits, to do business upon and the depositors do not realize a cent from it. . . . The country is now in the clutches of the bank combines and it may require a revolution to extricate it. Down with the banks!"[13]

Most of the complaints about the role the bankers played in economic life came from the farmers in the Midwest, who concentrated their critique on two essential points. First of all, the farmers felt that they were totally dependent upon East Coast banking monopolies whose directors did not care whether or not there was enough money available to lend to farmers at harvest time, when they needed it most. Second, the farmers believed that the inadequate supply of money in circulation was a situation maintained by bankers for their own profit. That money was not always readily available was considered to be grossly unfair by farmers since they considered themselves to be the citizens who had established the wealth of the country. As the historian of farmers' discontent, Theodore Saloutos, has explained: "For years they had been told that they were the backbone of the nation, that their calling was the most important, the most deserving, the most fundamental of all, the collapse of which would bring down the pillars of civilization itself."[14] To the farmers it did not make sense that the stature of farming had declined as America became increasingly industrialized, and that bankers, by giving or denying credit, were able to determine the success

or failure of agriculture as a business.

The farmers did indeed have a point: it was not easy for them to obtain sufficient credit. The American banking system—consisting of National and State banks—was not sympathetic. The national banks in particular could do little for farmers whose only collateral was land. They were not permitted to accept that sort of property for "fear that through the taking of this security in payment of debts due to them, they would become great holders of real estate."[15] Since funding from national banks was unavailable, farmers relied on other sources, for example, state banks which were allowed to accept real estate as security. Even better were savings banks, or trust and loan companies, both of which were specialized in lending money with real estate as collateral. The numbers of these banks grew considerably at the end of the nineteenth century and eventually they posed a competitive threat to the national banks: "The growth of state and private banks in the United States is not only a result of the increasing business and population, it is also a sign of the inadequacy of the national banking system under present laws to supply the banking facilities needed to carry on the enterprises of the present day. In the same way the growth of savings banks and trust and loan companies is another indication of the new conditions under which banking is now conducted."[16]

The difficulty of obtaining credit was not the only banking problem the farmers faced. In fact, their dependence on money from regions other than where they worked was a consequence of how land in the Midwest had been developed. The pioneers of the early nineteenth century had been able to develop new areas only because East Coast financiers had been willing to loan the money necessary for the purchase of farm equipment and supplies. Their large debts had the effect of putting many settlers in the position of tenancy. In addition, the small banks that were later established in these areas did not have enough money to lend during the harvest, when farmers needed additional funds to rent machinery, pay laborers, and generally set "the products in motion towards the consumer." In the early fall, when every farmer went to his bank to borrow money, the banks themselves had to borrow from the larger and more established banks in New York, Boston, or Philadelphia. The interest that country banks were obliged to pay on these loans was charged to the farmers, thus making it still more expensive for them to borrow money.

Paradoxically, during the first two decades of the twentieth century there was an agricultural boom and Midwest banks accumulated a great deal of wealth, yet the farmers were still unable to free themselves economically from the East: with few investment possibilities elsewhere, the banks were forced to invest in eastern institutions. These institutions in turn lent money to others, making it difficult or impossible for them to repay the original Midwest lenders when they asked for it. "The result is the tight money market we have in the centers every fall, and which seems to grow tighter and more threatening every year with the expansion of business."[17]

In view of this recurring problem, it is understandable that farmers suspected bankers of conspiring to limit the supply of money. Bankers, of course, disagreed, arguing instead that the problem resided with the farmers who were such bad borrowers. If only they would "regard their credit more sacredly," it was said, they could be assured of funding by the banks.[18]

Bankers realized that they had the power to influence economic and political life, but that they could not do this without the favor of their clients. In the first two decades of this century the realization would be transformed into a new concept of the banker's role in society, and as a consequence, of the service he should give to his clients. The bank building would play an important part in achieving the image of the bank as an institution essential to everyone's well-being.

The first and most basic change to occur involved the philosophy of banking. Until the end of the 1890s the banker prided himself on being a conservative businessman who would take as few risks as possible and avoid speculative investments.

Cautiously managing the capital entrusted to him, he followed the safest course in an attempt to make it grow. Capital might grow slowly, but one was sure of making profit.

Under pressure from the farmers' movements, bankers gradually realized it was not enough to sit safely on the sidelines, waiting for their capital to grow. They felt compelled to defend themselves against the accusations of being self-centered usurpers and discussed their responses in the meetings of their associations. Reports of the meetings held in the late 1890s testify to the new attitudes that emerged. Bankers argued that class distinctions did not exist as far as they were concerned. Banks were built by the thrift and industry of all the people who put their savings on deposit. Far from being against the people, bankers worked with depositors for the progress—a term pregnant with meaning—of all. As one American Bankers' Association member put it, everyone who deposits money, whether in large or small amounts, "constitute[s] the irresistible civilizing force which has moved like the benign influence of the Gulf Stream, silently tempering and converting the lands of snow and ice into waving fields of golden grain; waste places into humble homes; homes into palaces; and general doubt into general security."[19]

It was in this sense that bankers around the turn of the century began to refer to themselves as progressive: they contributed money to the constant advancement of people's well-being. Such an interpretation of the word "progressive" should have been acceptable to all bankers because it did not conflict with their innate conservatism. In fact, for a number of years both adjectives were used simultaneously without contradicting each other. "Conservative" referred to how to do business, whereas the word "progressive" said something about the role of the banker in society. Thus *The Banker's Magazine* could declare: "A bank, conservative and at the same time progressive, is the kind of financial institution that business demands to-day."[20] Bankers were not alone in emphasizing their progressive over their conservative tendencies. At the beginning of the twentieth century, this seeming contradiction between progressive and conservative attitudes was all-pervasive. It was even present in the philosophy of those reformers who organized the Progressive Movement. Concerned about increasing crime and social disorder in the cities, these reformers, led by Theodore Roosevelt, wanted to impose their own middle class moral values upon the urban masses. By fostering ethical standards, they hoped to change the lot of average people while safeguarding their own position within the social hierarchy.

In order to align himself with progressive principles, the banker had to redefine his role in the community in which he worked. He wanted to emerge from his strong box and humanize his institution; he would become a counselor to his clients and, acting as a friend, advise them on their financial problems. The bank, it was believed, should have a central position in the community, make connections with all inhabitants—rich and poor—and it should seek to influence all business dealings. In this way the bank would become the financial heart of the community and the banker would become responsible for the growth and wealth of the town in which he worked. In an advertisement on the occasion of its thirty-fourth anniversary the National Farmers Bank in Owatonna prescribed this role for itself: "The Bank is better than ever prepared to serve the financial interests of this community, both by extending proper credit to the worthy business enterprises and by conserving the wealth already existing here."[21] As will become clear below, many banks sought to express this new, communally oriented function by providing all sorts of innovative facilities in their buildings: community rooms, ladies' waiting rooms, meeting rooms, display cases for wheat or corn, and, in one case, even a podium to show prizewinning cows.

Providing good services would enable the banker to establish the special relationship with his clients that he needed in order to achieve a central place in the community. In the name of service, bankers entered fields which they had never seriously considered before. For example, they established agencies that gave advice to farmers about the kinds of crops or cattle that would sell best; they organized contests in a "campaign for better livestock and crop," and they gave domestic science lessons to the farmers' wives. Bankers were willing to take on these tasks because they realized that "when the farmer receives the cooperation of the banker, he usually is able to employ methods that increase the production capacity of his acreage. His earnings and deposits are therefore heavier."[22] While Midwest bankers concentrated their public relations efforts on farmers, they also devised special services to attract the savings of school children (thus creating good relations with those who will be the businessmen of the future), and, above all, of women.

Before the end of the nineteenth century, financial business was considered to be strictly a male enterprise. Women, it was argued, had no money and were therefore not expected to enter the bank. If they ventured to do so, they were usually treated so badly that they would not return. By the early twentieth century, as they increasingly freed themselves from the domestic sphere, more and more women wanted to deposit their savings in a bank (fig. 124). Nevertheless, bankers, reluctant to break with a custom, did not wish to mingle "female" business with their "real" business, and therefore created a separate room—the so-called ladies' waiting room—that was connected with the savings department through a teller's wicket. With two or three exceptions, all the banks that Sullivan designed had such a room.[23]

In the Midwest, agriculture had never been as profitable as it was in the two decades between 1900 and 1920. Here, too, many new banks were established and some of the wealthiest farmers acquired a measure of control as shareholders. The previous period of acrimony between farmers and bankers was all but forgotten. In 1905 *Bankers Monthly* reported of the situation in Kansas: "The farmers have turned their attention to banking naturally. They are making money so rapidly in the wheat business that they find it necessary to get into some other line in order to keep their capital moving. Our people are harvesting the biggest wheat crop ever raised in the western counties and a number of new banks will start up this fall."[24]

The wealth that the economic boom brought to the Midwest encouraged the leaders of many towns to dream that theirs would become a large city. Businessmen joined hands to develop methods of promoting the town in order to attract more economic activity. An important role in such town boosterism was played by various civic organizations including the Masons, Odd Fellows, Commercial Club, Rotary, or Lions, whose wealthy, progressive members wanted to do good for their community. Through these clubs businessmen induced one another to support the improvement of their town's appearance by campaigning for public parks and better roads.

One could find this booster mentality in each of the towns where Sullivan built a bank. As in Grinnell, there was in every case at least one person on the bank's board of directors who had greater aspirations, both for the bank and for the town in which it was located. In addition, civic groups strove to make the town's name better known in the surrounding area. As Edgar B. Wesley notes in *Owatonna: The Social Development of a Minnesota Community*, clubs composed of merchants and businessmen were organized to promote "the business welfare of the city. 'Owatonna Trade Days,' 'Buy Steele County,' 'Civic Week,' and other movements and slogans were started in order to attract business and build up civic pride."[25] A similar spirit was being fostered during this period in Cedar Rapids where, toward the end of 1908 the *Cedar Rapids Evening Gazette* described the town's great expectations for the coming year. Referring to the president of the Chamber of Commerce, the paper declared: "President Hall is showing his new confidence in the fact that Cedar Rapids is going to be a city. He believes that it is destined to be one of the largest cities in the Midwest."[26]

Bank buildings functioned as a means of demonstrating the community's prosperity and therefore

THEIR REALM NOW INCLUDES THE BANKS.

Figure 124 a
Women and Banking, Cartoon. From: The Chicago Tribune, *September 20, 1896, part IV, p. 25.*

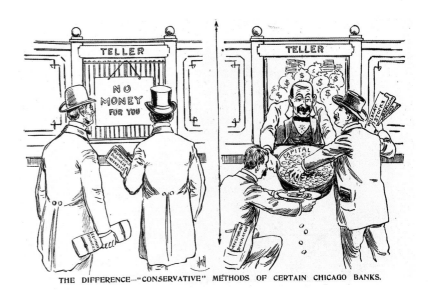

THE DIFFERENCE—"CONSERVATIVE" METHODS OF CERTAIN CHICAGO BANKS.

Figure 124 b
Conservative and Progressive Banking. Cartoon. From: The Chicago Tribune, *August 29, 1896, p.1.*

became an important part of the improvement programs initiated in these towns. Bankers recognized that their buildings were not adequate to the task of promoting the town as a business center. Indeed, prior to the early twentieth century, small town banks were not housed in buildings of their own, but occupied corner storefronts. It was not uncommon to find other businesses, such as stores and offices, on the ground floor of the same building as well as apartments on the upper floors. The mixture of functions did not allow banks to create an independent image, nor enable them to look particularly safe. A new building was the only solution for a banker who wanted to boost his bank and through it his town.[27] Moreover, a substantial and prosperous looking bank would presumably attract business. Clear, though indirect, evidence of this attitude can be gleaned from an advertisement placed in 1921 by the company responsible for the terra-cotta ornament on the National Farmers Bank in Owatonna. There it was proudly (if awkwardly) noted that Carl Bennett, director of the bank, "considers that the terra cotta used in their bank has contributed largely toward causing their building to still excite as much interest and commendation now, thirteen years after its construction, as when first built. The assets of the bank have increased from $700,000 to $2,800,000 within that period, and he ascribes a good share of the increase to the character of the building."[28]

Clearly, then, one can note that two contemporaneous developments were responsible for the growing desire among bankers to build a new building. One was the changing attitude of bankers toward the community and the altered place that the bank sought to occupy in society. A new bank building could give expression to these changes while at the same time suggesting that the bank nurtured the community's interests and that, thanks to the spirit of collaboration between them, both the bank and the community had prospered. That the tendency to move into new bank buildings was seen in terms of progressiveness becomes clear in light of an article in the Owatonna newspaper, *The People's Press*, which concluded with the follow-

ing remark: "It is to be hoped that the National Farmers bank will prosper in the measure in which it has shown its progressiveness."[29] The second development was directly related to the first. A new bank building testified to the health of the community. It helped to attract new business and additional assets to the town, resulting in greater wealth for all. Keeping in mind the broad social and economic factors that influenced bankers to build new structures during the first two decades of the twentieth century, let us now focus attention on those institutions that hired Louis Sullivan.

The history of the commission for the National Farmers Bank in Owatonna has been extensively described elsewhere,[30] but a summary will be helpful because what happened in Owatonna exemplifies the basic points set out above and thus helps explain why Sullivan was repeatedly chosen as architect of small town banks in the Midwest.

After its establishment in 1873, the National Farmers Bank managed to survive two economic depressions during the last three decades of the nineteenth century to become Owatonna's largest bank. At the turn of the century Owatonna was a county seat of approximately 5,000 inhabitants. Most of the business in the town and the environs involved farming which, according to a local historian, prospered with the agricultural boom around the country.

The growth of business activity had an effect on the National Farmers Bank, partly due to its location in the center of town on the northeast corner of Cedar Street and Broadway facing the town's square. Its building was a three-story Victorian structure[31] that, in addition to the bank, also housed a barbershop, a meat market, and some apartments. Eventually, the bank outgrew its quarters and apparently failed to meet standards of safety, so that by 1907 the bank's board of directors decided they needed a new building. In an advertisement in *The People's Press* of March 15, 1907, the bank proudly announced its plans for both "a larger banking room and more facilities for the convenience of customers."[32]

Undoubtedly, there was another reason that the

National Farmers Bank directors opted for a new building. Although theirs was the largest bank in town, it was not the only one. There were two competing institutions: the First National Bank of Owatonna and the Security State Bank. The latter, established in 1895, was the youngest of the three, but it had grown steadily and was, furthermore, housed in an impressively large three-story building on the northwest corner of Cedar Street and Broadway, directly across the street from the National Farmers Bank. Shortly after the National Farmers Bank announced its decision to build a new bank, an article in *The People's Press* announced that the Security State Bank had "every facility and ample room for modern banking."[33] The National Farmers Bank must have felt the pressure to modernize its building in order to maintain its leadership in the economic life of the town.

The National Farmers Bank was controlled by the family of Leonard L. Bennett, one of the original founders of the bank. His two sons held important positions in the bank: Carl was vice-president and Guy was cashier. In 1907, when the new bank building was being planned, Carl Bennett was in charge of day-to-day operations, and it was he who led the search for an architect. He is generally described as a quiet man who played a leading role in the life of Owatonna, not only because of his position at the bank, but also through his memberships in various civic institutions, including the Masons and the Commercial Club.[34] His education at Harvard University, combined with the artistic gifts that he is said to have possessed, must have marked Bennett as an unusual figure in Owatonna. We will see that in every town where Sullivan built a bank, there was at least one person like Bennett whose educational background and progressive interests encouraged him to foster a special design for his new bank building.

In an article published in *The Craftsman* in 1908, Bennett described how he came to chose Sullivan as his architect.[35] He explained that the bank needed additional space in order to accommodate new facilities for its growing business and then declared that the directors (principally Bennett himself) wanted "a simple, dignified and beautiful building." The directors, he further noted, "believed that a beautiful business house would be its own reward and that it would pay from the financial point of view in increased business." Bennett discovered, however, that it was not easy to find an architect who could design a beautiful bank building that would give expression to the special character of banking as an enterprise. After making an extensive study of existing bank buildings and a thorough search through architecture magazines, he finally decided to invite Sullivan to come to Owatonna to discuss the job.

Although he said that he loved Sullivan's "virile and astonishingly beautiful forms of expression" and declared that Sullivan was the man "to solve the problem of an adequate expression of banking," precisely why Bennett settled on Sullivan remains obscure. Prior to 1907 Sullivan had designed only three buildings in which banking facilities were housed (the Opera House Block in Pueblo, Colorado, 1890; the Union Trust Building in St. Louis, 1892–1893; and the Guaranty Building in Buffalo, 1894–1895), but in none of these structures was banking a principal function. Furthermore, at the time that Bennett made his study, Sullivan had few new buildings to his credit; the most recent work of interest was his Carson Pirie Scott Store which had been completed a few years earlier and for which Daniel Burnham was at that moment building an addition. There were also a few smaller projects, such as the Felsenthal Store, but a flourishing practice that could inspire confidence in the capabilities of the architect was lacking. Even the rejection of the "classic style," which Bennett described as a high priority in the selection process, cannot have been the main reason for choosing Sullivan, for he was not the only architect who designed buildings without reference to the past. In absence of other compelling evidence we can surmise that Bennett, who must have come to Chicago regularly on business, would have known the Auditorium, the Stock Exchange, or the Schiller Theater and must have been attracted by Sullivan's ornament.

We can only guess what he read, but the texts he examined probably included the articles Sullivan wrote in *The Craftsman* in 1905 and 1906.[36] Here Bennett would have found discussions of a new architecture that embodies the contemporary spirit of the people for whom it was built. Sullivan argued that architecture should be "a sane and pure accounting of Democracy, a philosophy founded upon Man, thereby setting forth, in clear and human terms, the integrity and responsibility and accountability of the Individual,—in short, a new, a real philosophy of the People."[37] Such a statement—exposing the creation of an architecture that would give form to the American spirit—must have been attractive to Bennett, who as the title of his article suggests, wanted to build a bank that would bring the very institution of banking closer to the people. In recognizing Sullivan's progressive spirit,[38] Bennett must have decided there was no architect better equipped to develop an architectural expression for the new role that the bank sought to play in serving to the community.

Although each of Sullivan's bank commissions had a background and a history proper to itself, certain aspects of the Owatonna story were common to every instance. There was, for example, always a desire for a well functioning, up-to-date building that would be readily recognized as a modern, progressive bank and that would, through its design, be distinguishable from the competition. Indeed, the Owatonna design's successful achievement of these objectives was itself an incentive for other bank directors to approach Sullivan.

That this was the case emerges clearly from an examination of the circumstances surrounding the commission for the People's Savings Bank in Cedar Rapids, which Sullivan received in 1909. Cedar Rapids, the largest of the towns in which Sullivan built banks, was rapidly growing in size as well as in prosperity (between 1880 and 1930 the population grew from 11,000 to 77,000).[39] Most of the businesses located here were engaged in the processing of agricultural products (for example, Quaker Oats), or the manufacture of farm machinery. Although the building he designed for this

bank was not particularly large, two years passed before it could be opened. The reason for the delay was that Sullivan's first design was too expensive, and a new, simplified scheme had to be devised. The contract was finally signed in the summer of 1910.[40]

The People's Savings Bank was founded in 1900 to serve people on the west bank of the Cedar River who, despite the town's rapid growth, did not have a bank in their own neighborhood. According to a contemporary report, the bank was operated on the principle that "the man who has a dollar to deposit is given the same polite attention as the man who has a hundred or a hundred thousand . . ."[41] The progressive attitude of the directors was also reflected in the active role that the bank played in the Westside Improvement League, which had been established to encourage business development there.[42] As a result of its commitment to such progressive projects, the bank gradually built up a large group of loyal customers with the result that, within twelve years, the bank's assets amounted to more than one million dollars.

The growth of the People's Savings Bank was greatly enhanced by its new building. Previously, the bank had been located in two other buildings: the first was on the site where the new building was later constructed (on the corner of Third Avenue and First Street, S.W.) and the second was half a block west, also on Third Avenue. Neither had been particularly well suited for banking, as they were no more than storefront houses, only part of which could be used by the bank. Moreover, neither of those earlier buildings were able to project an image of the bank as an institution in which one's savings would be in good hands.

In 1909 when the board of directors of the People's Savings Bank decided to construct a new building, it appointed a building committee under the direction of Fred H. Shaver, a member of one of the oldest Cedar Rapids families, owner of a biscuit factory, and member of the bank's board. Shaver was described at the time as someone "who had always shown a great deal of energy and whose judgement was always considered as exceptionally good.''[43] Although it is known that Shaver made a special effort to find the right architect, exactly how he located Sullivan remains a mystery. Presumably, Shaver made a tour to see various new bank buildings and he may have heard at that time about the bank in Owatonna. It is also possible that from the beginning Chicago architects figured prominently in Shaver's search, for there is evidence that Cedar Rapids bankers were well aware of Chicago architecture: in 1907 the Cedar Rapids National Bank had the interior of the building to which it was moving (on the corner of Second Avenue and Third Street) redone by Daniel Burnham. Burnham's style was probably considered to be too officious for a bank whose very title called up associations with "the people." In addition to architects from out of town, the Cedar Rapids firm of Josselyn and Taylor, which had already designed two banks in Cedar Rapids and had thus demonstrated expertise in the field, must have been considered as well. The same reasoning might have led Shaver to decide against Josselyn and Taylor since a building by their office would not have allowed the bank to acquire its own distinctive image. In the end, Shaver and his committee decided that Sullivan's originality as a designer would give their bank a structure suited to its particular needs.

That the People's Savings Bank was entirely satisfied with its architect is evident from the fact that Shaver warmly recommended Sullivan to the board of the St. Paul's Methodist Church in Cedar Rapids and to the director of the Van Allen Department Store in Clinton, Iowa. One passage in his letter to John D. Van Allen is of particular interest in the context of the present discussion. Writing just after the contract for the construction of the Cedar Rapids bank had been signed, Shaver declared: "I have had our bank plans examined by some of the best judges in the country and they consider them especially fine and we expect to get unlimited advertising throughout the country when the building is completed."[44] Shaver's expectations were not disappointed. As the bank's official historian later wrote: "At the annual meeting in January 1912, it was noted that the new accounts being obtained were averaging higher since the Bank moved into the new building . . ."[45]

Within a year of Shaver's recommendations, Sullivan secured the commissions for both the church and the department store;[46] and while working on them he became involved in the design of four more banks, two in Iowa, one in Ohio, and the last in Indiana. Although this may appear to have involved a great deal of work, in fact two of the four were extremely small. The history of the largest one, built in Grinnell, Iowa, in 1913–1914 was related earlier in this essay. At this point we are better able to appreciate the remark that George Hamlin, president of the bank in Grinnell, made to William Purcell who competed with Sullivan for the job. As Lathrop has noted, in 1913 Hamlin wrote Purcell "that he was interested in a building that 'was not too expensive' but still 'distinctive and possibly a little out of the ordinary as to appearance.'"[47] Hamlin made clear the bank's desire for a building whose striking appearance would not only emphasize the special role it played in the life of the town but also distinguish itself from the Grinnell Savings Bank, which had recently built a new structure diagonally across the street.

The first in the series of small bank buildings that Sullivan executed in 1913–1914 was the Henry C. Adams Building in Algona, Iowa (1913), which never actually functioned as a bank. Adams probably hoped—as did many of his contemporaries—to make his fortune as a banker during the economic boom, but he was unable to obtain a charter from the Comptroller of the Currency. He was therefore forced to turn his building, constructed while he was applying for the charter, into a real estate office, which came to be known as Land and Loan Office.[48] Adams's reasons for commissioning Sullivan are open for conjecture. No doubt the banks in Owatonna and Cedar Rapids contributed to Sullivan's reputation throughout the Midwest as a man who designed striking bank buildings yet, in Shaver's words, charged "no more than other architects."[49]

As with Sullivan's work in Algona, so with his Home Building Association of 1914 in Newark, Ohio: why the commission was given to Sullivan is not known. It is, however, possible to suggest how the project evolved: according to a local magazine the bank's president, E. M. Baugher, was endowed with a progressive spirit analogous to that which inspired other bank directors discussed above. Baugher was described as being "interested in everything that pertains to general progress and importance in Newark. He is numbered among the public spirited citizens."[50] The town, apparently, relied on people like Baugher to improve its reputation which around 1900 had been associated with crimes resulting from prohibition. After a "dry agent" was killed in Newark, the town was determined to forge a new and better image; a provocative, new bank building in the center of town was part of that campaign. "To bring the famous Louis Sullivan here to leave his mark would indeed add a measure of respectability to a town in sore need of it."[51] Once again, Sullivan was employed in an atmosphere of progressivism to boost the bank and, with it, the town.

The Purdue State Bank, which Sullivan built in 1914 in West Lafayette, Indiana, was his smallest commission among the banks. Neither its size nor its ornamental use of terra-cotta are particularly impressive. The bank's history, however, is interesting and merits discussion. Established in 1910, the Purdue State Bank was closely associated with Purdue University, whose President, W. E. Stone, was a member of the board of directors. Purdue, which had been founded after the Civil War, was growing considerably in the early twentieth century, yet one had to go all the way across the Wabash River to downtown Lafayette in order to find a bank. Once the Purdue State Bank was established, it rapidly gained a firm foothold in West Lafayette because, according to Indiana State law, banks located in Lafayette itself were not permitted to do business in the neighboring community.[52]

Having operated for four years out of a storefront, the bank desired a building of its own. With

this in mind, it purchased a triangular lot near the campus along the main artery connecting downtown Lafayette with the university. No evidence survives to explain how Sullivan was chosen to be the architect, but since Purdue was a strong intellectual force in the community, one can legitimately surmise that the president of the university played an important role in steering the commission to Sullivan.

There is a story about Sullivan's next bank commission, the People's Savings and Loan Association in Sidney, Ohio, that has been repeated in almost every book about the architect. Legend has it that during the course of Sullivan's presentation before the board of directors, one man remarked that he would like to see some columns in front of the facade. This so aroused Sullivan's anger that he refused to discuss the commission any further and left the meeting. The directors thereupon decided to go ahead with Sullivan's design and brought him back from the train station.[53] This episode has been used not only to illustrate how self-conscious and even arrogant Sullivan was, but also to indicate the conservativism of the bankers. Even if the former statement contains an element of truth, the latter was certainly not the case, at least not for all the directors of the Sidney bank. Lafayette M. Studevant was a very progressive board member who in 1886 conceived the idea of establishing a bank that would pay interest on deposits and thus "divide the earnings with the people who made the business possible."[54]

The bank was established on the first floor of a three-story structure in the center of town near the courthouse. However, a space in a building that was not owned by the bank was, in Studevant's opinion, not distinctive enough. He desired for his institution a beautiful new building of its own, "representing the THRIFT of the institution, that would be a joy to the Management and a credit to the city." In 1916 the bank made the largest gains "ever made in a single year," and in an advertisement described itself as the largest bank in Shelby County. This must have been a source of incentive to replace the original bank building with the structure designed by Sullivan. The architect must have come to Sidney by late March, for on April 4, 1917, the *Sidney Daily News* announced his plans for the new building and described in elaborate detail how the building was expected to look.

In spite of the story about the early history of the Sidney commission implying that the directors were conservatives who sought a conservative design to reflect their notion of banking, there is a reason to believe that Studevant was different. That he possessed a well-developed conception of the democratic character and progressive function of his bank, and could thus provide a detailed program to Sullivan, may be argued on the basis of a newspaper article about the new building. This article in the *Sidney Daily News* contains so precise an analysis not only of the superficial forms of the building, but also of its philosophical underpinnings that it could only have been written with the help of someone like Studevant:

The entire building, covering a space of 42 feet on Court Street by 112 feet on Ohio Avenue, will be occupied by the Association. It needs only to be added that the arrangement as perfected, is the result of carefully matured study of the needs of the institution as a going business (the working machine, so to speak) and the comfort and convenience of its patrons. The underlying idea and motive of the entire arrangement is SERVICE, and the building, its equipment and personelle [sic] may fittingly be characterized as a "service station" fulfilling its function as a public and social utility. The plan indeed, and in fact the entire arrangement and equipment may be described as "democratic" in the sense that the mystery and secrecy of the older banking room arrangements wherein the banker was high priest, hidden from view behind many doors, has given way to so complete an openness of arrangement with the executive officers in full view, as to remove social barriers, and thereby to facilitate the transaction of business, through freedom of access, and to encourage confidence through the influence of personal contact. The careful consideration in the provision of rest rooms for the comfort and conven-

ience of patrons, indicates a well defined tendency to make the institution, in a considerable degree, a social as well as a financial center.[55]

Sullivan's philosophy of a democratic architecture meshed seamlessly with Studevant's progressive ideas about banking.

Sullivan's last bank, designed in 1919, was also conceived in a progressive spirit. The Farmers and Merchants Union Bank in Columbus, Wisconsin, played an important role among the farmers of central Wisconsin. The president of the bank, J. Russell Wheeler, was for several years a member of the Agricultural Commission of the American Bankers' Association and was very much involved in the Banker-Farmer Movement, which was fostered by bankers around the turn of the century in order to promote better relations between the two professions.

The original bank building provided no sense of its commitment to the community. Apart from its central location across from the City Hall, there was little to distinguish the bank from other buildings on the same street. In addition, the building's interior was unsuitable for banking. It was too small to accommodate an expanding clientele, and the several different functions were not well arranged. Wheeler had planned to build a new bank for some years, and therefore made note of everything that was wrong with the original building: "And through a score of years, notes and sketches and plans grew as the needs manifested themselves. And not only so, but as other banks in this and other states were visited, the ever accompanying notebook made record of observed features of advantage and disadvantage. Now, among the many banks visited at various times, were some designed by the noted architect, Louis Sullivan."[56] These remarks seem to contradict Wheeler's account, related to John Szarkowski,[57] author of *The Idea of Louis Sullivan*, indicating that, when Wheeler once came home from a trip with a post card showing a bank designed by Sullivan, his wife convinced him to hire the Chicago architect, because this bank reminded her of Frank Lloyd

Wright's work, which she very much admired. Although one might conclude on these grounds that Sullivan received the commission thanks not to Wheeler but rather to his wife, this is not entirely correct. Presumably, Wheeler took the postcard home because he himself admired the bank for its spatial and functional arrangements. He must have recognized that Sullivan would be capable of designing a building that could house all the specific functions that Wheeler had in mind.[58] While he might have encountered some difficulty in appreciating Sullivan's idiosyncratic ornamental forms and was evidently afraid that the inhabitants of Columbus would reject them completely, it is nonetheless evident that Wheeler was sympathetic to Sullivan from the start.

It proved to be a wise choice, for the building Sullivan designed across the street from the old bank, and thus diagonally across from City Hall, assumed a very prominent position in the Columbus community. Both the *Columbus Democrat*[59] and Thomas E. Tallmadge writing for *The Western Architect*[60] emphasized the bank's community role. According to Tallmadge, "An examination of the plans shows, in addition to those features essential in a modern bank, a recognition of the bank's opportunity and duty as a factor in the communal life. We note the showcases—one for the exhibit of grains and produce, and the other for agricultural bulletins, maps, etc.—and more than these, the large assembly room in the rear, which, with its fireplace and conveniences, is dedicated to the uses of the community, and the social and intellectual uplift of the countryside."[61]

The history of the Columbus bank, in particular, demonstrates that by the late teens Sullivan had become the architect for the progressive banker. The commissions he received came from bankers who felt that historical styles were incompatible with the modern conception of banking as a service to everyone in the community. Sullivan's style, sustained by theories of democracy and functionalism, was expected to give expression to the banks' new role. Furthermore, his striking designs provided good publicity in the growing competi-

tion among banks in small country towns. Sullivan's work was readily identifiable and the banks he designed received an unusually large amount of attention, even before they opened.

Although initially Sullivan "did not care to follow up small bank prospects and was looking for strictly commercial work,"[62] he must have discovered rather early on that he could not maintain such an arrogant attitude because banks in small midwestern towns were virtually the only commissions he could get. Far from expressing an aversion, the letters he wrote in the teens often mention his attempts to find more work in this field. During one of his most desperate periods, when apart from the bank in Sidney he had no work at all, Sullivan would have done almost anything to secure another bank commission. He even considered hiring an agent who would promote him as a designer of banks. On August 10, 1917, he wrote to a former employee named Adolph Budina, "I am entering into negotiations with a party who knows the banking game, and is a high-grade salesman. We were brought together by a party in whom I have entire confidence. The idea is to commercialize my talent and reputation. We are only in the preliminaries; but if the deal goes through it may prove exceedingly important, and probably lucrative."[63] The plan, however, bore little fruit. After the People's Savings and Loan Association—on which he was working when he wrote to Budina— Sullivan received only one other commission for a bank and one for an alteration of a bank (in Manistique, Michigan). Several other prospects came to nothing. Just how important these jobs were to Sullivan emerges from a remark to Frank Lloyd Wright about the remodelling in Manistique: "It doesn't run heavily into money, but will keep the wolf away for a couple of months."[64]

In order to understand what was unique about Sullivan's banks, it is first necessary to determine what small country banks looked like at the beginning of the century and whether there was already an established type at the time Sullivan entered his field. Only a comparison of Sullivan's banks with those designed around the same time by others will indicate what Sullivan did to satisfy the desires of his clients and what features he contributed to the newly emerging bank type.

In the scholarly literature devoted to Sullivan's banks, two buildings have repeatedly been mentioned as sources, or at least as precursors: one is the design for the Security Bank in Minneapolis (fig. 125) that Harvey Ellis made in 1891 when he was working for the architect LeRoy Buffington, and the other is the village bank that Frank Lloyd Wright designed for a competition organized by *The Brickbuilder* in 1901. These are the earliest examples of small bank buildings designed by well-known architects. Both were conceived as one-floor buildings intended to house a single function. Both give expression to the function of banking through the use of closed, blocklike forms; no reference was made in either building to traditional styles. Nevertheless, it seems unlikely that these banks had an important influence on Sullivan, since a type existed already which Sullivan took as a basis for the elaboration of his design philosophy. Ellis's bank, for example, lacks the compactness that endows Sullivan's banks with a sense of security and strength. Thus, Ellis's Security Bank might be mistaken for a museum or art gallery—another building type that demands closed forms and that often exhibits the same symmetrical composition found in this bank.

Frank Lloyd Wright's bank, on the other hand, is compact and its tapering walls, reminiscent of Egyptian funeral monuments, suggest strength and safety (fig. 126a). Wright's use of ornament woven through the structural grid also shows his closeness to Sullivan's work in general, although the latitudinal organization of the interior space differs significantly from the ground plans of Sullivan's banks. As we will see, Sullivan's own longitudinal organization involved a continuation of a type that had already proven its functional value, and we should therefore look not to Frank Lloyd Wright as a source, but rather to bank buildings that already existed when Sullivan received his first bank commission.[65]

Bank buildings often were located at the intersection of two main streets, an advantageous situation that provided twice as much exposure as a site in the center of a block. In addition to its marketing potential, the corner location was preferable on functional grounds: it allowed for more windows in the building and in this period before the discovery of fluorescent light, natural light was very important for the day-to-day business of banking. The long row of windows almost always placed in one of the two outside walls had an enormous impact on the lay out of the banking room.

At the turn of the century there were two basic configurations for the floor plan of a bank and any variants were derived from one of them (fig. 127).[66] The so-called island plan stipulated that the tellers be grouped in a central block projected forward from the back of the room into the public space. The U-plan was organized in the opposite way: the tellers' and officers' spaces were placed along the walls which allowed the public lobby to reach as far as possible into the building. The U-plan was used more often than the island plan because it afforded greater convenience to the public, "as it puts all departments within easy view and reach."[67] In the U-plan the tellers were almost invariably placed below the row of windows, which would provide all the light they needed.

The vault was another item whose location in the bank was prescribed virtually from the outset. Situated at the end of the room on a direct axis with the bank's entrance, the vault and its gigantic open door would inspire confidence in the strength and security of the bank to incoming clients.

There were, in general, two possibilities for the placement of the director's office. Most often one would find it in the corner next to the entrance, a spot that allowed the director to see through a window between his room and the vestibule who was coming into the bank. If the director desired a quieter and more secluded space, his office would be located in the back of the building where it could be entered by a client only by special permission, although this latter solution all but disappeared in the era of progressive banking.

The placement of the other functions—ladies'

· DESIGN FOR SECURITY BANK MINNEAPOLIS ·

Figure 125
Harvey Ellis, Design for
Security Bank, Minneap-
olis, 1891. From Ameri-
can Architect and Build-
ing News *32, May 30,*
1891, n.p.

Figure 126
Frank Lloyd Wright,
Design for a Village Bank,
1901, Perspective and floor
plan. From The Brick-
builder *10, 1901, p. 160–*
61.

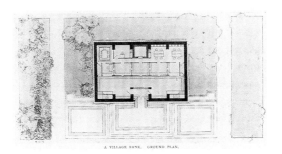

A VILLAGE BANK. GROUND PLAN.

waiting room, consultation room, and community room—varied from bank to bank. The ladies' waiting room often was located next to the entrance (across the vestibule from the director's office), so that the women scarcely entered the banking space. Connecting the ladies' area with the savings department was, however, more important than positioning it at the front of the building, so that the ladies' waiting room might well be found in other locations. Similarly, because the consultation room was frequently used by the bank officers, it was almost always located somewhere in the vicinity of their quarters.

This basic configuration may be found in the floor plan of the First National Bank in Stamford, Connecticut, which was described in *The Banker's Magazine* in 1906 (fig. 128).[68] The organization of the space is a mixture of the U-plan and the island plan. The first room one encountered upon entering the public space was the ladies' waiting room which had its own connection with the tellers. The tellers also had two counters facing the public lobby and another adjoining the bookkeepers' space, which was in turn projected forward into the lobby where two more counters could be approached by people in the lobby. The vault was not placed along the central axis, but rather in a corner at the back of the banking room, doubtless in order to increase the size of both the director's office and the reception room that was presumably available to clients making use of the safety deposit vaults. Since one entered the lobby on a diagonal, the vault was in full view as soon as one came into the bank and thus was still able to emphasize its symbolic meaning.

A similar floor plan was used by Walter Smedley in his design for the smaller Charter National Bank in Media, Pennsylvania (fig. 129a, b).[69] Upon entering the banking room, one could see the vault by looking across one of the tellers' counters that projected forward in a half-island. The vault's entrance was just off center, but, together with the open door, it would nevertheless command a great deal of attention. The president's office was located to the right of the entrance. Toward the rear of

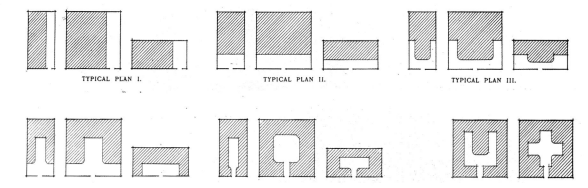

Figure 127
Six typical floor plans for
banks. From The Archi-
tectural Review 12, Feb-
ruary 1905, p. 28–29.

TYPICAL PLAN I.   TYPICAL PLAN II.   TYPICAL PLAN III.

the building, behind the vault, there was a room for safety deposit vault users, and another room reserved for the board of directors.

Smedley's bank in Media was one of the smallest and simplest versions possible. The New England Bank in Kansas City, Missouri by Wilder and Wight[70] had exactly the same layout, although it was a much larger institution located in an urban context rather than a country town (fig. 130 a, b). Immediately to the right and left of the vestibule were, respectively, the president's quarters and the ladies' department. All the remaining space was occupied by the public lobby and a surrounding counter for tellers and officers. In the center of the working space behind the tellers was the vault. Its entrance, on the central axis of the building, was easily visible through a teller's wicket located along this same axis.

These institutions built just after the turn of the century indicate that the organization of the bank's floor plan was more or less determined by that time and that variations were handled on an individual basis according to specific needs. Bankers must have had an idea of the configuration that would function best and conceived their building programs accordingly. Sullivan's floor plans did not differ significantly from those discussed above. He implied the importance of the bankers' contribution in response to Andrew Rebori's query about "how it happened that his preliminary sketches [for the Grinnell bank] were worked out in such a definite manner." Sullivan responded that "those

were the requirements as given, and it only remained to jot them down on paper."[71] With this in mind it is worthwhile to analyze how Sullivan arranged the interior of the Grinnell bank (figs. 131 and 132). After entering the bank through the vestibule, one found on the left side of a public space the special facilities: the women's room and the savings department, and the men's meeting room. On the right were, from front to back, the director's room (which also functioned as the consultation room), the raised platform occupied by the officers, and a space for two tellers. In the center at the rear were the money and deposit vaults, in front of which were a customers' room and another teller's space. Sullivan used this basic floor plan in all his banks, making only minor changes to allow for local requirements.

As far as the average exterior was concerned, bankers were less precise in defining their desires. In general there was a preference for architecture indicative of a classical style, which having survived for so many centuries, represented strength and security. There were, however, many variations within the range of classical architecture, all of which were equally available to an architect who wanted to appeal to the classical tradition. He might typically compose a façade with columns and a tympanum that vaguely referred to the architecture of a Greek or Roman temple. The same imposing effect, however, could also be achieved by reference to the revival of classical elements in Italian Renaissance architecture or French eight-

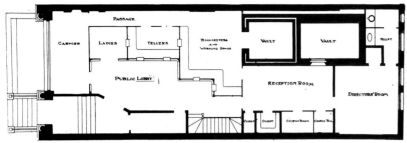

FLOOR PLAN, FIRST NATIONAL BANK, STAMFORD, CT.

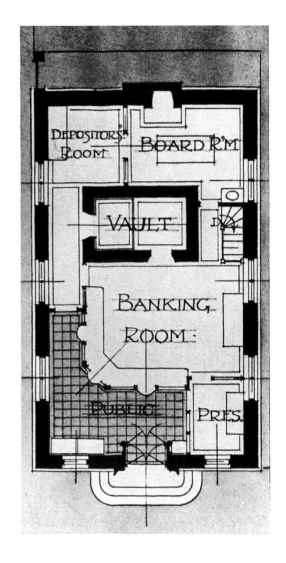

Figure 128
Floor plan of the First
National Bank in Stam-
ford, Connecticut. From
The Banker's Magazine
72, January 1906, p. 315.

eenth-century buildings. By considering a number of salient examples, it will be possible not only to understand the context in which Sullivan developed his ideas, but also to distinguish precisely what he contributed to the prevailing conception of bank architecture.

The Provident Savings Bank in Baltimore, built in 1904 by York and Sawyer, specialists in bank architecture, together with J. E. Sperry, was inspired by the Palazzo Strozzi in Florence (fig. 133).[72] If any structure ever deserved the metaphorical qualification of "strong box" or "jewel box" (metaphors used so often in relation to Sullivan's banks that they have almost lost their meaning), it was this building. Because of its cubical shape and use of large, rusticated blocks of stone, the building looks impenetrable while still inviting. The building thus demonstrated that it was possible to convey an impression of stability and security without resorting to the form of a classical temple.

That it was also unnecessary to rely on large size to inspire confidence in the building's safety can be seen in the simple, rather small cubic structure of the Marine National Bank in Wildwood, New Jersey, designed by Henry A. Macomb (fig. 134).[73] There the front and side elevations were divided by pilasters into respectively three and four equal planes. With the exception of the central plane in the front elevation where the architect placed the entrance, all other planes contained windows crowned by blind arches. The entrance was emphasized by square and half-round pilasters that projected forward of the wall surface on both sides of the door to support an architrave and

pediment. Above the blind arches there was a heavy cornice which bore the bank's name on the façade. Such a simple, classical composition, which made no reference to a specific style, was used for small town banks more often than the temple form.

An alternative solution for a bank façade which can be found in many country towns was used by architect Joseph C. Llewellyn in the First National Bank of Charlotte, Michigan (fig. 135).[74] There the narrow front consisted of little more than two Ionic columns that were attached to the corner

Figure 129 a, b
Walter Smedley, Charter
National Bank, Media
Pennsylvania, exterior and
floor plan. From The
Architectural Review *12,*
February 1905, p. 78.

piers and supported a heavy cornice. The space in between the columns was left open to accommodate the door and, above it was a huge window that allowed light to penetrate the building. Frank Lloyd Wright's First National Bank and Office of Frank L. Smith in Dwight, Illinois, built in 1904, was a stylized version of this oft-repeated type.

In the design of his bank exteriors Sullivan never made such obvious references to existing bank types as Wright had done in 1904. Instead, he sought to design a skin around the bank's space which would convey the institution's progressive image. An analysis of Sullivan's bank designs clarifies how, without resorting to historical references, he was nonetheless able to suggest the qualities of strength and security and thus inspire confidence on the part of a bank's customers as well as its directors.

The National Farmers Bank in Owatonna is located on an important site at the point where the main business street meets the town square (fig. 136). The building consists of two distinct parts: a

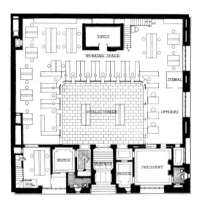

*Figure 130 a, b
Wilder and Wight, New
England National Bank,
Kansas City, Missouri,
exterior and floor plan.
From* The Architectural
Record *25, January 1909,
p. 37.*

*Figure 131
Louis H. Sullivan, Mer-
chants National Bank,
Grinnell, 1914, floor plan.
From reprint of* The
Western Architect *23,
February 1916.*

FIRST FLOOR PLAN

cubic banking room of one very tall story, and a lower, two-story building that originally housed a store and printing shop with its offices. The bank's height was obviously determined with reference to its urban environment. Together with the Kelly building, which housed the rival bank across the street and reaches the same height, the Sullivan bank forms a sort of gate between the square and the street. This effect is mirrored on the opposite side of the square by the county court-house and the fire department's building, which are also of equal height. Thus, the National Farmers Bank building accentuates the main axis that runs through the town.

The square part of the total structure reserved for banking is actually one huge, open space in which smaller rooms are created by means of partition walls (fig. 137). The rooms near the front of the building and the vault at the rear are the only spaces that are covered by a ceiling; all the others are open above, and arranged in a U-shape around a central lobby. The vestibule through which one

enters the banking room is in the center of the main street façade and, because it is low, it creates a tunnel-like effect in sharp contrast with the height and airiness of the principal space (fig. 139). To the left of the vestibule is the Farmers' Exchange, a sort of community room where the farmers could meet to discuss their common problems. Along the wall on the left are the women's room and the savings department, in addition to several coupon rooms. In the center, against the back wall, are the book and money vaults, in front of which the tell-

ers' counters project forward to form an island. The space along the right wall is occupied by the officers' desks and the consultation room. This room is connected both to the officers' area and the president's room, located to the right of the vestibule. The main banking room is very impressive because of its profusion of colorful ornament in plaster, terra-cotta, and cast iron, as well as its stained glass windows, mural paintings, and stencil work.[75] Sullivan's draftsman, George G. Elmslie, claims to have had an important part in

Figure 132
Louis H. Sullivan, Merchants National Bank, Grinnell, 1914, interior. Cervin Robinson, photographer.

Figure 133
York and Sawyer, in
collaboration with J. E.
Sperry, Provident Savings
Bank, Baltimore, Mary-
land. From The Architectural Record *16, August*
1909, p. 111.

the design of the ornament. Sullivan never had another chance to decorate a bank so elaborately; he himself spoke of the Owatonna interior as "a color symphony" and described his desire "to make out of doors-in-doors."[76]

The exterior skin around this room is also richly decorated, although not as elaborately as the interior. The façades are divided into three horizontal layers: a base of pink Port Wing sandstone pierced by several small square windows; a central layer of brick and terra-cotta surrounding a large, semicircular window; and a brick and terra-cotta cornice. The two façades can, however, also be read in a different way. On each side there is an upward, fan-shaped movement starting from the center (the door in front, and the small windows on the side), reaching out toward the brown terra-cotta cartouches in the upper corners, and finally cut off by the heavy cornice on top (fig. 138). In this way, Sullivan suggested that an organic source made the building grow, while at the same time he created a tension between upward movement and downward pressure which was reinforced by the contrast between the large window openings and the solid brick planes. By interrupting the green and blue terra-cotta borders that surround the brick planes, Sullivan suggested that the window intruded into this surface. He even intensified this suggestion by placing the enframed brick plane a few inches back, while keeping the arch around the window continuous with the sandstone base. By thus implying that the brick surface is stretched upward from the base far enough to slip in a large window, Sullivan likened the exterior surface to a skin tightly pulled around the inner space. This made the closed parts of the façades look even more closed and impenetrable, precisely the qualities one expects to find in a bank.

The exterior of the People's Savings Bank in Cedar Rapids is almost without ornament (fig. 140). The building is a low rectangular box, the center of which rises to form a clerestory above the public space, thus again suggesting upward movement. This is emphasized by the buttresses that are placed at intervals along the walls of the

Figure 134
Henry A. Macomb,
Marine National Bank,
Wildwood, New Jersey.
From The Architectural
Record *25, January 1909,*
p. 54.

clerestory and on top of which, like stylites, seated lions guard the business that transpires inside.[77]

Although this bank's exterior looks totally different from that of the Owatonna bank, its interior layout is more or less the same (fig. 141). The floor plan shows a simple division of functions around a public space: the tellers' space and women's room on the left; the officers' room, men's meeting room and two consultation rooms on the right; and the money and book vaults, together with the coupon rooms, in the back. The tellers' space and the men's and women's rooms are lit by small windows, but much more light enters into the building through clerestory windows in the upper part of the public space. There is little ornament in the building: apart from the columns supporting the clerestory, the only other decorations are above the public space where three mural paintings represent scenes from the life of a farmer and a fourth symbolizes the interrelationship of banking, industry, and commerce.

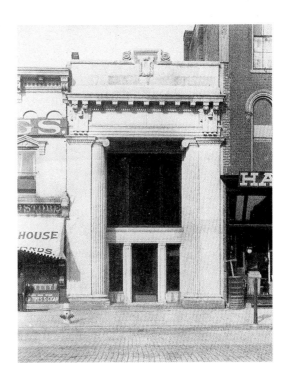

Figure 135
Jos. C. Llewellyn, First
National Bank, Charlotte,
Michigan. From The
Architectural Record *25,*
January 1909, p. 52.

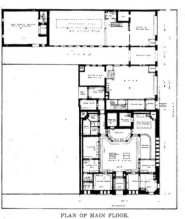

PLAN OF MAIN FLOOR.   PLAN OF UPPER FLOOR.

NATIONAL FARMERS' BANK OF OWATONNA, MINN.   Louis H. Sullivan, Architect.

Figure 136
Louis H. Sullivan,
National Farmers Bank,
Owatonna, Minnesota,
1906–1908. Cervin Robin-
son, photographer.

Figure 137
Louis H. Sullivan,
National Farmers Bank,
Owatonna, Minnesota,
1906–1908, floor plan.
From The Architectural
Record *24, October, 1908*
p. 25.

Figure 138
Louis H. Sullivan,
National Farmers Bank,
Owatonna, Minnesota,
1906–1908, detail. Cervin
Robinson, photographer.

Figure 139
Louis H. Sullivan,
National Farmers Bank,
Owatonna, Minnesota,
1906–1908, interior. Cer-
vin Robinson, photographer.

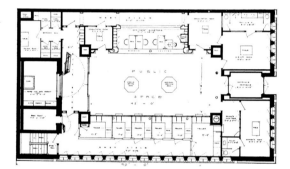

Figure 140
Louis H. Sullivan, People's Savings Bank, Cedar Rapids, Iowa, 1910–1911, exterior. Courtesy People's Savings Bank, Cedar Rapids.

Figure 141
Louis H. Sullivan, People's Savings Bank, Cedar Rapids, Iowa, 1910–1911, floor plan. From The Bankers' Magazine 84, March 1912, p. 416.

Only two other banks, those in Algona and Lafayette, match the one in Cedar Rapids for simplicity of design. The Henry C. Adams Building in Algona has on its long side a simple row of windows slightly accented by a modest amount of terra-cotta ornament (fig. 142 a, b). The main façade is somewhat more intriguing: the entrance is set behind a loggia so that the façade works like a screen, thus testifying to the enclosing quality of the brick wall. The plain door opening that expands into a large rectangular opening is actually similar to the more ornamented entrances Sullivan later designed for the Grinnell and Sidney banks. Like the façade composition in Owatonna, the door opening of the Algona bank suggests movement upwards. In Lafayette, on the other hand, where the front façade is little more than a door opening surrounded by terra-cotta ornament, there was no money for intricate design solutions (fig. 143). The trapezoidal building is equally simple; its rows of windows on two sides are reminiscent of those in Algona.

Although totally different in appearance, the Merchants' National Bank in Grinnell possesses certain features that can be traced to the National Farmers Bank in Owatonna. As demonstrated by the analysis of the floor plan above (see p. 178), this building too is a single open space in which certain functions are fenced off. However, the interior differs from the Owatonna bank in so far that it is only sparsely ornamented with terra-cotta and stained glass, set in an almost Wrightian environment of brick, plaster, and wood. The distinctive exterior is basically a plain rectangular brick box with a terra-cotta frieze and a heavily ornamented entrance. The long brick wall is interrupted by only two openings, both of which are cut sharply into the surface: a small window in the director's room and a large one above the tellers' and officers' spaces to light the banking room. The plainness of this exterior wall is continued on the front façade, where Sullivan allowed it to contrast with the elaborate ornament that he placed around the entrance.

As in Owatonna, the terra-cotta ornament conveys a sense of upward movement, suggesting the organic growth of the building (figs. 144 and 145). The door opening is put in between two "blossoming" columns joined by a cornice. Above the opening, and spreading ornament out around a circular window, are intermingled terra-cotta circles and squares through which forms derived from nature seem to burst forth. The ornament's simultaneous movement upward from the ground and forward from the wall surface creates once again a tension similar to that found in Owatonna with the flat wall planes which therefore feel like a tight and safe enclosure of the building's valuable contents. In addition, gilded griffins on either side of the door symbolize the bank's function of guarding valuable possessions. At the same time, they also respond to compositional considerations for leading the eye in the direction inherent in the ornament, and thus have essentially the same function as the big cartouches in the corners of the façade of the Owatonna bank. This explains why all the banks Sullivan built after Owatonna (except for Algona and Lafayette, which probably could not afford the expense) were decorated with heraldic figures as lions, griffins, or eagles.[78]

The Home Building Association (fig. 146) in Newark, Ohio, is very different from Sullivan's other bank buildings in the sense that it is the only one with two floors and a steel skeleton covered with greenish gray terra-cotta blocks. Why Sullivan decided to use a skeleton is not clear. The fact that he was forced to build two floors in order to create enough office space on the narrow lot cannot have been the reason, but cost may well have been a factor. The estimated cost of the Home Building Association was less than $50,000, whereas the Grinnell bank, for example, cost $60,000.[79] In the absence of an exact cost estimate for the Grinnell bank, it is hard to determine what accounts for the lesser price of the building in Newark, but the relatively cheap steel structure ($1600) and the resultant use not of brick but of terra-cotta ($5664) are doubtless two important factors.

The building's first floor is divided into two parts: a public space that runs from the vesti-

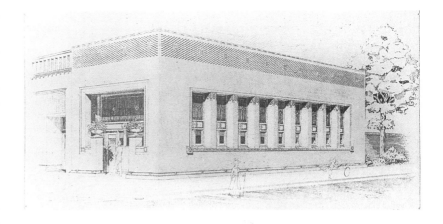

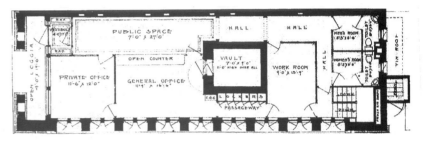

Figure 142 a, b
Louis H. Sullivan, Henry C. Adams Building, Algona, Iowa, 1913, exterior and floor plan. From The Architectural Record *39, May 1916, p. 46, 460.*

Figure 143
Louis H. Sullivan, Purdue State Bank, West Lafayette, 1914. Courtesy Bailey Collection, Tippecanoe County Historical Association, Lafayette, Indiana.

Figure 144
Louis H. Sullivan,
National Farmers Bank,
Owatonna, Minnesota,
1906–1908, front façade.
Cervin Robinson, photog-
rapher.

bule to the back wall and, parallel with it, a space for tellers, officers, and the consultation room. The vault is placed at the end of an aisle that runs behind the tellers' spaces. The second floor is divided into office spaces that are connected by a corridor (fig. 147).

This bank, too, stands out markedly in its environment because of its unusual terra-cotta ornament. The front elevation is divided into four equal planes, the top three of which are framed by an ornamental border and rest on a plantlike ornament whose stem seems to shoot directly out of the ground. These richly decorated planes contrast sharply with the door and window openings in the first floor, which have no ornament at all. The openings appear to have been cut out of the wall surface, which thus becomes highly visible.

While the principal façade suggests movement upward, the side façade, whose ornamental composition is more complex, is meant to show the relationship of the two floors. Its long elevation is divided into a simple base surmounted by a large, enframed plane, thus mirroring the proportions created by the ornamentation on the front of the building. The enframed plane is again connected with the ground by means of plantlike ornaments that in this case do not support the frame from below, but cut through it and seem therefore to pull the plane itself downward. This same plane is interrupted by another rectangle—a smaller enframed field surrounding the windows of the first and second floors. Instead of clarifying the relationship between the floors by making the first story grow upward, as if naturally, into the second, the frame makes this field appear to float on the wall: the pull downward is not contrasted by a complementary upward movement. As a result of the different design solutions for the front and side façades, the Newark bank is less unified than Sullivan's other banks.

The banks in Sidney and Columbus both continue the type used in Owatonna and Grinnell in the sense that they all emphasize the contrast between plain brick walls and heavy terra-cotta ornamentation. The People's Savings and Loan

Figure 145
Louis H. Sullivan, Merchants National Bank, Grinnell, Iowa, 1914, front façade. Cervin Robinson, photographer.

Association in Sidney (fig. 148) is located on the corner of a square in the center of which stands the courthouse, a huge structure in Second Empire style, built in 1881. Diagonally across the street from the bank is the Monumental Building, another large, heavy looking structure, erected in 1876 as a memorial to those who died in the Civil War. Its Victorian Gothic style is reminiscent of Frank Furness's work and must therefore have looked familiar to Sullivan.

It was not easy for Sullivan to compete with these two large and impressive buildings, especially since his bank was the same height as the other buildings around the square, almost all of which were two stories high. Yet, the colorful windows and the use of glass mosaic as well as terra-cotta ensure that the building will be noticed within the context of the square.

The ornamentation of the Sidney bank again emphasizes the tautness of the skin around the inner space. Although the front façade exhibits the same upward movement we found in his other banks, here Sullivan offered yet another variation of the familiar theme. The façade is divided into two parts by a terra-cotta band that runs around the building and indicates the height of the spaces that divide the large banking room inside. Around the door, terra-cotta ornament reaches the height of that band at which point it culminates in a blue half-circle. The two nodes that connect the vertical

Figure 146
Louis H. Sullivan, Home Building Association, Newark, Ohio, 1914. Courtesy Burnham Library, The Art Institute of Chicago.

Figure 147
Louis H. Sullivan, Home Building Association, Newark, Ohio, 1914, floor plan. From The Architectural Record *39, May 1916, p. 450.*

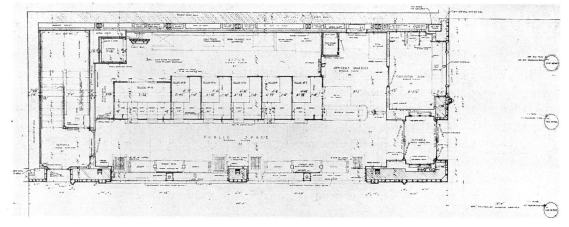

"stem" formed by the door are each marked by a griffin; similarly, the points where the half-circle touches the band are emphasized by flowerlike cartouches which lift the pressure of the arch from the windows directly below. In the center of the cornice on the front is another floral cartouche which leads the eye from the arch to the top of the building, thus creating a movement in the shape of an ogive arch. Sullivan had already used this shape much earlier in the design of a mantelpiece for the Selz house, built in Chicago in 1883 (fig. 149).[80] There on either side of the fireplace are two squat columns that support a marble plate, above which is a semicircular mirror set in a rectangular wooden frame. At the top of this half-circle the mirror's border extends upward into a flowerlike ornament that has the same function as the cartouche in the cornice of the Sidney façade: to organize visual movement upwards and focus it on a single, culminating point.

The side façade of the Sidney bank is much simpler (fig. 150). The terra-cotta band delineates a baselike element that is pierced by two small windows. Above the band is a row of nine more windows through which light enters the banking room. These windows, as well as a large horizontal mosaic bearing the name of the bank, are each surrounded by terra-cotta frames that together suggest an enormous grid clinging to the plain brick façade by means of the naturalistic ornament. In a manner similar to the way ornament functions on the front, two huge ornamental forms at the bottom of the grid alleviate the pressure that the heavy terra-cotta grid would otherwise exercise on the unadorned windows in the base, thus making the whole façade appear airy and weightless.

The bank's interior is much like the others (fig. 151): on one side are the women's room and tellers' spaces; on the other a space for the officers, a consultation room, a stenographer's room, and an additional office. The vault is located in the back with its entrance just off center so that the huge round door, which stands open during the day, is exactly along the central axis. Behind the vault are the director's office and the men's meeting room.

Sullivan developed an innovative air-conditioning system for this building: air that was cooled in the basement was blown into the banking room through ducts hidden in the four piers at the corners of the public space. The ornamental vases on top of these piers serve as light reflectors. The interior decoration is sober and limited to discrete areas of plaster ornament on the four piers just mentioned as well as on the horizontal band that runs continuously above the counters and desks.

The Farmers and Merchants Union Bank in Columbus (fig. 152 a, b) is built on a narrow corner lot with the result that instead of a central public lobby surrounded by the workspace, the floor plan is divided into two equal and parallel spaces, one of which forms the vestibule and public lobby, while the other is occupied by a consultation room, spaces for officers and tellers, and the vault. Behind the vault, in a slightly lower part of the building, are found the assembly room and "women's retiring room." Special features of this bank interior are formed by the two show cases—one for grains and the other for publications—both of which are placed against a wall in the public lobby.

The bi-partite layout of the interior is made visible in the building's exterior by door and window openings of equal width. On top of them is an enormous lintel surmounted by a semicircular window, the whole comprising a challenging composition that seems to defy the laws of gravitation. However, the terra-cotta ornamental forms, consisting of stems and leaves that spread out to the side, are placed like clamps at the points where one would expect the lintel to break. As in Sidney, an ornament in the center of the cornice—in this case a brooding eagle—pulls the eye to the top of the building.

As in most of Sullivan's banks, the side elevation at Columbus is totally plain except for some ornament around a row of windows located in between two buttresses (fig. 153). Instead of fulfilling their conventional function of supporting the building's ceiling, these buttresses are used to counterbalance the arched windows, as if to keep them in place. The terra-cotta ornament that completely covers

Figure 148
Louis H. Sullivan, People's Savings and Loan Association, Sidney, Ohio, 1917–1918. Cervin Robinson, photographer.

Figure 149
Louis H. Sullivan, Mantelpiece from the Selz House, Chicago, 1883. Richard Nickel, photographer. Courtesy Richard Nickel Committee.

the abutments of these windows also helps to neutralize the pressure on the windows.

By using ornament both to create a sense of motion that annihilates any feeling of downward pressure and to contrast with the flat brick surface, Sullivan again succeeded in conveying the idea that the walls are tight skins enclosing a volume, while the richness of the ornament helps to indicate the importance of the business inside. In addition, the design ensures that the bank will stand out at the town's main intersection where the business street meets the boulevard coming from the station and enables it to claim a central place in the community alongside the city hall and the public library. Thus the Farmers and Merchants Union Bank, Sullivan's last contribution of this type, restates his solution for a progressive bank in a small town environment.

Historians have in the past considered Sullivan's banks to be the products of an architect who, at the end of his career, sought to disguise his diminished

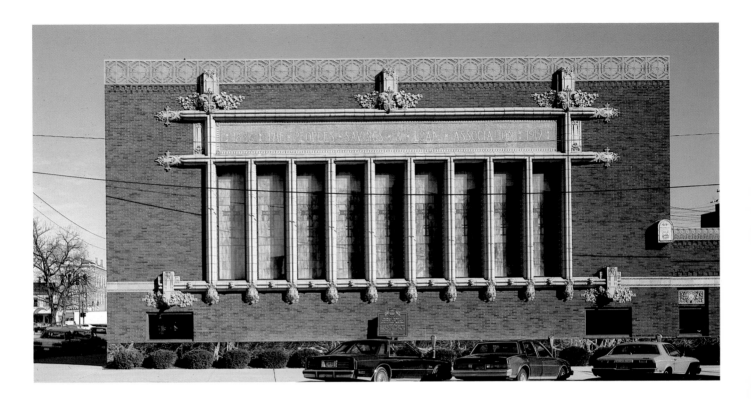

creativity by an unbridled use of decoration. But it is more the case that Sullivan's modern, unmonumental buildings actually fulfilled the wishes of progressive bankers: they drew attention to the new role by means of which the bank sought to promote itself as an institution looking after its clients' well being while at the same time promoting the town as a desirable locale for new business. How well Sullivan's designs responded to the bankers' innovative policies is also indicated by the influence they exercised on other architects working in the Midwest. Although not large in number, the banks that follow Sullivan's example clearly demonstrate that his solution to the problem of the progressive bank building was not an isolated case. Several were designed by Purcell and Elmslie, and by Parker Berry, all architects who had started their careers as draftsmen for Louis Sullivan.

Sullivan's influence can be seen clearly in the Merchants Bank of Winona (fig. 154), built in 1911 by the firm of Purcell and Elmslie. William

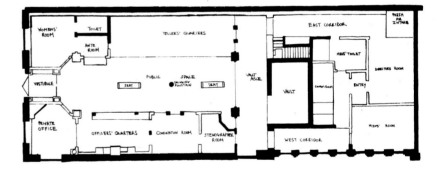

Figure 150
Louis H. Sullivan, People's Savings and Loan Association, Sidney, Ohio, 1917–1918, side view. Cervin Robinson, photographer.

Figure 151
Louis H. Sullivan, People's Savings and Loan Association, Sidney, Ohio, 1917–1918, floorplan.

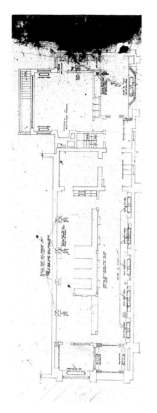

Figure 152 a, b
Louis H. Sullivan, Farm-
ers and Merchants Union
Bank, Columbus, Wiscon-
sin, 1919–1920. Cervin
Robinson, photographer.
Floorplan, Courtesy Farm-
ers and Merchants Union
Bank.

Figure 153
Louis H. Sullivan, Farm-
ers and Merchants Union
Bank, Columbus, Wiscon-
sin, 1919–1920, detail.
Cervin Robinson, photog-
rapher.

G. Purcell had worked for Sullivan only briefly in 1903 but George G. Elmslie had been his chief draftsman for twenty years before joining Purcell in 1909. Although before that time Purcell had already designed several small town banks, none of those early projects had been realized. Upon his arrival, Elmslie redirected Purcell's preference for Wrightian interlocking shapes toward more Sullivanesque façade compositions and ornament. In a manner reminiscent of Frank Lloyd Wright's Unity Temple, the heavy corner piers are slightly set back and separated from two slender columns by thin strips of stained glass, making the columns appear to be the only supports for the heavy cornice and making the piers seem to have no other function than enclosing the façade. Indebted to Sullivan, on the other hand, is the placing of the stained glass windows and ornament, as well as the way in which the semicircular pediment above the door intrudes into the glass surface. In the banks Purcell and Elmslie subsequently designed at Le Roy and Hector, Minnesota, Sullivan's influence supercedes that of Wright.[81]

Sullivan's impact was not confined to those who had once worked for him but can be found as well in designs by little-known architects. The most direct imitation of a Sullivan bank is undoubtedly the Farmers Bank and Trust Company in Poseyville, Indiana, built in 1924 by Edward Thole.[82] The windows and surrounding ornament in its two façades are undisguised copies of the large window in Sullivan's People's Savings and Loan Association in Sidney. Another equally unabashed example of borrowing can be found in *Radford's Stores and Flat Buildings* catalog, a publication of The Radford Architectural Company that sold plans to the "man who has a moderate sum to invest" (fig. 155).[83] This 1909 catalogue includes three designs for banks "with the banking room on the ground floor and offices above," one of which exhibits a striking similarity to Sullivan's work in the way that planes interlock and door and window openings protrude into the brick and terracotta surfaces.

Even certain banks designed in more traditional styles show the influence of Sullivan's work. For example, the way in which the arches of the Cosmopolitan State Bank in Chicago (fig. 156), designed by Schmidt, Garden, and Martin in 1920, break through a horizontal limestone band to reach a heavy cornice crowned with two eagles is very similar to the way Sullivan employed arches in his banks in Owatonna, Sidney, and Columbus. Furthermore, the contrast one can see in the Chicago bank between the ornament and the plain brick surfaces was earlier used by Sullivan to emphasize the enclosing quality of his banks' walls.

During the 1910s and early 1920s a small but nonetheless significant number of architects saw the value of Sullivan's solution for the midwestern bank. His characteristic design became a model for others, underscoring the fact that Sullivan continued to make important architectural contributions even near the end of his career. In the 1920s, as a declining agriculture economy began to have an impact on banking, fewer banks were built and the progressive type Sullivan had developed ceased to be used. Subsequently a taste for streamlined modernism emerged in the United States, with the result that architects became incapable of understanding or appreciating Sullivan's banks. It was

Figure 154
William G. Purcell and George G. Elmslie, Merchants National Bank, Winona, Minnesota, 1911. Courtesy Northwest Architectural Archives, University of Minnesota, St. Paul

Figure 155
Design for a Bank. From
Radford's Stores and Flat
Buildings, *ca. 1909, p. 11.*

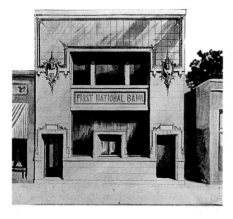

DESIGN NO. 4016.

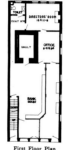

First Floor Plan

Size: Width, 24 feet; Length, 60 feet.

Blue Prints consist of basement plan; first and second floor plans; all elevations and necessary interior details.

Specifications are typewritten and contain all information necessary for the proper construction of the building.

Price of Plans and Specifications...........$15.00

Bank Building of brick with handsome front of White Glazed Terra Cotta. Has fireproof vault and private office and Directors' Room on first floor in additions to the space required for banking purposes. Second floor has five well arranged offices with plenty of light and air. Adapted to city, town or village.

Estimated cost of construction .under favorable conditions $5000.00 to $5750.00.

11

Second Floor Plan

Figure 156
*Schmidt, Garden & Martin, Cosmopolitan State Bank, Chicago, 1920.
From* American Architect and Building News *109, April 1921, p. 443.*

only fifty years later, in 1980, that Chicago architects Ben Weese and Tom Hickey again borrowed elements from Sullivan's work in their design for the Community Bank of Lawndale in Chicago,[84] thus paying homage to the architect who had developed a successful building type for the progressive banker in the Midwest (fig. 157).

1. Many people have contributed to the research and development of this article. Most of all I am grateful to David Van Zanten who invited me to participate in this project and generously shared his vast knowledge of Sullivan's work. I would also like to thank Robert Bruegmann who in initial discussions helped to clarify the direction this essay has taken, and Russell Lewis who made important bibliographical suggestions. Susan Ball, Owen Gregory, Neil Harris, and Edward N. Kaufman read the manuscript and offered valuable editorial advice. Patty Stern was an energetic and resourceful research assistant. My wife Nancy Troy was an indispensable critic of my writing; without her support this article would have had a far less "progressive image."

2. *The Grinnell Herald* (January 5, 1915), p. 1.

3. *The Grinnell Register* (December 28, 1914), p. 1.

4. See Willard Connelly, *Louis Sullivan, The Shaping of American Architecture* (New York: Horizon Press, 1960), pp. 272–75, and Bruce Brooks Pfeiffer, ed., *Frank Lloyd Wright, Letters to Architects.* (Fresno, CA: The Press at California State University, 1984) pp. 1–43.

5. See David Gebhard, "A Guide to the Architecture of Purcell and Elmslie," *Prairie School Review* 2, no. 1 (1965); H. Allen Brooks, *The Prairie School, Frank Lloyd Wright and His Midwest Contemporaries* (New York, London: W. W. Norton & Company, 1972); and Craig R. Zabel, "The Prairie School Banks of Frank Lloyd Wright, Louis H. Sullivan, and Purcell and Elmslie," Diss. University of Illinois at Urbana-Champaign, 1984.

6. Andrew Rebori, "An Architecture Of Democracy, Three Recent Examples From The Work of Louis H. Sullivan," *Architectural Record* 39, (1916): 437–65; and Alan Lathrop, "The Prairie School Bank: Patron and Architect," *Prairie School Architecture* (St. Paul, MN: Minnesota Museum of Art at Landmark Center, 1982), p. 59.

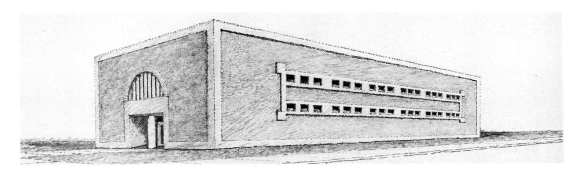

Figure 157
Ben Weese and Tom Hickey, Community Bank of Lawnsdale, Chicago, 1980. Courtesy Weese Hickey Weese, Chicago.

7. Obituary *Grinnell Register-Herald*, August 7, 1950. According to this message, Ricker lived from 1868–1950.

8. I thank Professor Joseph Wall of Grinnell College for this information.

9. Lathrop, p. 59.

10. *The Grinnell Register* (December 28, 1914), p. 1.

11. *The Grinnell Herald* (April 24, 1914), p. 1.

12. For recent literature on Sullivan's banks, see: H. Allen Brooks, *op. cit.*; Kenneth W. Severens, "The Reunion of Louis Sullivan and Frank Lloyd Wright," *The Prairie School Review* 12, no. 3 (Third Quarter, 1975): 5–21; Narciso G. Menocal, *Architecture as Nature, The Transcendentalist Idea of Louis Sullivan* (Madison, Wisc.: The University of Wisconsin Press, 1981), pp. 128–45; Alan K. Lathrop, *op. cit.*; Richard Guy Wilson and Sidney K. Robinson, *The Prairie School in Iowa*, Ames, Iowa: The Iowa State University Press, 1977; and Craig R. Zabel, *op. cit.*

13. "The Banking Evil," quoted in: "Populistic Views About Banking," *The Banker's Magazine* 52, no. 5, (May 1896): 647.

14. Theodore Saloutos and John D. Hicks, *Agricultural Discontent in the Middle West, 1900–1939* (Madison, Wisc.: University of Wisconsin Press, 1951); see also Richard Hofstadter, *The Age of Reform, From Bryan to FDR* (New York: Knopf, 1955).

15. "National Banks and Real Estate Loans," *The Banker's Magazine* 46, (March 1892): 691.

16. *The Banker's Magazine* 54, (May 1897): 665.

17. George E. Roberts, *A Central Bank of Issue*, Delivered before the Nebraska State Bankers' Association, Omaha, September 19, 1907, p. 2.

18. "Congress and the National Banks," *The Banker's Magazine* 46 (February 1892): 607.

19. Myron T. Herrick, "The Effect of Banks on the People's Progress," *The Banker's Magazine* 59 (October 1899): 539. Since a social history of banking does not exist, most of these observations are based on publications in bankers' journals; *The Banker's Magazine* appeared the most helpful for my research.

20. "The Commercial National Bank of Houston, Houston, Texas," *The Banker's Magazine* 77 (January 1905): 97.

21. *The People's Press* (June 28, 1907): n.p.

22. Shaw Banking Service, *Advertising and Service* (Chicago, New York, London, A.B. Shaw Co., n.d.), p. 195.

23. The exceptions are Algona, Newark, and probably Lafayette; the floor plan of the Purdue State Bank in Lafayette was never published, but because of the bank's small size we assume that there was not enough space for a ladies' waiting room.

24. "Kansas Farmers as Bankers," *Bankers' Monthly* 31 (August–September 1905): 106.

25. Edgar B. Wesley, *Owatonna: The Social Development of a Minnesota Community* (Minneapolis: The University of Minnesota Press, 1938), p. 99.

26. "Prospects Great for 1909," *Cedar Rapids Evening Gazette* (November 10, 1908): 5. Architect Edward Bennett's plan for the river front improvement in Cedar Rapids reflects the same spirit.

27. A typological study on the bank building does not exist; all observations are made on basis of bankers' journals.

28. "To My Friend The Banker," advertisement for the American Terra Cotta and Ceramic Company, *Bankers Monthly* 38 (March 1921): 105.

29. "Farmers Bank Has Moved," *The People's Press* (July 17, 1908): 1.

30. Paul E. Sprague, "The National Farmer's Bank, Owatonna, Minnesota," *The Prairie School Review* 4, no. 2 (1967) 5–21; Robert R. Warn, "Part I: Bennett & Sullivan, Client & Creator," *The Prairie School Review* 10, no. 3 (Third Quarter, 1973): 5–15; Robert R. Warn, "Part II: Louis H. Sullivan, '. . . an air of finality,'" *The Prairie School Review* 10, no. 4 (Fourth Quarter, 1973): 5–19; Larry Millett, *The Curve of the Arch, The Story of Louis Sullivan's Owatonna Bank* (St. Paul, Minn.: Minnesota Historical Society Press, 1985).

31. For a photo, see Millett, *op. cit.* p. 11.

32. *The People's Press* (March 15, 1907): n.p.

33. *The People's Press* (May 3, 1907): 1.

34. For a good description of Bennett's personality, see Larry Millett, chapter 1.

35. This and the following quotations are from Carl K. Bennett, "A Bank Built For Farmers: Louis Sullivan Designs A Building Which Marks A New Epoch In American Architecture," *The Craftsman* 15, no. 2 (November 1908): 176–84.

36. Louis H. Sullivan, "What Is Architecture?–A Study Of The American People of Today," *The Craftsman* 10 (May 1906): 143–49: (June 1906): 352–58; (July 1906): 507–513.

37. *Ibid.* 10 (June 1906): 358.

38. On Sullivan's progressiveness and his leading role in the Architectural League of America, whose motto was "Progress Before Precedent," see Sherman Paul, *Louis Sullivan, An Architect in American Thought* (Englewood Cliffs, NJ: Prentice-Hall, 1962), pp. 54–59; and H. Allen Brooks, *op. cit.*, pp. 37–42.

39. Janette S. Murray and Frank G. Murray, *The Story of Cedar Rapids* (New York: Stratford House, 1950), p. 90.

40. See: *Peoples Bank: The First 75 Years* (Cedar Rapids, Iowa: Peoples Bank and Trust Company, 1978), pp. 18–19.

41. *Cedar Rapids Evening Gazette*, January 2, 1907, quoted in *Peoples Bank*, p. 15.

42. Interview with Mr. Wm. C. Crawford, former director of the Peoples Bank on June 25, 1985.

43. "The Peoples Savings Bank, Cedar Rapids, Iowa," *The Banker's Magazine* 84 (March 1912): 425.

44. Letter from Fred. H. Shaver to John D. Van Allen and Son in Clinton, Iowa, dated September 29, 1910, in Burnham Library, Art Institute of Chicago; I thank John Zukowsky for bringing this letter to my attention.

45. *Peoples Bank*, p. 24.

46. For the history of these two projects see: Hugh Morrison, *Louis Sullivan, Prophet of Modern Architecture* (New York, London: Norton, 1962), pp. 213–17; and Connelly, *op. cit.*, pp. 252–60.

47. Lathrop, p. 59–60.

48. Morrison, p. 217.

49. Letter from Shaver to Van Allen, September 29, 1910.

50. Quoted from "an early Newark history" in: Jay Hoster, "Trying to Save a Masterpiece," *Columbus Monthly*, n.d., p. 138. I am grateful to Holly Dankert who, in a Spring 1985 seminar at Northwestern University led by David Van Zanten, collected material on the Newark bank.

51. Ibid. Hoster quotes here an article by Mary Lynn Stevens, executive director of the Licking County Historical Society.

52. Information provided by Mr. J.A. Posthauer, president, Purdue National Bank, during an interview on July 19, 1985.

53. See Morrison, p. 180, and Connelly, p. 268.

54. This and the following quotations are from the *Sidney Daily News* of May 30, 1918, p. 2; January 2, 1917 and January 16, 1917.

55. Ibid.

56. Fred A. Stare, "New Building Constructed," *The Columbus Journal-Republican* (August 31, 1961), n.p.

57. John Szarkowski, *The Idea of Louis Sullivan* (Minne-

apolis, MN: University of Minnesota Press, 1956).

58. The minutes of the directors' meeting on September 4, 1919 mention: "Resolved that the bill of Claude and Starck, Architects, [from Madison] amounting to $150.00 covering plans for the new bank building is hereby authorized to be paid." Whether they were asked to make a design or acted as consulting architects is not known. See: Gordon Orr, "The Collaboration of Claude and Starck with Chicago Architectural Firms," *The Prairie School Review* 12, no. 4 (Fourth Quarter, 1975): 5–12.

59. "New Farmers and Merchants Bank Building to Open Monday June 14," *Columbus Democrat*, June 9, p. 1; also June 16, photo caption.

60. Thomas E. Tallmadge, "The Farmers' and Merchants' Bank of Columbus, Wisconsin," *The Western Architect* 29 (July 1920): 63–65.

61. Ibid., p. 64–65.

62. From a letter by Carl K. Bennett to William G. Purcell, quoted in: Robert R. Warn, "Part II: Louis H. Sullivan, '. . . an air of finality,'" p. 5.

63. A holograph of this letter is in the collection of the Burnham Library of The Art Institute of Chicago; see also Connelly, p. 272.

64. Letter from Louis Sullivan to Frank Lloyd Wright dated January 20, 1919, published in Bruce Brooks Pfeiffer, pp. 12–13.

65. A study of the history of the bank building does not exist; my analyses are based on bankers' and architects' magazines.

66. Philip Sawyer, "The Planning of Bank Buildings," *The Architectural Review* 12 (1905): 24–31.

67. Alfred Hopkins, "Some Ideas on Bank Buildings—Artistic and Practical," *The Architectural Forum* 36, no. 1 (January 1922): 3.

68. W. J. Hoggson, "Laying out a Banking Room," *The Banker's Magazine* 72 (January 1906): 313–16. Because I had to base my study on material available in journals, I was not always able to make comparisons between Sullivan's banks and other midwestern banks. Probably, the small banks in residential areas in Chicago were the ones that Sullivan used as his examples. There is, however, no documentation available about these banks and we do not know what their interiors looked like. As I will show, we may assume that these banks in residential neighborhoods had the same floor plan as the ones described here.

69. Published in *The Architectural Review* (1905): 78.

70. Published in *The Architectural Record* 25 (January 1909): p. 37.

71. Andrew Rebori, "An Architecture of Democracy," p. 438.

72. This bank was published very often in architectural magazines; see, for example, *The Architectural Review* 12 (1905): 81.

73. *Architectural Record* 25 (January 1909): 54.

74. *Architectural Record* 25 (January, 1909): 52.

75. For a more elaborate description of the bank's interior, see: Millett, *The Curve of the Arch*, chapter 4.

76. Letter from Sullivan to Bennett dated April 1, 1908, quoted in *Prairie School Review*, 10, no. 3 (1973): 5.

77. At a later time, lions were also placed next to the entrance.

78. The planters in the door opening of the Algona bank actually have the same function; the probable reason that no heraldic figures can be found in Owatonna is, according to Tim Samuelson, that Elmslie did not like them and, therefore, kept them out of the ornamental program.

79. Cost estimate in collection of Mrs. Jane Tammen in Newark; for costs of the Grinnell bank, see *The Grinnell Herald*, January 5, 1915, p. 1.

80. I am grateful to John Vinci for showing a photo of this mantelpiece to me; the top of this mantelpiece is in his collection.

81. Zabel, passim.

82. I am grateful to John Stamper who brought this bank to my attention.

83. *Radford's Stores and Flat Buildings* (Chicago, New York: The Radford Architectural Company, ca. 1909).

84. Maurizio Casari and Vincenzo Pavan, eds. *New Chicago Architecture* (New York, Chicago: Rizzoli, Inc.), p. 196.

Enigma of Modern Architecture
An Introduction to the Critics

Rochelle Berger Elstein

PROPHET OF MODERN ARCHITECTURE AND OLD master, father of functionalism and decorator, derivative designer and master theoretician, poet and protestant, progenitor of the business building and mystic, triumphant innovator and romantic failure—Louis H. Sullivan has been described by critics and historians as all of these things and many others as well. Among the other characterizations has been a curious kind of religious imagery, curious in part because Sullivan himself was not an orthodox believer, but appropriate because there is in Sullivan's writings the suggestion of a self-anointed messianism. Moreover, to some he seemed to possess a status as exalted as a great religious leader. Many writers talked of "pilgrimages" to visit his small town banks, but pilgrimage was clearly intended to be metaphorical. "Prophet" was a term often applied to Sullivan—Hugh Morrison merely borrowed and popularized it—but its religious implications were irrelevant. "Forerunner" would have been as appropriate. Yet there is, even in Morrison, intimation of the theological when he says that what Sullivan had was not a theory or even a philosophy, but a religion of architecture. The depiction of Louis Sullivan as a Christlike figure sometimes went beyond metaphor. Sheldon Cheney, in a careful selection of words, accused Sullivan's adversaries of crucifying him, and Frank Lloyd Wright compared the architect to that "consummate radical" and messiah who would banish death, Jesus Christ.[1]

More than any other American architect, Sullivan has been characterized in terms that are varied and indeed contradictory. Attempts to assess his genius and calculate his contributions to our architectural heritage have been undertaken by his colleagues and followers, by contemporary critics and later historians, by scholars from a variety of disciplines from literature to photography to history. Sullivan's work, both his buildings and his writings, has engendered more diverse criticism than any other architect and, over the century, he has defied categorization and easy evaluation. What various writers at various times have seen in Sullivan's work reflects both the objective reality and the conceptual "lens" through which his work was perceived. Briefly surveying the panorama of Sullivan criticism will therefore introduce us not only to the works of this great architect and his place in American architecture, but also to several frameworks for architectural criticism as well.

Louis Sullivan, in a period in which he was still optimistic about the prospects for the future of architecture, was negative toward the criticism of his day. "Why have we not more of vital architectural criticism? . . . They write merely in the fashion."[2] What he failed to see was that critics, as much as architects, were imbedded in as well as shapers of their milieu. In his view the architect both captured and created the essential values and truths of his time. In like manner, the architectural critic influenced and was influenced by the values and truths—the *zeitgeist*—of his era. Architectural movements and intellectual currents shaped architectural criticism as much as they shaped architecture. What George Edgell noted about change in the art of building may be equally applied to the art of interpreting and evaluating building, namely that "[that] which to-day is regarded as unprogressive, a generation from now may be in the van[guard.]"[3]

Sullivan's achievements have never been seen in isolation but in the context of architectural and historical trends, and often philosophical and critical ones. Sullivan and the Chicago School came of age in a century saturated with historicism. It was against that approach that they rebelled. The dominant role of nature in the education of the young architect and in the organic unity of the buildings, both of which are major themes in Sullivan's writings, was a corrective to the nineteenth century's preoccupation with historic precedent. By the third decade of the twentieth century, their great revolution had been fought and won. Impatient with the reaction—the triumph of neoclassicism that began with the World's Columbian Exposition in Chicago in 1893—a new generation of designers, critics, and historians was ready to embrace a new architecture. An innovative wave, functionalist, modernist, undecorated, and uncompromisingly structural—in short, the International Style—swept in. Revisionist critics saw Louis Sullivan as progenitor of this new approach, citing his dictum "form follows function" and pointing to the unornamented warehouses and factories of Dankmar Adler and Louis Sullivan as antecedents for the European functionalists. Two decades later, in reaction to the austere and pristine structures of the transplanted Bauhaus architects, another reaction emphasizing social and humanistic values denigrated the significance of Sullivan as a pure structuralist. Rather it stressed his personalizing ornament and his buildings' dynamism as an embodiment of American ideas and values. Contemporaneous with this were books celebrating technical innovativeness and, later, some important works which adumbrated Sullivan's romantic and transcendental roots, unifying the idea and practice of architecture.

Early Critics

The two decades of Sullivan's great productivity coincided with the burgeoning of the architectural press in the United States. Critics and editors of *Architectural Record, Engineering Magazine,* and *Inland Architect and News Record* often wrote about Sullivan. These men, for example, Montgomery Schuyler, Barr Ferree, and Robert C. McLean, stressed that the skyscraper was an American invention, born and raised in Chicago, and given form by Adler & Sullivan who first applied ancient aesthetic canons to the vertical building.[4] A favorite topic was the Guaranty Building (fig. 154) whose highly-decorated surfaces led critics to debate whether Sullivan was a decorator or an architect. Schuyler wrote: "I know of no steel-framed building in which the metallic construction is more palpably felt through the envelope of baked clay," but, for Ferree, who had acclaimed the judicious Wainwright ornament, the fecund foliage of the Buffalo variation was more problematical.[5] A resolute admirer of Sullivan, Schuyler neutralized doubt about the inordinate richness of some Sullivan decoration by pointing to unornamented façades and praising the interplay of their strong masses: "The Auditorium (fig. 155) alone would suffice to refute that unjust limitation [that he was a decorator only], for the largeness, and simplicity and liberality of the general scheme are eminently architectonic."[6] Schuyler and fellow critic Harry Desmond advised readers to study Sullivan's work; they judged that Sullivan was a heroic architect, persisting in grappling with complex and troubling problems, inventive and original and, because of his avant-garde solutions, and the public's undeveloped taste, isolated—a lone genius who throughout his career was endlessly fascinating.[7]

Architect contemporaries who knew Sullivan wrote about him in ways that emphasized both his talent and his flaws. John Root, who died before Sullivan matured, judged him to be a promising designer who sometimes ignored the large issues

Figure 159
Adler & Sullivan, Audi-
torium, Chicago, Illinois,
1886–1889. Courtesy Chi-
cago Historical Society
ICHi–18768.

of composition.[8] Dankmar Adler both admired and criticized him, acknowledging his partner's "pre-eminence in the artistic field" but later finding fault with Sullivan's philosophy. He attacked "On Inspiration," and he amended Sullivan's dictum that "form follows function" to read that function and environment together determine form. "The architect is not allowed to wait until, seized by an irresistible impulse from within, he gives the world the fruit of his studies and musings. He is of the world as well as in it. The world of today has greater need of his aid than had any previous period, and he is pressed into its service and must work for it and with it, no matter whether or not urged by the spirit within him."[9] Frank Lloyd Wright provided a gloss on his "Lieber Meister's" text: since a building, to be functional, must be integral with the environment, with a seamless continuity between materials and purpose, in actuality, "form and function are one."[10]

Sullivan's younger colleagues—to call them disciples would violate their insistence that what Sullivan most emphatically modelled was individuality—were in essential agreement about his achievements and his enduring contributions. (Only George Elmslie, the assistant who had known, aided and defended him, refrained from putting all his thoughts on paper.)[11] Wright, and young architects Andrew Rebori and Claude Bragdon concurred that he was a prophet, without honor in his own land.[12] It was not that Sullivan had failed, they thought, but rather that society had

failed to appreciate him, whom they identified as both engineer and architect and in whose most embellished designs they found practical aspects.[13] His facility as a conceptualizer impressed those who worked under him; Wright repeatedly told the story of how Sullivan threw the design of the Wainwright Building on his desk and the sky-scraper sprang forth fully formed, after the briefest of gestation periods.[14] On the ornament, however, they differed, with Rebori praising it unstintingly. Thomas Tallmadge, a Chicago architect and con-temporary of Wright, perceived inconsistency between a democratic aesthetic and an aristo-cratic ornament; and Bragdon urged restraint: "Mr. Sullivan works most unerringly when most restrained by practical limits" but he is sometimes betrayed by the very "fecundity of invention."[15] But no excess of ornament prevented his build-ings from fully embodying and expressing their civilization: the place, the time, and the society they shared.

Beyond Chicago's boundaries, foreign visitors had spread Sullivan's reputation to Europe, espe-cially to France where the Transportation Building was lauded and where his architecture was perma-nently exhibited.[16] To the critic for the *Gazette des Beaux Arts* he was a pupil of Vaudremer who would have seen Sullivan's buildings as aston-ishingly heretical. The American, however, expressed his own culture and society brilliantly and audaciously, if not in the Beaux-Arts manner.[17]

The Critics' Debate in the 1920s and 1930s

The near unanimity of opinion of the early critics fragmented in the 1920s and especially in the 1930s, as theories proliferated regarding the func-tion and aim of architecture, and a new architec-tural style gained a critical following. It would be a mistake to think that seeing Sullivan as the progenitor of functionalism was a European phe-nomenon or that all the critics who were enthusi-astic about the International Style accepted the

Chicago architect as its ancestor. Arrayed on the pro-functionalist side were Hugh Morrison, George Edgell, Sigfried Giedion, and Sheldon Cheney; among those who argued the multi-plicity of anti-functionalist positions were half a dozen opponents whose arguments were grounded in organic architecture, ornamentalism, empathy, aestheticism, and just plain antipathy to Sullivan's work.

Proponents of the modernist perspective—Morrison, Edgell, and Giedion—offered a view of Sullivan as synthesizer of engineering and architecture, romanticism and realism; and then they bolstered their argument by reviewing his critical acceptance in the United States and abroad.[18] By illustrating the severe and unornamented Wirt Dexter Building (fig. 160) they highlighted Sullivan's "modernity" and they rationalized the Guaranty's terra-cotta as fire-proofing. For this group, Sullivan's bequest to his century, to both Europeans and Americans, was a theory that enshrined honesty in structure and raised utility above fine art; his "system of thinking" "rendered possible the development of a true architectural style in the present day."[19]

Not all International Style partisans agreed on Sullivan's role; to the Museum of Modern Art architectural critic Henry-Russell Hitchcock, he was only "half-modern" and his "paranoiac" ornament was simply derived from Henry Hobson Richardson's.[20] Hitchcock's and fellow Museum of Modern Art curator Philip Johnson's assessments of Sullivan were published twenty-seven years apart, but they concurred that Sullivan produced one original building, the Wainwright, which he then just repeated. Its quality was equalled by McKim, Mead and White and surpassed by Richardson, Root, and Wright.[21] On the extent of his influence and his value as a designer, however, the two critics differed: Hitchcock praised a few buildings but saw him as a second-rate architect; Johnson was more positive: Sullivan excelled at doing tall office buildings, in fact as a "model of the importance of *design*, . . . he made the tall office building into art" and his ornament was very relevant to architects in 1956.[22] In this he echoed the argument of Henry Hope who in 1947 had written that ornament was a manifestation of the spiritual function of architecture, and that "the proper evaluation of Sullivan's architecture will include his ornament."[23]

Lewis Mumford did for Louis Sullivan's posthumous reputation what Montgomery Schuyler had done for him earlier. While admitting his flaws,

Figure 160
Adler & Sullivan, Wirt Dexter Building, Chicago, Illinois, 1887. Rochelle Elstein, photographer.

Mumford extolled and defended Sullivan, concluding that, although Sullivan failed to achieve everything, he accomplished something so worthwhile and enduring that he must be accorded a unique place in architectural history.[24] Mumford decided that despite Sullivan's numerous shortcomings, he was, in the last analysis, the cornerstone of organic architecture and the first truly American architect.

Sullivan was the first American architect to think consciously of his relations with civilization. . . . [He] knew what he was about, and what is more important, he knew what he ought to be about. . . . Sullivan saw that the business of the architect was to organize the forces of modern society, discipline them for human ends, express them in the plastic-utilitarian forms of building.[25]

Comprehending his country, epoch, and civilization, Sullivan fully understood that architecture was the social art—that buildings are outward manifestations of internal values and what their buildings convey is the truest expression of what the people are. If he was overwhelmed by the destructive forces of the age, he nevertheless was "a real beginning" in the genesis of modern architecture in America and ultimately the world.

Critics of the 1970s and 1980s

Among the commemorations of the Sullivan centennial were an exhibition at The Art Institute of Chicago and a column in *The Architectural Record*. The former, although sparsely attended, included both philosophy and ornament; the latter was noteworthy as the last exposition of the Sullivan-as-first-modernist argument.[26] Within a few years that view was superseded by the one that defined Sullivan as a Romantic and a Transcendentalist. He was seen as an architect whose ideas and architecture were inseparable, each building an attempt to achieve through art a communion with the cosmos, a union with nature. Because every design is the reification of his philosophy, the "remarkable bond between his concept of architecture and his architectural conception" required that critics and historians apprehend the message for which architecture is the medium.[27] Narciso Menocal's book is devoted to Sullivan's writings, and to the multiplicity of sources, both American and European, which he used, albeit often in unsystematic and fragmentary ways. Menocal emphasizes Sullivan's place in intellectual history, if not in the history of architecture, because he sees Adler as the partnership's architect and regards Sullivan as an ornamentalist, an articulator of surfaces. Louis Sullivan was a nineteenth-century man, with an outdated philosophy and a way of working unsuited to corporate America, coupled with a messianism which made him immune to change. Therefore, the modernists and functionalists were wrong, but what Mumford had intuited was correct: "A strong correspondence between his poetic idea of America and his practice . . . is perhaps the most salient of Sullivan's achievements and places him in a category almost his own."[28]

William Jordy's conclusions about Sullivan contain elements of the Menocal position but include Romanticism as one of many factors shaping his architecture and his place in history. Other factors which Jordy considers important include composition ("the block") and detailing (the ornament). It was on Sullivan's architecture that Jordy focuses his attention, expanding the definition of function to encompass the spiritual and no doubt agreeing with Paul Sprague about the metaphysical function of ornament. "It was ornament for Sullivan that represented the most effective means of expression of those non-material functions that stood behind and gave artistic meaning to the work of art."[29] Jordy's vocabulary—"scintillating, evanescent, exuberant"—conveys the energy that enlivens Sullivan compositions, and directs the reader back to the buildings. "The thrust of the philosophical speculation toward the architecture, and of the architectural form toward the philosophy, is reciprocal," but the philosophy was diffuse and the style effusive, whereas the architecture was "forthright and lucid."[30] If in the end Sullivan failed, Jordy concludes, it was because his was the most ambitious of programs: to carry the dialectic of opposites to a synthesis that was permanent and true, national and cosmic, artistic and social.

As a brief postscript to the lengthy and substantive Sullivan criticism, two recent studies that review architectural historiography and criticism can be mentioned, although neither sheds new light on Sullivan. Wichit Charenbakh's is a patchwork of quotations interspersed with factual data about the critics; it emphasizes technological innovation (and borrows much of Carl Condit's text). To Charenbakh, Louis Sullivan was the father of the skyscraper, who shaped the metamorphosis of the new engineering into a new architectural mode. Sullivan was never defeated: he "strove, sought, found and never yielded. . . . [Root, Sullivan, and unnamed other Chicago architects] strongly believed that they had created a new style of architecture by means of a new kind of thinking about it"; and Charenbakh obviously thinks so too.[31] In the second recent work, Deborah Pokinski debunks the "legend" of the Chicago School, identifying the errors widely propounded by its historians.[32] She sees Sullivan as neither the father of functionalism nor the progenitor of the skyscraper but essentially as a decorator. In a subsequent study, with a different emphasis, she modified her argument and concluded that America had an indigenous modernism, was receptive to the new architecture, and that "modern" did not connote a style but a principle.[33]

Carson's and the Critics

To recapitulate the history of Sullivan criticism, it is possible to compare treatments of a single structure, and, in so doing, investigate a variety of critical modes. The Schlesinger & Mayer Building, which later became Carson Pirie Scott & Company (fig. 161), was one of Sullivan's most significant buildings, historically because it was his last major commission; because he worked on it without Adler, from whom he had parted in 1895; and because stylistically it was a departure from his earlier skyscrapers in that it was not soaringly vertical, but a dynamic equilibrium of vertical and horizontal forces. Critically, too, it is a key monument. Modernist critics have focused on the upper stories and ignored or dismissed the exuberant foliate ornament of the first two floors, while partisans of Sullivan's decoration have praised the ironwork and terra-cotta, their psychological functionalism and their structural integration.

The first assessment of the newly completed building in the national architectural press was written by Lyndon P. Smith who worked on the Bayard Building in 1897 and was therefore familiar with Sullivan's architecture and his philosophy.[34] Smith's balanced critique praised both the department store's uniqueness and its value as a model. He devoted space both to its structure and to its ornament, the latter full of "vitality, of movement, grace . . . organic." Form followed utilitarian function in the extent of the fenestration; it followed psychic function in the delicacy of the ornament. Smith deemed it a feminine building, in contrast to the Guaranty Building in Buffalo whose assertive and purposeful elements made it masculine. The building was outstanding not only for its architectural excellence but because it was founded upon a "comprehensive theory." The master's theory had yet to be completely expounded in print by Sullivan in 1904, but one principle to which Smith alludes is Sullivan's Swedenborgian dichotomizing of masculine and feminine, rationality and emotion, wisdom and love which would unfold in *A System of Architectural Ornament According with a Philosophy of Man's Powers*.[35] Smith's four key elements were, first and foremost, that Sullivan was considered as an architect and a decorator, a planner and builder

Figure 161
Louis H. Sullivan, Carson
Pirie Scott Store, Chicago,
Illinois, 1899/1903–1904.
Courtesy Chicago Historical
Society ICHi–01571.

as much as an ornamenter; secondly, that function-alism embraced psychological and social factors as well as structural and technical ones; thirdly, that the building was an expression of a coherent and total design philosophy; and, finally, that the orna-ment was integral and essential.

Seventy years later William Jordy "read" the Carson Pirie Scott Store in much the same way. In a chapter entitled "Functionalism as Fact and Symbol: Louis Sullivan's Commercial Buildings, Tombs, and Banks," the department store building is discussed as an entity in which structure and decoration are mutually reinforcing and in which function extends to the psychological, practical, and formal aspects of the work.[36] Jordy is less convinced than Smith that the ornament succeeds in defining and enhancing the underlying function and forces of structure. However, he does conclude that in this building, if less so in others, ornament is an essential part of the totality. Sullivan's theory and his architecture were integrated although the former was more derivative and synthetic. Between Smith's critique and Jordy's was a period of seven decades and an architectural movement that established a new design vocabulary. Apolo-gists for Sullivan's role as progenitor of the Inter-national Style have been discussed; here it suffices to say that William Jordy was only partially persuaded that they were correct. Rather he thought that much of the similarity seen by "mod-ernist didacts" between Sullivan and the European modernists resulted from misreading misleading photographs. In studying Carson's entry, he con-cluded that practical and historical factors were determinants of the design of the rounded corner; its formal role was to contrast with the planarity of the walls and to create an original and beautiful change of direction.[37] His analysis of this building meshes with his formulation of Sullivan's philos-ophy. The reconciliation of opposites—of the vertical and the horizontal, the State Street and Madison façades, structure and ornament which is so clearly embodied in the entrance to Carson's—is finally what he saw as the essence of Louis Sulli-van's aesthetic and indeed his *Weltanschauung*.

Hugh Morrison, who wrote the first monograph on Sullivan, which appeared in 1935, stressed the practical advantage of a rounded, multi-doored pavilion to facilitate entrance and egress.[38] Not a word about the dynamic relationship between the corner and the walls; nothing about ornament! Precedent and practicality were the determinants of form for Morrison, reflecting his propensity to view Sullivan as presaging the new European architecture. Sullivan's ornament was baffling and best ignored.[39] Somewhat later, Sigfried Giedion extolled the Carson's building for its "expressive strength" and precision, but criticized the same corner (which Jordy would later admire) as a manifestation of Sullivanesque schizophrenia, a curved element discordant with the sharp planarity of the façades.[40] Giedion attributed it to the clients' demands and to French precedents.[41] Overall, Giedion saw the Carson Pirie Scott Store as pioneering a "neutral spatial network," a clear break with the repeated verticality of Sullivan's skyscrapers. This snippet of Giedion's criticism encapsulates his thesis that American architecture must be seen in relation to European and suggests that in Giedion's hands, Carson Pirie Scott became a proto-International Style building. Where is the ornament? one might ask. Ornament is irrelevant, a regrettable remnant of the nineteenth century.

While the functionalist apologists seemed to carry the day from 1930 to 1965, they were not without opposition.[42] Vincent Scully's lively interpretation of Sullivan criticized his predecessors for ignoring the ornament, condemning it as obsolete, or dismissing it as solipsistic, a form of art for the artist's sake. Scully's thesis, restating Geoffrey Scott, was that the humanistic purpose of architecture was to make invisible forces tangible and comprehensible.[43] Buildings were to be described as living and "locomoting," since they moved the observer to see in them the same vital force that animates the universe. When Scully described buildings, he used a vocabulary not hitherto employed.[44] Carson's composition complements the powerful velocity of street life; the upper stories float; and the entrance corner

was a kind of living membrane; the distended walls, being forced apart by internal pressure, bulge into a dynamic curve. This empathic description goes beyond structural logic and ornamental geometry into an experience that can only be called kinesthetic.

To a critic who preceded Scully, Sullivan was the creator not of empathic but of organic architecture. Lewis Mumford thought that Sullivan sometimes used ornament like an intoxicant and his late buildings suffered from Adler's absence; the rounded glass bay of Carson's began as a "legitimate accent," "a clean logical solution . . . [and] decisive in every way" but unfortunately he compromised it with the elaborate ornament.[45] On balance, Mumford admired Carson's and he noted that two decades would have to pass before its excellence was equalled and, then, it was in Europe not in America.

Willard Connely saw the ornamented entrance as transforming women's shopping into a ceremonial and aesthetic experience, commerce becoming celebration, function encompassing the psychological and economic as well as structural.[46] Carl Condit's books had a technological emphasis and his discussion of the State and Madison corner was of a harmonious transition between two elevations, whose ornament was delicate, profuse, and original.[47] He discussed the foundations, the framing and production of the ornament, but went beyond these data to Sullivan's writings, especially those that bared his psyche.[48] Condit's interpretation is a variation on the theme of the intrinsic relationship between Sullivan's architecture and his writings. For Narciso Menocal and William Jordy, the writings represented Sullivan's philosophy; for Condit, the writings revealed (sometimes obliquely) Sullivan's self. If the forces that shaped the architect and the urges and techniques shaping his architecture were not always absolutely clear to Condit, Condit's evaluation of Sullivan is absolutely intelligible to us. Carson's is the ultimate Chicago School building and its architect an unparalleled genius.[49]

Critics and historians have been engaged in interpreting Louis Sullivan for more than 100 years and a final assessment has proven to be elusive. It is not that he built so much—his output was about 180 buildings—nor that his development was so complicated, although there were clear breaks between the early works and the Auditorium, and the buildings of the 1880s and the Wainwright Building. Why, then, has Louis Sullivan proven to be such an enigma? His buildings integrate burgeoning foliate ornament with rational, geometric structure. By sundering them, critics have been able to see him as progenitor of both organic and functionalist architecture.[50] As an author he was romantic, florid, and eclectic, as a builder more controlled and original. Wright argued that Sullivan's two modes of expression were disparate: "He may have been ridiculous when he wrote. . . . He was miraculous when he drew." By integrating his writings and his buildings, critics have been prone to see him as a tragic failure who aspired to create a perfect synthesis between idea and form, an aspiration so ambitious that it was doomed to founder. Even those who are steeped in architectural forms and concepts have been forced to turn to other arts finally to convey the essence of his work. Frank Lloyd Wright said of his designing that "music [is] its only paraphrase and Peer."[51] Sullivan himself defined the architect as "a poet who uses not words but building materials as a medium of expression."[52] One of his heroes was Walt Whitman and like Whitman he aspired to create out of simple materials an art that was American and enduring.

Poetry is that most complex art form, using the most shared of media—mere words—in unique and unprecedented ways. It employs imagery, metaphor, rhythm, and allusion to create works that are both intensely personal and universally comprehensible. As individuals, we read poems and understand them, yet our appreciation of them is enhanced as interpreters make unapprehended nuances available to us. Each poem contains multiple layers of meaning, and succeeding generations of readers and critics must discover for themselves the readings that speak to them. As our milieu changes, as new frameworks emerge for comprehending works of architecture, art, and literature, as new styles evolve for which precedents must be ascertained, new formulations of the meanings implicit in Sullivan's creations will also evolve.

American architectural critics' passionate involvement in that most passionate of architects, Louis H. Sullivan, may well continue for the next 100 years because his contribution to our architectural heritage is so vast and complex that essential aspects of it have yet to be unravelled.

1. Hugh Morrison, *Louis Sullivan: Prophet of Modern Architecture* (New York: Museum of Modern Art and W. W. Norton & Co., 1935). Sheldon Cheney, *The New World Architecture*, (New York: Longmans, Green & Co., 1930), p. 274. Frank Lloyd Wright, "Louis H. Sullivan—His Work," *Architectural Record* 56 (July 1924): 32. For an early use of the term "prophet," see Harry W. Desmond, "Another View—What Mr. Louis Sullivan Stands For" *Architectural Record* 16 (July 1904): 61.

2. Louis H. Sullivan, "What is Architecture—A Study in the American People of Today," *The Craftsman* 10 (June 1906): 354.

3. George Edgell, *The Architecture of To-day* (New York: Charles Scribner's Sons, 1928), p. 3.

4. Montgomery Schuyler, "Architecture in Chicago: A Critique of the Work of Adler & Sullivan," *The Architectural Record* Great American Architects Series 2 (December 1895): 12. Montgomery Schuyler, "The Skyscraper Up to Date", *The Architectural Record* 8 (January–March 1899): 250. Barr Ferree, "The High Building and Its Art," *Scribner's Magazine* 15 (March 1894): 303. Barr Ferree, "The Modern Office Building," pt. 3, *Inland Architect and News Record* 27 (June 1896): 45.

5. Schuyler, "Architecture in Chicago," p. 33. Ferree, "The High Building," p. 314.

6. Schuyler, "Architecture in Chicago," p. 23.

7. Sometimes thwarted, sometime flawed, "there is no denying that a new work by Louis Sullivan is the most interesting event which can happen in the American architectural world today." Montgomery Schuyler, "The People's Savings Bank of Cedar Rapids, Iowa," *The Architectural Record* 31 (January 1912): 45.

8. John Root, "Architects of Chicago," *Inland Architect and News Record* 16 (January 1891): 92.

9. Dankmar Adler in "The Influence of Steel Construction and Plate Glass upon the Development of Modern Style," *Inland Architect* 28 (November 1896): 35.

10. Frank Lloyd Wright, "Sullivan Against the World," *The Architectural Record* 105 (June 1949): 298.

11. Elmslie was not altogether silent; he provided much of the information on which Morrison's book was based and it was dedicated to him. He wrote an article on the ornament; and, although he never intended it for publication, he sent a letter to Wright to clarify his role in Sullivan's work and to correct Wright's own overdrawn self-assessment. Morison, *Louis Sullivan: Prophet of Modern Architecture*, pp. xix–xx. George G. Elmslie, "Sullivan Ornamentation," *Journal of the American Institute of Architects* 6 (October 1946): 155–158. Mark L. Peisch, Letter of George Grant Elmslie to Frank Lloyd Wright, 12 June 1936, *Journal of the Society of Architectural Historians* 20 (October 1961): 140–141.

12. That Sullivan's contributions were acknowledged by English and especially French critics was often pointed out and Wright speculated that the American public had been so habituated to clichéd architecture that they could not see Sullivan's for what it was. Wright, "Louis H. Sullivan—His Work," p. 32. Claude Bragdon, *Architecture and Democracy* (New York: Alfred W. Knopf Co., 1918), p. 141. Andrew Rebori, "Louis H. Sullivan," *The Architectural Record* 55 (June 1924): 587.

13. Bragdon emphasized that the ubiquitous ornament of the Guaranty Building, which he poetically described as "fine as lace and strong as steel," was skillfully crafted to capture dust which served to emphasize the patterns of which the surface was composed. Claude Bragdon, "Architecture in the United States," pt. 3: "The Skyscraper" *The Architectural Record* 26 (August 1909): 92. Claude Brag-

don, "An American Architect, Being an Appreciation of Louis H. Sullivan," *House and Garden* 7 (January 1905): p. 52. See also Andrew Rebori, "Louis H. Sullivan," 586–87. Wright, "Louis H. Sullivan—His Work," pp. 28–32. Frank Lloyd Wright, *Genius and the Mobocracy* (New York: Duell, Sloan and Pearce, 1949), p. 90.

14. Wright, "Louis H. Sullivan—His Work," p. 29. Wright, *Genius and the Mobocracy*, p. 95. Purcell agreed about Sullivan's fluency in sketching and in formulating ideas, citing his practice of using all the familiar draftsman's tools *except* the eraser. William G. Purcell, "Sullivan at Work," *Northwest Architect* 8 (January–February 1944): 11.

15. Bragdon, "An American Architect," p. 54. A. N. Rebori, "An Architecture of Democracy," *The Architectural Record* 29 (May 1916): 436. Thomas Tallmadge, *The Story of Architecture in America* (New York: W. W. Norton & Co., 1927), p. 226.

16. Lauren S. Weingarden, "Louis H. Sullivan: Investigation of a Second French Connection," *Journal of the Society of Architectural Historians* 39 (December 1980): 300.

17. Jacques Hermant, "L'Art a l'Exposition de Chicago," *Gazette des Beaux Arts* (3 parts) 3rd. series, 10 (September 1893): 237–53; (November 1893): 416–25; (December 1893): 441–61.

18. Morrison even argued that Tallmadge had recanted and would have revised his chapter title to "Louis Sullivan and the Cause Triumphant." *Louis Sullivan: Prophet*, p. xviii.

19. Ibid., pp. 279–80.

20. Henry-Russell Hitchcock, *The Architecture of H. H. Richardson and His Time* (Cambridge: M.I.T. Press, 1966), p. 196. Ibid., 301. That Henry-Russell Hitchcock and Philip Johnson were partisans of the International Style is amply demonstrated by their Museum of Modern Art exhibition and catalogue; that they were not prone to see Sullivan in their camp is implied in the title of a chapter of that catalogue: "A Third Principle: The Avoidance of Applied Decor," and, if further proof need be adduced, one can turn to p. 69 and read how easy it is "to defend the claim [that] the best buildings since 1800 are the least ornamented." Henry-Russell Hitchcock and Philip Johnson, *The International Style: Architecture Since 1922*, (New York: Museum of Modern Art, 1932), p. 69.

21. Henry-Russell Hitchcock, *Modern Architecture: Romanticism and Reintegration* (New York: Payson and Clarke, Ltd., 1929).

22. Philip Johnson, "Is Sullivan the Father of Functionalism?" *Art News* 55 (December 1956): 45–46; 56–57.

23. Henry R. Hope, "Louis Sullivan's Architectural Ornament," *Architectural Review* [London] 102 (October 1947): 117. Among the critics who evaluated his ornament and found it *retardataire* were Walter Behrendt and Nikolaus Pevsner, the former because personal expression in architecture was a nineteenth-century aim, the latter because it was a variant of art nouveau whose source was Gothic Revival forms. Sullivan qualified to be a "pioneer" because he first expressed the structural grid, although he occasionally compromised it with fanciful ornament. Colin Rowe carried this line of thought further, agreeing with Pevsner about the cellular frame but disagreeing about art nouveau which he identified as an idea rather than a style, and which he rejected as being the basis for the atheoretical structural revolution in Chicago. Rowe was not in the Morrison camp either; in buildings of the International Style, "autonomous structure perforates abstract space," while for Sullivan, space and structure were inseparable. Fiske Kimball's ability to see Sullivan as the first structural innovator since the Middle Ages and the man whose "free and functional mode of design" set the stage for decades of soaring skyscrapers might imply that Kimball should be grouped with Giedion and Morrison and to a certain extent that is true. But he tempered Sullivan's functionalism, when he concluded that Sullivan "achieved unity of form arbitrarily." Walter C. Behrendt, *Modern Building* (New York: Harcourt, Brace & Co., 1937), p. 121. Nikolaus Pevsner, *Pioneers of Modern Design*, (Middlesex: Penguin Books, 1960), p. 29, 97. Colin Rowe, "The Chicago Frame," *Architectural Review* 120 (November 1956): 287. Fiske Kimball, "Louis Sullivan: An Old Master," *The Architectural Record* 57 (April 1925): 289, 303. Fiske Kimball, *American Architecture*, (New York: Bobbs-Merrill, 1928), pp. 158, 168.

24. The flaws included structural dishonesty (the extra piers on the Wainwright façade were for show, not for support); disunity (in the late works, form and feeling conflicted, masculine and feminine aspects separated); unsuccessful ornament (excess sometimes ruined the logic of the design, and immoderate decoration was self-indulgent and old-fashioned); and, finally, the rhetoric and the architecture were contradictory. Also, Sullivan was not a gifted planner; his habits were disreputable, his writing style bombastic. Mumford, *Brown Decades: Study of the Arts in America, 1865–1895*, (New York: Dover Pubs., Inc., 1955, copyright 1931), pp. 152, 149, 155. Mumford, *The Roots of American Architecture*, (New York: Reinhold Pub. Corp., 1952), pp. 18, 21, 433.

25. Mumford, *Brown Decades*, pp. 162–63.

26. *Louis Sullivan and the Architecture of Free Enterprise* edited by Edgar Kaufmann, Jr. (Chicago: Art Institute of Chicago, 1956). "Sullivan Seen by his Contemporaries; In his Centennial Year, Another Look," *Architectural Record* 120 (September 1956): 18, 416, 420, 422.

27. Narciso Menocal, *Architecture as Nature: The Transcendentalist Idea of Louis Sullivan* (Madison: University of Wisconsin Press, 1981), p. 151.

28. Ibid.

29. Paul E. Sprague, "The Architectural Ornament of Louis Sullivan," (Ph.D. diss., Princeton University, 1968), p. 40.

30. William H. Jordy, *American Buildings and Their Architects*. V. 3. *Progressive and Academic Ideals at the Turn of the Twentieth Century* (Garden City, NY: Anchor Books, 1976), p. 174.

31. Wichit Charenbakh, *Chicago School Architects and their Critics*, (Ann Arbor, MI: UMI Research Press, 1981), p. 166.

32. The skeleton frame was not intended as a new form of expression; "form follows function" was not a utilitarian dogma; and modern architecture was not born in Chicago. Deborah F. Pokinski, "The Legend of the Chicago School of Architecture: A Study in the Historiography of Modern American Architecture," (M.A. thesis, Cornell University, 1973), pp. 127ff.

33. There was an important tradition of modern architecture in America from the early 1890s; the foundation for it was new methods of construction but it was expressed as a continuity with the past; the European avant-garde played a role but there were uniquely American contributions. Deborah F. Pokinski, *The Development of the American Modern Style* (Ann Arbor, MI: UMI Research Press, 1984), pp. 79ff.

34. Lyndon P. Smith, "The Schlesinger & Mayer Building; An Attempt to Give Functional Expression to the Architecture of a Department Store," *The Architectural Record* 16 (July 1904): 53–60.

35. Louis H. Sullivan, *A System of Architectural Ornament According with a Philosophy of Man's Powers* (New York: American Institute of Architects, 1924). For a discussion of the influence of Swedenborg on Sullivan, see Narciso

Menocal, *Architecture as Nature* pp. 24ff. Sherman Paul wrote a study (which Menocal's complements) of Sullivan's literary sources, focusing on his place in American intellectual history. Sherman Paul, *Louis Sullivan: An Architect in American Thought*, (Englewood Cliffs, NJ: Prentice-Hall, Inc., 1962).

36. Jordy, *American Buildings 3, Progressive and Academic Ideals*, pp. 135–44.

37. Ibid., p. 139.

38. Morrison's *Louis Sullivan: Prophet of Modern Architecture* appeared in 1935, the same year in which he organized a Sullivan exhibition at the Museum of Modern Art. Three years earlier, a pioneering show at the same museum presented the new architecture to Americans for the first time in a major setting. The influential and widely distributed catalogue was by Henry-Russell Hitchcock and Philip Johnson, *The International Style: Architecture Since 1922* (New York: Museum of Modern Art, 1932).

39. Morrison, *Louis Sullivan: Prophet*, p. 200.

40. Sigfried Giedion, *Space, Time, and Architecture: The Growth of a New Tradition* (Cambridge: Harvard University Press, 1954), pp. 387–88. Giedion gave a series of lectures on architecture at Harvard University which were collected and published as *Space, Time and Architecture: The Growth of a New Tradition*, first appearing in 1941 and in several subsequent editions. In Giedion's book, William LeBaron Jenney became the Peter Behrens of Chicago, a comparison which would have vexed the early critics and Sullivan himself because they saw in Chicago a movement to create an indigenous architecture.

41. For the other side, the influence of American architects on Europe, see Leonard Eaton, *American Architecture Comes of Age: European Reaction to Henry Hobson Richardson and Louis Sullivan* (Cambridge: Harvard University Press, 1972).

42. The Morrison and Giedion view had a remarkable longevity and was propounded again in the mid-1960s by a man who was trained as an architect in Germany, steeped in Bauhaus principles and later taught in Chicago with Mies van der Rohe at Illinois Institute of Technology. For Ludwig Hilberseimer, Louis Sullivan was most noteworthy for the Auditorium and the Carson Pirie Scott Store, whose entrance Hilberseimer criticized, arguing that the structural integrity of the building was vitiated by rounding the corner. A more conventional but bolder right angle would have been the preferable solution. Hilberseimer's attitude toward the ornament was more positive than Morrison's or Giedion's; he saw it as an idiosyncracy of the architect but praised its organic essence. Despite Sullivan's occasional lapses, like failing to make the Auditorium three separate structures, Hilberseimer saw Sullivan's achievements and his significance as comparable to Schinkel's, whom the writer praised for translating a new purpose into a new architecture. Hilberseimer, Ludwig, *Contemporary Architecture: Its Roots and Trends* (Chicago: P. Theobald, 1964), p. 99.

43. Scully, Vincent, Jr., "Louis Sullivan's Architectural Ornament: A Brief Note Concerning Humanist Design in the Age of Force," *Perspecta* 5 (1959): 73–80.

44. In Scully's article, the style reinforces the substance; his language has a rhythm which makes the argument all the more persuasive. The prose is lucid yet embellished, the flow lively but never out of control, especially in contrast with Sullivan's perfervid and often overblown style.

45. Lewis Mumford, *The Brown Decades*, pp. 155–56.

46. Willard Connely, *Louis Sullivan as He Lived: The Shaping of American Architecture*, (New York: Horizon Press, 1960), p. 235.

47. Carl W. Condit, *The Chicago School of Architecture: A History of Commercial and Public Building in the Chicago Area 1875–1925* (Chicago: University of Chicago Press, 1964), pp. 163–164.

48. Ibid., pp. 167–71. Louis H. Sullivan, *Kindergarten Chats and Other Writings*, edited by Isabella Athey (New York: Wittenborn, 1947 [reprint, 1968]). *The Autobiography of an Idea*, (New York: American Institute of Architects, 1924). The autobiography went through several editions. For a complete bibliography of Sullivan's writings, see Menocal, *Architecture as Nature*, pp. 203–206.

49. Condit, *The Chicago School of Architecture*, pp. 165, 220.

50. Wright wrote that Sullivan's unique bequest was that he modelled the striving for the complete integration of ornament and structure — "of-the-thing-not-on-it," was the way he phrased it. Frank Lloyd Wright, *Genius and the Mobocracy*, p. 77. Wright, "Sullivan Against the World," *Architectural Review* 105 (June 1949): 296.

51. Wright, *Genius and the Mobocracy*, p. 72.

52. "Louis Sullivan, the First American Architect," *Current Literature* 52 (June, 1912): 707.

Chronology

The following list of the most significant events in Louis Sullivan's personal and professional life does not include his architectural work (see "Louis H. Sullivan's Major Designs") or his numerous places of residence, mostly in Chicago. For more complete information see Robert Twombly, *Louis Sullivan: His Life and Work* (New York: Viking Penguin, 1986).

1856
September 3: born in Boston, Massachusetts

1870
June: graduates from Rice Grammar School, Boston

1870–1872
Attends English High School, Boston

1872
October: enters Massachusetts Institute of Technology's Building and Architecture Department as a special student

1873
June: leaves MIT, joins the firm of Furness & Hewitt, Philadelphia

November: leaves Furness & Hewitt, enters William Le Baron Jenney's office in Chicago

1874
July 10: sails from New York for Liverpool

August: arrives in Paris, lives at 17, rue Racine

October 22: admitted to the Ecole des Beaux-Arts, Paris, as a second year (beginning) student in architecture

1875
April–May: tours southern France, northern Italy, Rome

May 24: arrives in New York from Liverpool

Summer: begins work as a free-lance designer/draftsman in Chicago

1876
May: extensive press coverage of his controversial frescoes—his first executed architectural designs—for Moody's Tabernacle and Sinai Synagogue, Chicago

1879
Free lancing includes work for "Dankmar Adler, Architect"

1881
Becomes partner in "Dankmar Adler & Company"

1882
August 12: first newspaper interview, in the Chicago *Inter-Ocean*, on Hooley's Theater remodeling

1883
May 1: becomes principal in "Adler & Sullivan"

1884
November 17: founding member of the Western Association of Architects

1885
January: founding member of the Illinois State Association of Architects

October: first public speech, "Characteristics and Tendencies in American Architecture," second Western Association of Architects convention, St. Louis

1886
November 17: "Essay on Inspiration" read to third Western Association of Architects convention, Chicago

1887
April 2: "What is the Just Subordination, in Architectural Design, of Details to Mass?" read to Illinois State Association of Architects monthly meeting

October 21: elected fellow of the American Institute of Architects

1888
ca. February: Frank Lloyd Wright enters Adler & Sullivan's office

1889
April 9: "Style" read to Chicago Architectural Sketch Club

Summer: suffers nervous exhaustion from overwork on the Chicago Auditorium Building

Fall: Adler & Sullivan move to 1600 Auditorium Tower office

1890
March 1, 4: purchases eleven acres of beachfront property for a winter home in Ocean Springs, Mississippi

March: designs homes for himself and James Charnley in Ocean Springs, Mississippi

1891
December: "The High Building Question," proposing the set-back skyscraper, published in *The Graphic* magazine, Chicago

1892
April: purchases 41.5 beachfront acres in Ocean Springs, Mississippi

May: moves into home at 3030 Lake Park Avenue, Chicago, owned by his brother, Albert, which he had designed for his mother, Andrienne, who died on May 15

August: sells the 41.5 acres in Ocean Springs, Mississippi

"Ornament in Architecture" published in *Engineering Magazine*

1893
Spring: Frank Lloyd Wright leaves Adler & Sullivan

August 5: "Polychromatic Treatment of Architecture" read to World Congress of Architects, Chicago World's Fair

1894
October: "Emotional Architecture as Compared with Intellectual: A Study in Objective and Subjective" read to American Institute of Architects convention, New York City

1894–1897
Member of Board of Directors, American Institute of Architects

1895
July 11: Dankmar Adler leaves architectural profession terminating the Adler & Sullivan partnership

1895–1896
Serves on executive committee, Board of Directors, American Institute of Architects

1896
March: "The Tall Office Building Artistically Considered" published in *Lippincott's* magazine

Summer: Albert Sullivan takes over 3030 Lake Park Avenue home ending the relationship with his brother, Louis

1897
August 23: mortgages Ocean Springs, Mississippi, land to secure $3000 loan from Joseph Rose, Chicago

1898
March 1: repays loan and regains title to his land

1899
January: "An Unaffected School of Modern Architecture: Will it Come?" published in *The Artist*

June 3: "The Modern Phase of Architecture" read to founding convention of the Architectural League of America, Cleveland

July 1: marries Mary Azona Hattabaugh at St. Paul's Reformed Episcopal Church, Chicago

1900
June: "The Young Man in Architecture" read to second Architectural League of America convention, Chicago

1901
February 16–February 8, 1902: "Kindergarten Chats" published in 52 installments of Interstate Architect & Builder, Cleveland

1902
May 30: "Education" read to fourth Architectural League of America convention, Toronto

1903

October: unable to repay $10,000 loan from Ellis Wainwright, St. Louis

1905

August: mortgages home and land at Ocean Springs, Mississippi, to secure $5000 loan from Gustave Hottinger, Chicago

December: fails to secure lectureship at University of Michigan School of Architecture

1906

January: "What is Architecture?: A Study of the American People of Today" published in *American Contractor*

1908

fall: completes manuscript of "Democracy: A Man-Search," written since 1905 under the title, "Natural Thinking: A Study in Democracy"

1909

January: "Is our Art a Betrayal Rather than an Expression of American Life?" published in *The Craftsman*

November 29: personal and professional possessions sold at Williams, Barker & Severns Company auction showrooms, Chicago

December 6: Mary Sullivan leaves to live with Davies Edward Marshall in New York City

1910

January 6: sells six acres of Ocean Springs land to Gustave Hottinger for $1

May 1: sells remaining five acres of Ocean Springs land and his home to Gustave Hottinger for $8500

1916–1917?

Mary and Louis Sullivan divorce

1917

December 31: looks for civil service job with federal government

1918

February: unable to pay rent, leaves Auditorium Tower office for 431 S. Wabash Avenue

April: fails to land Department of Construction job with federal government

May: unable to pay rent, gives up 431 So. Wabash Avenue office

October: in new office at 1808 Prairie Avenue

Attempts unsuccessfully to publish "Kindergarten Chats" as a book with Alfred Knopf

1920

December: learns he will not be appointed director of Alfred Loos' Free School of Architecture in Vienna

1921

November: in new office at 1701 Prairie Avenue

1922

June–September 1923: publishes *The Autobiography of an Idea* in fifteen installments of the American Institute of Architects *Journal*

1923

February: "The Chicago Tribune Competition" published in *The Architectural Record*

April: "Concerning the Imperial Hotel, Tokyo, Japan" published in *The Architectural Record*

1924

February: "Reflections on the Tokyo Disaster" published in *The Architectural Record*

Early April: receives bound copies of his books, *The Autobiography of an Idea* and *A System of Architectural Ornament* from publisher

April 14: dies in his Warner Hotel room of kidney disease and myocarditis

April 16: buried in Graceland Cemetery, Chicago

Louis H. Sullivan's Major Designs

Between 1876 and 1922, Louis Sullivan produced at least 238 architectural designs, most of them in association with Dankmar Adler from 1879 to 1895. Of these, some 158 were designed between 1883-to-1895 Sullivan was a principal in the Adler & Sullivan partnership. The following entries are important architecturally or as milestones in Sullivan's career, and unless otherwise indicated were intended for Chicago. Dates were established by consulting primary sources.

S: Building was standing in 1986
PC: Project was partially constructed
P: Project was not constructed
No symbol means the erected commission has since been demolished.

For a complete list of Sullivan's and Adler & Sullivan's designs see Robert Twombly, *Louis Sullivan: His Life and Work* (New York: Viking Penguin, 1986), Appendix A.

I *Free-lance designer, 1876 to mid-1881, including work for "Dankmar Adler, Architect," beginning in 1879*

1876
Chicago Avenue Church ("Moody's Tabernacle"), interior frescoes, Johnston & Edelmann, architects

Sinai Synagogue, interior frescoes, Johnston & Edelmann, Burling & Adler, associated architects

1879
Central Music Hall, interior decorations (?)

1880
John Borden Block
John Borden residence
Grand Opera House, interior remodeling, decorations

1880–1881
Max M. Rothschild Building

II *Partner in Adler & Company, mid-1881 to April 30, 1883*

1881
John M. Brunswick & Julius Balke Factory (S)

1881–1882
Jewelers' Building (S)
Revell Building

1882
Academy of Music, Kalamazoo, Michigan
John M. Brunswick & Julius Balke Warehouse (S)
Hooley's Theater remodeling
Charles F. Kimball residence
Marx Wineman residence

1883
Aurora Watch Company (PC, S), Aurora, Illinois
Ferdinand & William Kauffmann store and flats (S)
J. H. McVicker's Theater (P)
Max M. Rothschild flats
Charles M. Schwab residence
Morris Selz residence

1884
Solomon Blumenfeld flats
Ann Halsted flats (S)
J. H. Haverly Theater remodeling
Frank A. Kennedy Bakery
Richard Knisely Factory
Martin A. Ryerson Building
A. F. Troescher Building

1885
Dankmar Adler residence
Chiltenham Improvement Company pavilion
Eli B. Felsenthal residence
Ann Halsted flats (S), addition to 1884 structure
Interstate Exposition Building, partial interior remodeling
Fanny Kohn residence
Benjamin Lindauer residence
J. H. McVicker's Theater remodeling
J. M. Scoville Factory, additions and alterations
Zion Temple

1886
Chicago Opera House, auditorium remodeling
Richard T. Crane Factory and addition
Illinois Central Railroad Station, 39th Street
Milwaukee Exposition Building, interior remodeling
Martin A. Ryerson Charities Trust Building
West Chicago Clubhouse

1886–1889
Chicago Auditorium Building (S)

1887
Chicago Nursery & Half Orphan Asylum
Wirt Dexter Building (S)
Martin A. Ryerson Tomb (S)
Selz, Schwab Factory
Standard Club

1888
Victor Falkenau flats
Illinois Central Railroad Station, 43rd Street
Walker Warehouse

1889
Inter-Ocean Building, addition and alterations
Kehilath Anshe Ma'ariv Synagogue (P)
Opera House Block, Pueblo, Colorado

1889–1890
Carnegie Hall (S), New York City, consultants
Kehilath Anshe Ma'ariv Synagogue, revision of 1889 project

1890
James Charnley residence (S), Ocean Springs, Mississippi
Chicago Cold Storage Exchange Warehouse (PC)
Carrie Elizabeth Getty Tomb (S)
Grand Opera House, Milwaukee, Wisconsin, interior remodeling
Ontario Hotel (P), Salt Lake City, Utah
Opera House Block (P), Seattle, Washington
Louis H. Sullivan residence (S), Ocean Springs, Mississippi
Wainwright Building (S), St. Louis, Missouri

1890–1891
Dooly Block, Salt Lake City, Utah
J. H. McVicker's Theater reconstruction

1891
James Charnley residence (S), Frank Lloyd Wright principal designer

Illinois Central Railroad Station, New Orleans, Louisiana
Mercantile Club Building (P), St. Louis, Missouri
Odd Fellows (Fraternity) Temple Building (P)
Schiller Building
Albert W. Sullivan residence
Transportation Building, Chicago World's Fair
Charlotte Dickson Wainwright Tomb (S), St. Louis, Missouri

1892
William Mayer Warehouse
Portland Building (P), St. Louis, Missouri
St. Nicholas Hotel, St. Louis, Missouri
"Trust & Savings" Building (P), St. Louis, Missouri, name and date conjectural
Victoria Hotel, Chicago Heights, Illinois

1893
First Regiment Armory conversion to Trocadero Amusement Park
Chicago Stock Exchange Building
"Trust & Savings" Building (P), second version: see 1892
Union Trust Building (S), St. Louis, Missouri

1894
Burnet House Hotel (P), Cincinnati, Ohio
Chemical National Bank Building (P), St. Louis, Missouri, date is uncertain

1894–1895
Guaranty Building (S), Buffalo, New York

IV Independent Practice, July 1, 1895 to 1922

1896
Schlesinger & Mayer Store (P), 10 stories, 141–43 Wabash Avenue

1897
Bayard (Condict) Building (S), New York City
Hippodrome, St. Louis, Missouri, consultant

1898
Gage (McCormick) Building façade (S)
Schlesinger & Mayer Store (P), nine-story version, State and Madison streets
Schlesinger & Mayer Store (P), ten-story version, State and Madison streets
Schlesinger & Mayer Store (P), twelve-story version, State and Madison streets
Schlesinger & Mayer Store (S), nine-stories, Madison Street

1899–1900
Holy Trinity Cathedral (S)

1901
Presbyterian Hospital woman's pavilion (P)

1902
Schlesinger & Mayer Store (S), twelve-stories, State and Madison streets
Schlesinger & Mayer Store (P), twenty-story version, State and Madison streets

1906
National Farmers' Bank (S), Owatonna, Minnesota

1907
Henry Babson residence, Riverside, Illinois
Island City (Petty's Island) Amusement Park (P), Philadelphia, Pennsylvania

1908
Chicago Auditorium Building remodeling as hotel (P)

Chicago Auditorium Building remodeling as offices (P)

1909
Josephine Crane Bradley residence (S), Madison, Wisconsin

1909–1911
People's Savings Bank (S), Cedar Rapids, Iowa

1910–1911
St. Paul's Methodist Episcopal Church (PC, S), Cedar Rapids, Iowa

1911
Carl K. Bennett residence (P), Owatonna, Minnesota

1913–1914
Merchants' National Bank (S), Grinnell, Iowa

1916
District High School (P), Owatonna, Minnesota

1917
People's Savings & Loan Association Bank (S), Sidney, Ohio

Index